AGING AND IMMUNITY

DEVELOPMENTS IN IMMUNOLOGY

AGING AND IMMUNITY

Proceedings of an International Symposium, London, Ontario, Canada,
May 10 and 11, 1979

Editors:

S. K. SINGHAL AND N. R. SINCLAIR
*Department of Microbiology and Immunology, The University of
Western Ontario*

C. R. STILLER
Department of Medicine, The University of Western Ontario

ELSEVIER/NORTH-HOLLAND
NEW YORK • AMSTERDAM • OXFORD

Published by

Elsevier North Holland, Inc.
52 Vanderbilt Avenue, New York, New York 10017

Sole distributors outside USA and Canada

Elsevier/North-Holland Biomedical Press
335 Jan van Galenstraat, PO Box 211
Amsterdam, The Netherlands

Library of Congress Cataloging in Publication Data

Main entry under title:

Aging and immunity.
    (Developments in immunology; v. 5 ISSN 0163-5921)

    Bibliography: p.
    Includes index.
    1. Immunity—Congresses. 2. Aging—Congresses. 3. Immunologic
diseases—Age factors—Congresses. I. Singhal, S.K. II. Sinclair, Nicholas
R. St.C. III. Stiller, Calvin R. IV. Series. [DNLM: 1. Aging—Congresses.
2. Immunity—In old age—Congresses. W1 DE997WM v. 5 / WT104.3
A2673 1979]
QR185.3.A35   616.07'9   79-16556
ISBN 0-444-00346-0

Manufactured in the United States of America

Contents

Preface

Aging cells, organs and organisms undergo a number of changes in metabolic function which tend to decrease their overall capacities compared to those found earlier in their life spans. Many of these changes are considered to be the hallmarks of old age; however, they may be the result of damaging, but correctable pathologic processes commonly associated, but not a part of, the aging process. The separation of events constituting the aging process from correlated changes which are not really part of the aging process requires the analysis of appropriate fundamental models. Areas such as Immunology, Cell Biology, Virology and Pathology contribute to our knowledge concerning the constitutents of the aging process. Many of the contributions in this particular proceedings involve a study of the immune system, a model suitable to the investigation of aging because its components have been defined and because these components are subject to changes during aging. Also, the role which the immune system plays in either conferring resistance or increasing susceptibility to damaging processes during aging represents an important factor determining the overall response of cells, organs or individuals to the passage of time.

The aging process may be interpreted at many levels of scientific thought. These range from the biochemical and physiologic on one hand to the sociological and religious on the other. This book will deal with the biomedical end of this broad spectrum.

In order to contribute to basic knowledge concerning the aging process, an International Symposium on Aging and Immunity was held under the auspices of the University of Western Ontario at London, Ontario, Canada, May 11th and 12th, 1979. The results of that symposium, both the submitted papers as well as transcripts of the informal discussions which occurred after the presentation of papers, are presented in this publication. Contributions came from individuals representing a wide variety of basic and clinical biomedical research. We hope that the results of these two days of deliberations will help others interested in this broad and complex field to formulate ideas and areas in which to pursue their own research.

We wish to extend our great appreciation to all the many investigators who have contributed both their energies and their intellects in making this conference and the publication of these proceedings a worthwhile effort. None of this effort could have been possible without the generous support of a number of organizations. We also wish to extend our appreciation to the Elsevier North Holland Publishing Company for their patience and help in producing a prompt and accurate publication of these proceedings.

S.K. Singhal

C.R. Stiller

N.R.StC. Sinclair

List of Participants

Abdou, N.I.	University Kansas Medical Center, Kansas, Missouri
Acres, Bruce	Ontario Cancer Institute, Toronto, Ontario
Austin, T.W.	Victoria Hospital, London, Ontario
Bailey, Linda D.	Pennsylvania State University, University Park, Pennsylvania
Baines, Malcolm	Queen's University, Kingston, Ontario
Ball, J.	University of Western Ontario, London, Ontario
Banerjee, Diponkar	University of Western Ontario, London, Ontario
Bash, J.A.	University Cincinnati Medical Center, Cincinnati, Ohio
Bell, D.	University of Western Ontario, London, Ontario
Boyd, Stephen	Ortho Pharmaceutical, Don Mills, Ontario
Burns, Christine	Pennsylvania State University, University Park, Pennsylvania
Cape, R.D.	University of Western Ontario, London, Ontario
Chan, F.P.H.	University of Western Ontario, London, Ontario
Chiller, J.	National Jewish Hospital and Research Center, Denver, Colorado
Cinader, B.	University of Toronto, Toronto, Ontario
Clark, David, A.	McMaster University, Hamilton, Ontario
Colby, W.D.	University of Western Ontario, London, Ontario
Cunningham, A.J.	Ontario Cancer Institute, Toronto, Ontario
Delovitch, Terry	University of Toronto, Toronto, Ontario
de Veber, L.L.	War Memorial Children's Hospital, London, Ontario
Drozdowicz, Carla Kim	Pennsylvania State University, State College, Pennsylvania
Ebers, G.	University Hospital, London, Ontario
Edmonds, Merrill	Victoria Hospital, London, Ontario
Eskew, Mary Lou	Pennsylvania State University, University Park, Pennsylvania

Essani, N.) Essani, K.)	University of Western Ontario, London, Ontario
Ferguson, Frederick G.	Pennsylvania State University, University Park, Pennsylvania
Fisman, M.	London Psychiatric Hospital, London, Ontario
Flinchum, Sherry Dupere	Ohio State University, Columbus, Ohio
Flintoff, W.	University of Western Ontario, London, Ontario
Fyson, Raina E.	University of Ottawa, Ottawa, Ontario
Gambel, Phillip	Pennsylvania State University, University Park, Pennsylvania
Goldstein, S.	McMaster University, Hamilton, Ontario
Good, R.A.	Memorial Sloan-Kettering Cancer Center, New York, New York
Gorczynski, R.M.	Ontario Cancer Institute, Toronto, Ontario
Habicht, Gail	State University in New York, Stonybrook, New York
Harth, M.	University of Western Ontario, London, Ontario
Hartmann, D.P.	Georgetown University, Washington, D.C.
Hattori, Masakazu	University of Colorado, Denver, Colorado
Hazlett, Linda D.	Wayne State University, Detroit, Michigan
Heller, David	Pennsylvania State University, University Park, Pennsylvania
Hewetson, John	Medical College of Pennsylvania, Philadelphia, Pennsylvania
Hussain, Rabia	Johns Hopkins University, Baltimore, Maryland
Inch, W.R.	Ontario Cancer Foundation, London, Ontario
Injevan, Julita	University of Toronto, Toronto, Ontario
Johnson, David	Parkwood Hospital, London, Ontario
Kay, M.	Veterans Administration Center, Los Angeles, California
Kolodziej, Bruno	Ohio State University, Columbus, Ohio
Leon, Myron	Wayne State University, Detroit, Michigan
Low, Mike	University of Western Ontario, London, Ontario

Macpherson, C.	University of Western Ontario, London, Ontario
MacSween, J.M.	Dalhousie University, Halifax, Nova Scotia
Makinodan, T.	Veterans Administration Center, Los Angeles, California
McCain, Glenn	University of Texas, Dallas, Texas
McCourtie, David	St. Joseph's Hospital, London, Ontario
McCredie, J.A.	Ontario Cancer Foundation, London, Ontario
McGarry, Ronald	University of Western Ontario, London, Ontario
Merskey, Harold	London Psychiatric Hospital, London, Ontario
Morrell, Roger	Veterans Administration Medical Center, Allen Park, Michigan
Morris, Vincent	University of Western Ontario, London, Ontario
Nakano, Katsuji	University of Toronto, Toronto, Ontario
Nawrocki, John	University of Michigan, Ann Arbor, Michigan
Pancer, Larry	University of Western Ontario, London, Ontario
Park, Byung Hak	State University in New York, Buffalo, New York
Patterson, Christopher	Parkwood Hospital, London, Ontario
Paty, D.	University Hospital, London, Ontario
Pease, Larry	University of Michigan, Ann Arbor, Michigan
Pechan, Peter	University of Gutenberg, Mainz, West Germany
Pinto, Angelo	Pennsylvania State University, University Park, Pennsylvania
Pross, Hugh	Queen's University, Kingston, Ontario
Rigby, Russell	Victoria Hospital, London, Ontario
Ritchie, Joan	Pennsylvania State University, University Park, Pennsylvania
Rode, Harold	McGill University, Montreal, Quebec
Rozanis, Jacob	University of Western Ontario, London, Ontario
Sabiston, Brian	Defence and Civil Institute of Environmental Medicine, Downsview, Ontario

Shek, P.N.	D.C.I.E.M., Downsview, Ontario
Sinclair, N.R.StC.	University of Western Ontario, London, Ontario
Singhal, S.K.	University of Western Ontario, London, Ontario
Stiller, C.	University of Western Ontario, London, Ontario
Strejan, G.	University of Western Ontario, London, Ontario
Szewczuk, M.R.	McMaster University, Hamilton, Ontario
Talal, N.	Veterans Administration Hospital, San Francisco, California
Tanner, Robert	Memorial Sloan-Kettering Cancer Center, New York, New York
Thompson, John	University of Western Ontario, London, Ontario
Tugwell, M.	University of Western Ontario, London, Ontario
Turpie, Irene	McMaster University, Hamilton, Ontario
Turker, Mitchell	Indiana University, Bloomington, Indiana
Ward, M.	University of Western Ontario, London, Ontario
Weksler, M.	Cornell University, New York, New York
Wilkie, Bruce	Ontario Veternary College, University of Guelph, Guelph, Ontario
Wisniewski, H.	Institute for Basic Research in Mental Retardation, Staten Island, New York
Wright, Peter	University of Guelph, Guelph, Ontario
Yamamura, Yasuhiro	Allegheny Singer Research Corporation, Pittsburgh, Pennsylvania
Zarkower, Arian	Pennsylvania State University, University Park, Pennsylvania
Zavery, O.	Victoria Hospital, London, Ontario
Zuberi, R.	University of Western Ontario, London, Ontario

Acknowledgments

Our sincere thanks are due to the following for generous support: A.H. Robins Canada Ltd.; Bristol Myers Pharmaceutical Group; Burroughs Wellcome Ltd.; Canadian Society for Immunology; Chelsey Park Corporation; Ciba-Geigy Canada Ltd. (Sponsor Dr. R.A. Good); Eli Lilly & Company Ltd.; Frank W. Horner Ltd.; Glaxo Canada Ltd.; Hoechst Pharmaceuticals; Hoffman-La Roche Ltd.; Medical Research Council of Canada; Merck Frosst Laboratories; Novopharm Ltd.; Ontario Ministry of Health; Pfizer Company Ltd. (Sponsor Dr. M. Wexsler); Sandoz Pharmaceuticals; Upjohn Company of Canada; and The University of Western Ontario F.R. Eccles Fund (Sponsor Drs. H. Wigzell and N. Talal), and Faculties of Medicine, Dentistry, Science and Graduate Studies.

SESSION 1

Regulation and Genetics of Immune Response

Chairman: T.L. Delovitch
University of Toronto,
Toronto, Ontario

Published 1979 by Elsevier North Holland, Inc.
Singhal, Sinclair, Stiller, eds. Aging and Immunity

AUTO-ANTI-IDIOTYPIC IMMUNITY: APPLICATIONS AND PROBLEMS

HANS BINZ* AND HANS WIGZELL**
*Institute for Medical Microbiology, University of Zürich, Postfach, 8028 Zürich,
Switzerland;**Department of Immunology, Uppsala University Biomedical Center,
Box 582, S-751 23 Uppsala, Sweden

INTRODUCTION

The immune system is composed of a variety of celltypes and humoral agents
which interact in a positive or negative manner when reacting towards foreign
immunogenic substances. Our understanding how the immune response does occur
has been greatly helped by the use of inbred strains of animals, the use of
serological markers to define subsets of cells and a rapid development of
technology allowing the assessment of function of these cells. Several pieces
of important information are still lacking, however, before we can safely
state that we even know of all the cells involved in the generation of an
immune reaction. Our ignorance is even more deeper when it comes to the actual
functions of the participating cells in any detail. It is thus obvious that
attempts to in a predictive manner manipulate such a complex and largely ob-
scure system will suffer from great inherent difficulties. This manipulation
is still a matter of great theoretical and practical interest and we will
here discuss approaches attempting to achieve specific decreases or increases
of immune reactivity in adult individuals using auto-anti-idiotypic immune
reactions.

It has been known since several years that we are not tolerant towards
our own antibody molecules, in particular to the antigenic or idiotypic determinants being present on the variable regions of the immunoglobulin molecules[1]. Reactions involving idiotypic and anti-idiotypic determinants have
been considered to constitute a maybe major driving force in the actual control of the immune response, where administrations of antigen may only function to perturb an existing equilibrium in a network of idiotypes and anti-
idiotypes[2]. Results which support such a concept in a comparatively direct
manner have been published[3,4,5]. Likewise, it has gradually become clear
over the years that T lymphocytes play a dominating role in the actual control of most specific immune responses. It is thus obvious that before
auto-anti-idiotypic approaches are made to control an immune response one must first scrutinize the actual knowledge of idiotypes on immunocompetent T cells.

Idiotypes on T cells

It is by now well established that immunocompetent T cells express their immunocompetence via a display of antigen-specific, idiotypic receptors[6,7]. Such receptors represent the actual product of the cells as shown via internal labelling procedures in combination with specific fractionation procedures to obtain morphologically and functionally distinct subsets of lymphocytes[8]. Idiotypic markers have thus been found on T lymphocytes involved in the initiation of MLC or Graft-versus-Host reactions[9], on helper T cells as well as their suppressor counterparts[7,10,11,12] and on cytolytic T cells at the effector cell stage[13]. Likewise, it has been possible to demonstrate the presence of idiotypic markers of "B cell type" on helper or suppressor T cell factors [14,15]. It would thus seem safe to conclude that antigen-specific receptors present on competent T lymphocytes or their corresponding specific factors are all expressing idiotypic markers.

Idiotypi is a feature of antigenic markers present on the variable region of immunoglobulin molecules and were initially thought to represent unique features of that particular immunoglobulin molecule[16]. Though this has since been shown to be a too restricted definition idiotypic markers do still serve as useful antigenic determinants in the analysis of the genetics of immunoglobulins. There exist in a simplified concept three kinds of idiotypic groups on a classical immunoglobulin molecule: Those requiring the participation of both heavy and light chain variable regions, those determined by the heavy variable region only and those coded for by the variable region of the light chain. Whereas it is clear from the definition that B cells display all three kind of idiotypes within their possible spectrum of idiotopes it has so far only been possible to define V_H-coded idiotypic determinants on the T cell receptors[8,17]. This has been ascertain in several ways: a) By inheritance of T cell carried idiotypes where in no case detectable contribution of light chain immunoglobulin genes were observed. b) By actual immunization procedures using either heavy chain-light chain Ig hybrid molecules as inducers of anti-idiotypic antisera and where only animals immunized with the "correct" heavy but not light chains produced anti-T cell reactive anti-idiotypic sera. Likewise, immunization with purified heavy chains only but not light chains could be shown to induce auto-anti-idiotypic antibodies reactive with the individuals own T cells with the relevant specificity. c) By in vitro inhibition experiments using as target the idiotypic T cells and where binding of the anti-idiotypic antibodies could be blocked by intact idiotypic IgG antibody molecules and with heavy but not light chains produced from such IgG molecules.

The above data in combination with the preliminary findings as to the biochemistry of the T cell receptor polypeptide composition from several groups
18, 19, 20 have suggested that there may indeed be no conventional light chains
of Ig type in these receptors. It is in fact not clear if the T cell receptor
molecules necessarily is composed of more than one chain of polypeptides at
least in the MLC and CTL reactive T cell compartments. Here, it has been found
in the rat [8,18] that a polypeptide chain slightly larger than 70.000 daltons
may constitute the sole part of the receptor, either in a single or more likely
dimeric stage. However, whereas these receptors so far have failed to express
a content of additional types of polypeptide chains results with antigen-specific
"factors" of T cell origin have indicated the presence of additional chains,
most likely carrying serological markers of MHC type[19,21]. Limited data available from the "factor" work does suggest, however, that the larger chain is the
antigen-specific chain and there is no evidence as yet to suggest that this
additional, hypothetical "MHC" chain is necessary for the creation of antigen-
binding specificity of the T cell receptors[21]. It is also possible to consider
that the occurrance of an additional, self-MHC chain together with the idiotypic
chain may occur for reasons of partial self-reactivity of that chain[22]. Only
additional data from cloned immunocompetent T cells or their corresponding T
cell hybridomas will probably yield enough clearcut results to finally solve
this question. It is, however, already clear that IgT chains do exist, drawing
from the same V_H-gene pool as their corresponding B cell Ig partners. Whether
there exist specific IgT molecules for T cells with varying functions is entirely
possible but no size differences in chains have been noted in biochemical studies
of T cell chains from mixtures of MLC reactive and killer T cells[17,18].

Of practical importance in regulatory reasonings are the findings that it is
possible to selectively kill idiotype-positive T cells with anti-idiotypic antibodies and complement in vitro [8]. Likewise, anti-idiotype reactive T cells with
lytic ability can be shown to occur demonstrating the ability of both humoral
and cellular anti-idiotypic immunity to be able to function in an eliminatory
manner towards idiotypic lymphocytes.

Immune regulation via controlled auto-anti-idiotypic reactions

Several systems exist where s.c. dominating clones of antibodies constitute
a major part of the antibody response against a particular antigenic determinant.
In these situations it has also been possible to achieve a significant depletion of immune responsiveness using anti-idiotypic antibodies[5,23,24,25] sometimes in
combination with antigen resulting in long-lived immune unresponsiveness caused

mainly by suppressor T cells. It is thus possible to induce auto-anti-idiotypic suppressor cells in adult individuals via the administration of anti-idiotypic antibodies where such suppressor T cells may then function for prolonged periods of times in vivo. In most of these systems there will, however, normally with time be a development of clones of B cells lacking the relevant idiotype but with antigen-binding specificity. This would then at a later stage allow an immune response of normal vigour towards the same antigenic determinant (s) but now using antibodies with different idiotypic determinants. It is clear that such sneaking through with time of at least B cells with "new" idiotypes may constitute a major problem when attempting auto-immune regulation using anti-idiotypic immune reactions. Likewise, highly heterogenous immune responses, where many diverse idiotypes are present on the respective responding B and T cells would also be correspondingly more difficult to regulate using anti-idiotypic measures.

We will here mostly deal with studies on immune reactions involving T cells with specificity for allo-MHC antigens. It is possible that such antigens constitute unique target structures for T lymphocytes in the sense that normal helper and killer T cells seem to function in vivo with specific reactivity for self-MHC structures being seen in conjunction with foreign material[26,27]. Our data would, however, indicate that allo-MHC reactive T cells contain self-MHC reactive T cells[22], a finding which has also been suggested by earlier workers in this field[28,29,30]. Thus, it is likely that besides providing information of potential relevance for transplantation immunologists studies on the regulation of such allo-MHC reactive T cells should also tell about the basic functions of normal T cells against "conventional" antigens.

In the systems involving anti-allo-MHC antigens one typical feature is the very high frequency of specific, participating normal responder T cells[31,32,33], amounting to several percent of the total population. When attempting to cause auto-anti-idiotypic immunity against such allo-MHC reactive T cells we were thus initially concerned about the possibility that possible auto-anti-idiotypic T cells may have been eliminated in vivo because of the high concentration of these idiotypes in the normal animals. However, using either idiotype-positive T cell receptor molecules or IgG allo-MHC antibodies in either intact form or as isolated heavy chains as auto-immunogen it was found possible both in rat and mice to induce detectable auto-anti-idiotypic immunity[34,35]. The success in these experiments is, however, irregular and can not be produced in a highly predictable manner indicating our ignorance as to several of the parameters involved in the induction of such auto-anti-idiotypic responses. Still, the results has provided us with significant insight as to how an auto-anti-idiotypic immune reaction can function when being induced in an efficient manner. Table 1 summarizes the findings observed using either as immunogen the indicated material or as an alternative antigen-specific T blasts being obtained in a purified form from MLC:s. As seen, the production of auto-anti-idiotypic immunity in "successful" animals (= we have had many "negative" animals being normal in immune responsiveness to the relevant allo-MHC antigens but so far never encountered animals displaying positively increased responsiveness against these antigens subsequent to attempted auto-anti-idiotypic immunization procedures) can be expressed in a "positive" or active form and a "negative" or eliminatory form.

TABLE 1

A SUMMARY OF RESULTS INDICATING IN A POSITIVE OR NEGATIVE MANNER THE POSSIBILITY OF INDUCING AUTO-ANTI-IDIOTYPIC IMMUNITY IN MICE OR RATS TOWARDS AUTOLOGOUS ALLO-MHC REACTIVE LYMPHOCYTES

Positive evidence in auto-idiotype immunized animals

1. Production of auto-anti-idiotypic antibodies able to

a) In the presence of complement wipe out GvH and MLC reactive T cells, effector killer T cells and idiotype positive lymphocytes.
b) In the absence of complement stain T cells and allow their specific enrichment of elimination via chromatography fractionation.
c) Allow the enumeration of idiotypic T cells in normal or immune populations.
d) In the absence of complement in vitro allow the induction of specific MLC proliferating and cytolytic T cells.

2. Production of auto-anti-idiotype reactive T lymphocytes as shown by

a) Presence of cytolytic T cells with specificity towards autologous idiotype-positive T blasts.
b) Presence of suppressor T cells with the ability to suppress the relevant allo-MHC reactivity in normal syngeneic recipients.

Negative evidence of auto-anti-idiotypic immunity

1. Physical disappearance of idiotype-positive T cells from the lymphoid organs.
2. Specific elimination of T cell reactivity towards the relevant allo-MHC antigens as shown in GvH, MLC, CTL and graft survival experiments.

The active signs of auto-anti-idiotypic immunity involve the production of auto-anti-idiotypic antibodies capable of eliminating specific immune reaction in responder T cells against the relevant antigen[36]. Furthermore, they also include the demonstration of auto-anti-idiotype reactive T cells as shown in direct cytolytic assays against ^{51}Cr-labelled idiotype-positive T cells[37] or as speci-

fic suppressor cells of responsiveness using transfers of cells to normal syngeneic recipients[37]. Negative signs of auto-anti-idiotypic immune reactions
involve the disappearance of idiotype-positive lymphocytes from the circulation
of the immunized individuals coupled with a parallel reduction in specific
allo-MHC reactivity of T cells from such immunized animals[35]. Grafting experiments involving skin grafts or heart grafts have shown that such suppressed
animals may express a highly significant increase in their survival time of
the relevant but not third party MHC grafts[38]. No negative reactions have been
observed in the suppressed animals as to immune complex deposits in their kidneys and the suppression once induced would seem to be quite long lasting. However, several questions remain to be solved and sorted out as discussed in the
next paragraph.

Problems involved in inducing transplantation tolerance via auto-anti-idiotypic
immunity

The dominating problem in the present allo-MHC system in relation to auto-
anti-idiotypes and tolerance induction is the low frequency of success or rather
the highly unpredictable behaviour of the procedure. Whereas several laboratories
have been able to use one of the above described procedures to produce auto-
anti-idiotypic antibodies which can be found to function in the expected manner[35,
39-41] many groups of research workers have found the frequency of success much
too low to be useful both for practical and theoretical studies. One of the
complexities involved is heterogeneity at the level of the allo-MHC antigens,
where both antigens of H-2/Ag-B and Ia type are involved. Here it has been
possible to show that auto-anti-idiotypic immune responses against killer T
cells (specific for H-2K/D) or proliferating T cell (specific for Ia) have
different specificities. To obtain a complete suppression
in a system across a complete MHC haplotype barrier it would
thus be necessary to achieve auto-anti-idiotypic suppression
against several sets of idiotype positive T cells with specificities for diverse alloantigenic determinants.

That such a dichotomy of suppression indeed may occur when attempting to
achieve transplantation tolerance by auto-blast immunization procedures has been
shown when comparing the degree of MLC suppression in relation to the unresponsiveness induced when testing in GvH systems or graft survival. Table 2 gives
some summary results of such a study in the rat allo-MHC system. As can be seen
sizeable variation in reduction may be observed when comparing lymphocytes from
the same auto-immunized donor with regard to MLC and GvH reactivity. Likewise in

TABLE 2

EXAMPLES WHERE UNEQUAL SUPPRESSION OF FUNCTIONS MAY ENSUE FOLLOWING AUTO-BLAST
IMMUNIZATION PROCEDURES. SYSTEM: LEWIS RATS IMMUNIZED WITH LEWIS-ANTI-DA MLC
T BLASTS

A. Comparison of residual GvH, MLC and CTL activities of individual donors
   in % of control)

Rat no	GvH-anti-DA	MLC-anti-DA	CML-anti-DA
1	67	4	27
2	33	3	29
3	0	27	29
4	2	15	29
5	19	15	not done
6	55	22	not done

B. Survival of LewisxDAF$_1$ versus LewisxBNF$_1$ heart grafts (all Lewis
   recipients suppressed to more than 85 % in their anti-DA MLC reactivity

Recipients	LewisxDA F$_1$ grafts	LewisxBN F$_1$ grafts
Auto-anti-DA Lewis	9,10,10,11,12,42, >180,>180,>180,>180	9,9,9,9,10,10,10 10,11 and 11 days
Normal Lewis rats	8,9,9,9,10 days	9,10,10,10,11 days

a group of 10 Lewis rats being auto-immunized with Lewis-anti-DA T blasts and
tested as to expressing more than 85 % specific suppression for MLC activity
towards DA alloantigens only 5 rats expressed highly significant increases in
DA graft survival whilst the other five animals had normal rejection times. It
is thus clear that the measure of MLC unresponsiveness that can be induced in
some auto-blast immunized animals in itself does not constitute a guarantee
that a subsequent in vivo graft of relevant allo-MHC type will be tolerated.

Another problem besides the low and varying frequency of induction of close
to complete MLC unresponsiveness is the requirement for adjuvants. If auto-
blasts are used as immunogen (a likely source of idiotype receptors in possible
clinical situations where anti-idiotypic immunosorbants will be lacking)
suppression via auto-anti-idiotypic reactions have only been noted when using
Freund´s complete adjuvant. Attempts to use Freund´s incomplete adjuvant, glutar-
aldehyde-fixed or alum precipitated blasts have all failed to induce significant anti-idiotypic immunity. In a possible future clinical approach Freund´s
complete adjuvant would be impossible to use for reasons of danger of induction
of myelomas. Here some recent studies using synthetic adjuvants of the dimuramyl
peptide classes have suggested a possible alternative, as some of these deriva-
tives have been found to function in inducing significant auto-anti-idiotypic
immunity in mouse experiments (H.Binz, unpublished observations).

A third problem that we have yet not observed in the present anti-MHC system
but which has been found in several other idiotypic-anti-idiotypic systems have
been the possibility of a stimulating rather than a depressing reaction subsequent to an attempt to induce an anti-idiotypic immune reaction of the suppressive type. Despite the fact that we have not observed such an opposite
reaction in toto it may well be that our immunization approaches have induced
stimultaneous positive versus negative reactions leaving the animals in a
"neutral" stage. We have in fact been able to show that the very same reagent
(auto-anti-idiotypic antibodies) which in the presence of complement may lead
to an efficient selective ripe out of the relevant immunocompetent cells in
the absence of complement may cause the opposite, namely stimulation[13,42].

TABLE 3

C57BL/6-anti-CBA T LYMPHOCYTES OF LYT-1^+2^- and 1^-2^+ PHENOTYPE HAVE DIFFERENT
IDIOTYPES AND FUNCTION. SUMMARY OF FINDINGS

A. Consequences of immunization with MLC blasts
   a) Immunization with syngeneic C57BL-anti-CBA Lyt-1^+2^- blasts will cause
   a specific reduction of anti-CBA reactivity as measured both at MLC and
   CTL levels.
   b) Immunization with the corresponding Lyt-1^-2^+ blasts will cause a selective
   elimination of CTL anti-CBA reactivity.

B. Consequences of absorption of a C57BL-anti-(C57BL-anti-CBA) serum with MLC
   blasts
   a) Absorption with Lyt-1^+2^- will remove the capacity of the antiserum to
   in the presence of complementwipe of MLC anti-CBA activity but will leave
   antibody activity against anti-CBA CTL:s intact.
   b) Absorption with Lyt-1^-2^+ blasts will remove anti-CTL antibodies whilst
   leaving ability to wipe out MLC activity against CBA intact.

C. Consequences of stimulating C57BL normal T cells with CBA spleen cells or
   C57BL-anti-C57BL-anti-CBA idiotypic serum in vitro in absence of complement
   a) Stimulation with CBA spleen cells will lead to proliferation of normal
   C57BL T cells as well as induction of CTL activity against CBA targets.
   Lyt-1^-2^+ T cells will not be stimulated into CTL:s by allogeneic cells.
   b) Stimulation with anti-idiotypic serum will induce proliferation of normal
   C57BL T cells and induction of CTL activity against CBA targets. Lyt-1^-2^+
   T cells will be stimulated into efficient CTL:s against CBA targets.

Table 3 summarizes the finding obtained in the present system using subsets of
T cells as well as whole T cell populations. As can be seen normal T cells
carrying the relevant idiotypic receptors can be stimulated into proliferation
and induction of cytolytic function by anti-idiotypic antibodies in the media
in vitro. It can thus be seen that anti-idiotypic antibodies may constitute
highly potent immunogens as "pure" normal C57BL/6 Lyt-1^-2^+ T cells could be

induced by auto-anti-idiotypic antibodies but not by relevant allogeneic cells to become specific CTL:s . Likewise, the data in table 3 provide direct proof that Ly1$^-$2$^+$ and 1$^+$2$^-$ T cells have different idiotypes. It would thus seem clear that matters such as varying concentrations of complement in the tissue fluids in vivo may cause diametrically opposite results of the presence of the very same reagent, the anti-idiotypic antibodies. Whereas the antibody in the situation of complement being present does function as a complement fixing lytic antibody it will in its absence act like the allo-MHC antigen in a molecular mimicry model and stimulate the allo-MHC reactive lymphocytes into function. It remains to be established whether this finding represents a general "law" of anti-idiotypic antibodies and, if so, if changes in complement concentrations in vivo during critical phases of the induction of auto-anti-idiotypic immunity may lead to predictable changes in the outcome of such an immunization procedure.

Applications of auto-anti-idiotypes: Some general thoughts

Possible uses of auto-anti-idiotypic immune reactions are plentifold. They can as already extensively discussed be used in transplantation immunology either as treatment of the recipient in kidney graft situation whereas in cases of grafting of immunocompetent cells like for bone marrow the donor would have to be treated. Regulation of auto-immune reactions is another possibility as an already existing immune state is not an absolute hinder for auto-anti-idiotypic immunity to function as an abrogatory element[36]. Reactions with anti-idiotypic specificity against tumors of B type has by several groups been shown to result in the rejection or delayed outgrowth of the syngeneic tumors. It is thus possible that auto-anti-idiotypic immune reactions could provide an adjunct in the treatment of such diseases if the number of target cells is kept low enough. Here one should note that several percent of the normal T cell pool carrying idiotypic markers can be eliminated by the auto-anti-idiotypic immunity in the allo-MHC system[6] thus showing that tolerance towards autologous idiotypes may not be induced until quite high levels of idiotypic material are around in the tissues. Finally, anti-idiotypic immunity may in fact extend beyond the normal considerations of the boundaries of the immune system. It is thus known that in the same manner as anti-idiotypic antibodies in the allo-MHC system can function like allo-MHC antigens in the absence of complement so can anti-anti-insulin antibodies mimic insulin in binding and functional properties. A mindboggling possibility of using molecular mimicry in situations where the steric configurations of certain molecules

12

are responsible for biological activity can thus be assumed to exist. If any
of these possibilities will resist the hard challenge of both theoretical and
clinical reality, however, only time will tell.

ACKNOWLEDGEMENTS

   This work was supported by Swedish Cancer Society, by Swiss Cancer Society
135-AK-79, by Swiss National Science Foundation grants 3.688-0.76 and 3.194-0.77,
and by NIH grant AI 13485-03.

REFERENCES

1. Rodkey, L.L. (1974) J. Exp. Med. 139, 712.
2. Jerne, N.K. (1974) Ann. Immunol. (Inst. Pasteur) 125, 373.
3. Oudin, J. and Cazenave, P. (1971) Proc. Nat. Acad. Sci., U.S. 68, 2616.
4. Eichmann, K., Coutinho, A., and Melchers, F. (1977) J. Exp. Med. 146, 1436.
5. Woodland, R. and Cantor, H. (1978) Eur. J. Immunol. 8, 600.
6. Binz, H. and Wigzell, H. (1975) J. Exp. Med. 142, 197.
7. Eichmann, K. and Rajewsky, K. (1975) Eur. J. Immunol. 5, 661.
8. Binz, H. and Wigzell, H. (1977) Progr. Allergy, 23, 154.
9. Binz, H., Lindenmann, J., and Wigzell, H. (1974) J. Exp. Med. 140, 731.
10. Black, S.J., Hämmerling, G.J., Berek, C., Rajewsky, K., and Eichmann, K.
    (1976) J. Exp. Med. 143, 846.
11. Cozensa, H., Julius, M.H., and Augustin, A.A. (1977) Immunol. Rev. 34, 3.
12. Pincus, S.H., Singer, A., Hodes, R.J., and Dickler, H.B. (1979) Cells of
    Immunoglobulin Synthesis,ed. B. Pernis and H. Vogel, Acad. Press, in press.
13. Binz, H., Frischknecht, H., Shen, F.W., and Wigzell, H. (1979) J.Exp. Med.
    149, 910.
14. Mozes, E. (1978) Ir genes and Ia antigens, ed. H.O. McDevitt, Acad. Press,
    p. 475.
15. Kontiainen, S., Simpson. E., Bohrer, E., Beverly, P., Herzenberg, L.A.,
    Fitzpatrick, W.C., Vogt, P., Torano, A., McKenzie, I.F.C., and Feldman, M.
    (1978) Nature, 274, 477.
16. Oudin, J. (1974) Ann. Immunol. (Inst. Pasteur), 125, 309.
17. Eichmann, K. (1978) Adv. Immunol. 28, 195.
18. Binz, H. and Wigzell, H. (1975) Scand. J. Immunol. 4, 591.
19. Theze, J., Kapp, J.A. and Benacerraf, B. (1977) J. Exp. Med. 145, 839.
20. Krawinkel, U., Cramer, M., Imanishi-Kari, T., Jack, R,S., Rajewsky, K.,
    and Mäkelä, O. (1977) Eur. J. Immunol. 7, 566.
21. Taussig, M.J. and Holliman, A. (1979) Nature, 277, 308.
22. Binz, H., Frischknecht, H., Mercilli, C., Dunst, S., and Wigzell, H. (1979)
    submitted for publication.
23. Hart, D.A., Wang, A.L., Pawlek, L.L., and Nisonoff, A. (1972) J. Exp. Med.
    135, 1293.
24. Cozensa, H. and Köhler, H. (1972) Proc. Nat. Acad. Sci., USA, 69, 2701.
25. Eichmann, K. (1974) Eur. J. Immunol. 4, 296.
26. Paul, W.E., Shevach, E.M., Thomas, D.W., Pickerel, S.F., and Rosenthal, A.S.
    (1976) Cold Spring Harbor Symp. Quant. Biol., 41, 571.
27. Zinkernagel, R.M. and Doherty, P.C. (1975) J. Exp. Med. 141, 1427.
28. Shearer, G.M. and Schmitt-Verhulst, A.M. (1977) Adv. Immunol. 25, 55.
29. Bevan, M. (1977) Proc. Nat. Acad. Sci., USA, 74, 2094.
30. Finberg, R., Burakoff, S.J., Cantor, H., and Benacerraf, B. (1978)
    Prof. Nat. Acad. Sci., USA, 75, 5145.

31. Wilson, D.W., Blyth, J.L., and Nowell, P.C. (1968). J. Exp. Med. 128, 1157.
32. Ford, W.L., Simmonds, S.J., and Atkins, R.C. (1975) J. Exp. Med. 141, 681.
33. Binz, H., Bächi, T., Wigzell, H., Ramseier, H., and Lindenmann, J. (1975) Proc. Nat. Acad. Sci., USA, 72, 3210.
34. Binz, H. and Wigzell, H. (1976) J. Exp. Med. 144, 1438.
35. Andersson, L.C., Binz, H., and Wigzell, H. (1976) Nature, 264, 778.
36. Aguet, M., Andersson, L.C., Andersson, R., Wight, E., Binz, H., and Wigzell, H. (1978) J. Exp. Med. 147, 51.
37. Binz, H. and Wigzell, H. (1978) J. Exp. Med. 147, 63.
38. Binz, H. and Wigzell, H. (1979) Transplant. Proc. 11, 914.
39. Krammer, P.H. (1978) J. Exp. Med. 147, 25.
40. Braun, M. and Saal, F. (1977) Cell. Immunol. 30, 254.
41. Sell, K.W., Ahmed, A., Strong, D.M., Goldman, M.H., Leapman, S.B., Smith, A.H., and Grawith, K. (1979) Transplant. Proc. 11, 704.
42. Frischknecht, H., Binz, H., and Wigzell, H. (1978) J. Exp. Med. 147, 500.
43. Sege, K. and Peterson, P. (1978) Proc. Nat. Acad. Sci., USA, 75, 2443.

14

DISCUSSION

LAWTON: How many clones of self-reactive T cells do you predict in terms of their identity with allo-reactives?

WIGZELL: I would say it is actually up to people to prove that helper T cells and killer T cells are not all self-MHC-restricted or self-MHC-reactive. In other words a very high number, the exact figures I couldn't tell you. I think that the suppressor T cell stories with regard to the binding specificity would suggest that the suppressor T cells may not express the same degree of obsession with regard to self-MHC reactivity. So if you asked about the suppressor T cells with regard to self-MHC reactivity in clones, I would say they may be quite limited, but the helper killer T cells very high in number.

CHILLER: In the Binz experiment where you get cross-reactivity with self antigen, why do you think that cross-reactivity is limited to just the H-2I gene product rather than say the equivalent of H-2K and H-2D?

WIGZELL: I think that's an artifact. I think that the anti-idiotypic antiserum we used to select for the T cell receptor was biased in the sense that it selected predominantly for anti-Ia reactive T cell receptors and a minority was for anti-A or B. My prediction would be that if we selected for anti-A or B reactive T cells we would see these components.

CHILLER: There is no reason why initially that anti-idiotype should have been thought to be important here.

WIGZELL: We simply don't know that with the antiserum used, but there is one reason why it is biased: because the majority of the T cell receptors in the population we extracted are anti-Ia reactive. So it could be a function at the level of both the anti-idiotypic serum and the T cell receptor used for making immune absorbent.

DELOVITCH: I'd like to ask two related questions, one is of a speculative nature, but first - do you feel that there is really a qualitative difference between the Ly-1 and Ly-2,3 idiotypic determinants in that they really do not share determinants on T cell sub-populations?

WIGZELL: There exists data in the literature which would suggest that idiotypes of similar nature may be expressed on Ly-1 and Ly-2 positive cells in using some soluble antigens although these results have never shown directly the presence of the idiotypes on the cells. It has been shown by indirect functional means. I am referring to the work of Eichmann and Rajewsky.

DELOVITCH: And secondly, do you feel that the Ly-1 and Ly-2,3 cells each synthesize the idiotypic determinants that they express, and is this synthesis regulated by the MHC receptors that they each bear?

WIGZELL: It is like this. The specificity of the T cell receptor is in part selected for, of course, by the thymic epithelium. In other words if you introduce the thymic graft of another MHC you would select for that reactivity. However, at the same time you could show that the T cells that come out of such a chimera will fail to react against itself in a strong allo-activity which, of course, must mean that they are actually eliminating also in a parallel way, allo-reactive like receptors for self. So in that way they are influenced, but I don't think I could answer whether, let's say, the Ly-1 or the Ly-2 cells directly would be influenced by selected groups of receptors because they would display different MHC components on the surface. That's possible but has no strong evidence for it. Cytotoxic T cells, you know, can express Ia.

ABDOU: Is there any direct solid evidence that, in a spontaneous auto-immune state you fail to detect auto-anti-idiotype and the opposite in a normal state?

WIGZELL: I would answer it in another way. Whenever you have induced a conventional immune response and you really look for it, you should normally detect auto-anti-idiotypic antibodies or auto-anti-idiotypic reactive cells, but the relative distribution of the idiotype-positive versus the anti-idiotypic-positive factors, should vary with time of the immune response.

Published 1979 by Elsevier North Holland, Inc.
Singhal, Sinclair, Stiller, eds. Aging and Immunity

COMMUNICATION AMONG IMMUNOLOGIC CELLS AND AUTOIMMUNITY

HARVEY CANTOR[+] AND RICHARD K. GERSHON[++]
[+]Harvard Medical School/Farber Cancer Institute, 44 Binney Street, Boston, MA
02115; [++]Director, Laboratory of Immunology, Howard Hughes Medical Institute,
Yale University Medical Center, 310 Cedar Street, New Haven, CT 06510

After a certain optimal age, the immune system begins to break down. This
is not surprising since in keeping with the general deterioration of tissues
and organ systems associated with senescence. What strikes some people as
paradoxical is that this decline is often accompanied by an increase in autoantibody production. However, with the general recognition in the past few
years that there are sets of T cells which act to suppress the immune response,
a hypothesis linking a selective decline of T-cell function with increasing
autoantibody production has been suggested. Support for this thesis has been
found in the observation that athymic nude mice have more autoantibodies
than do their littermate controls which have a thymus[1] and that several inbred
strains that spontaneously develop autoimmune disease harbor defects in the
ability of T-cell sets to communicate with one another.

The alternative idea holds that, with age, "forbidden" clones arise and
react against the host. This latter point is based on the idea that each
immunological cell carries at its membrane surface a "receptor" capable of
binding to particular chemical determinants or antigen. Exposure of immunological cells to molecules that fit well with its receptors induces these
cells to multiply rapidly and to give rise to "clones" of thousands of daughter
cells, each marked by the same surface receptor. According to this idea,
the intensity, duration and type of immune response depends mainly on the
numbers of clones that might be mobilized by a particular antigen. Absence
of severe immune reactions to an individual's own tissues, according to this
view, depends on elimination, at birth, of immunologic cells carrying receptors
that might bind to "self" molecules. According to this notion, occasional
immunologic reactions against "self" are due to renegade cells carrying "forbidden" receptors that have somehow escaped elimination during development of
the immune system.

The purpose of this article is to summarize experimental evidence supporting
a different view of the immune system: that immune reactions are primarily
determined by messages passed among different types of immunologic cells that

regulate the intensity and duration of an immune reaction. Each cellular member of this communication network expresses characteristic surface markers associated with its genetically assigned physiologic function. So far, three categories, or types have been examined--categorized as inducer cells, regulatory cells and effector cells. Communication among these immunologic cell sets determines not only the intensity and type of immune response after perturbation of the system by foreign materials; in addition, it may be essential for preventing autoimmune reactions and associated diseases.

The peripheral T-cell pool contains at least three separate T-cell sets. We refer to them in shorthand as the Ly123 set, the Ly1 set, and the Ly23 set. They compose respectively 50%, 30% and approximately 5-10% of the peripheral T-cell pool.[2] These findings indicate that, according to the criterion of selective expression of gene products on the cell surface, the T-cell pool is divisible into at least three groups of cells, each following a different set of genetic instruction. The question then becomes whether these individual differentiative programs include information that decides what the function of each T-cell set should be, as judged by analysis of the functional activity of these sets in vitro and in vivo. These studies have defined three major populations of immunologic cells.

1) Inducer Cells. Evidence to date indicates that cells of the Ly1 set are genetically programmed to help or amplify the activity of other cells after stimulation by antigen. Cells of this set are most aptly termed inducer cells since they will induce or activate other effector cell sets to fulfill their respective genetic programs: Ly1 cells induce B cells to secrete antibody[2,3]; they induce macrophages and monocytes (and other inflammatory leukocytes) to participate in delayed-type hypersensitivity responses;[4] they can, under appropriate circumstances, induce precursors of killer cells to differentiate to killer-effector cells.[3] Ly1 cells also induce a set of resting, non-immune T cells to generate potent feedback inhibitory activity.[5-7] Analysis of isolated Ly1 inducer cells from non-immune donors indicates that these cells are already programmed for helper/inducer function before overt immunization with antigen; this function is independent of the ability of Ly1 inducer cells to interact with antigen.[8] The ability of Ly1 cells to induce other cell sets to fulfill their respective genetic programs is not limited to cells of the immunologic system: they also induce osteoclasts to resorb bone and CFU to differentiate into mature erythroid elements (Glimcher, Shen and Cantor, ms. in preparation).

2) <u>Mature Cytotoxic and Suppressor Cells</u>. By contrast, cells of the Ly23 set are specially equipped to develop both alloreactive cytotoxic activity as well as to suppress both humoral and cell-mediated immune responses following immunization.[2,3,9-11] Whether cytotoxicity and antigen-induced suppression are two manifestations of one genetic program or whether they represent the phenotype of two separate genetic programs is not yet clearly established. However, at least some cells in the Ly23 suppressor set express an antigen coded for in the I-J subregion of the MHC;[12] this gene product has not been found on killer cells or their precursors. This suggests that although similar in many characteristics, mature killer and suppressor cells are separable. That specific suppression is not due solely to cytotoxic elimination of relevant clones of cells is also consistent with the following observation: after isolation of suppressed cells in mice depleted of a T-cell system (by thymectomy, lethal irradiation and repopulation with T-cell depleted bone marrow cells) a return of antigen reactivity of the previously functionally inert suppressed cells occurred within 3-6 weeks.[13]

3) <u>Regulatory Cells</u>. Cells of the Ly123 phenotype have been the least well-defined of the various T-cell sets. It is likely that at least some Ly123 cells represent a store of receptor-positive intermediary cells that regulate the supply and function of more mature Ly1 and Ly23 cells. This view is based in part on experiments showing that (a) after stimulation with chemically-altered syngeneic cells, some Ly123 cells give rise to Ly23 progeny[8,14] and (b) experiments indicating that purified populations of Ly123 cells can give rise to Ly1 cells after polyclonal activation by Concanavalin A and antigen-specific helper cells after in vitro stimulation with Strep A (McVay-Boudreau, Shen and Cantor; McDougal and Shen, ms. in preparation). The notion that at least a portion of Ly123 cells represents a precursor pool is also supported by earlier observations that cells of the Ly123 subclass are detectable in the spleens of mice within the first week of life, while both Ly1 and Ly23 cells do not reach maximal numbers until adult life (8-12 wks of age).[2] Development of mature, functional Ly1 cells from gradient purified "post-thymic" Ly123 precursors, using chromosomally marked cells also supports this view.[15]

On the other hand, we have not yet established whether some Ly123 cells may exert immunoregulatory effects without giving rise to mature Ly1 or Ly23 progeny. It is of more than theoretical interest to identify a stable, fully differentiated Ly123 effector cell set which does not have a precursor function. In this regard, we must find out if, during the differentiative history of an Ly123 precursor cell, expression of a new genetic program responsible for functional potential of the cell ("luxury genes") involves simultaneous acquisition of a new function and surface phenotype or whether the following might ensue: $Ly1^+23^+$ precursor → expression of a new genetic program → immature $Ly1^+23^+$ inducer → maturation leading to more efficient expression of the newly-activated gene program → $Ly1^+23^-$ inducer.

DEFINITION OF FEEDBACK INHIBITION AMONG IMMUNOLOGIC CELLS

Antigen-stimulated Ly1 cells,[5-7] or supernatants of activated Ly1 cells (ms. in preparation), in addition to inducing B cells to secrete antibody can induce or activate resting Ly123 cells to develop profound feedback inhibitory activity. The term "feedback" is used because (a) the degree of suppressive activity exerted by a fixed number of non-immune Ly123 cells increases in direct proportion to the numbers of antigen-activated Ly1 inducer cells and (b) one target of suppression is the inducer cell itself. This Ly1:Ly123 interaction has also been shown to govern the duration and intensity of immune reactions in vivo.[6] These findings indicate that, like the formation of antibody, the generation of immunologic suppression after stimulation by antigen is not an autonomous function; both are markedly dependent on induction by Ly1 cells. Although at least a portion of the suppressive effects of activated Ly123 cells reflects an Ly123→Ly23 differentiative step, whether all suppressive activity reflects induction of an Ly123→Ly23 differentiative step is not yet established.

Analysis of the role of these T-T interactions in the immune response to antigen in vitro and in vivo has suggested that the following events ensue after stimulation of the immune system by foreign materials: activated antigen-specific Ly1 cells induce B cells to form antibody and also induce resting Ly123 cells to suppress T-inducer cell activity. Reduction in T-inducer activity is accompanied by decreased induction of B cells as well as progressively decreasing induction of resting Ly123 cells; the net result is progressive decrease in both antibody secretion and suppressor cell formation.

SEPARATION OF SETS OF INDUCER CELLS BY ANTI-Qal SERA

The ability of Ly1 inducer cells to activate various effector cell systems on the one hand, as well as suppressive systems on the other, plays a pivotal role in the type and intensity of an antibody response. It was therefore important to find out whether cells of the Ly1 set that induce suppressive activity represented a specialized subgroup of Ly1 cells that differed from cells that, for example, induced B cells to produce antibody. A direct approach to this question came from the finding that a portion of Ly1 cells also express a newly-defined antigen called Qa1[16,17] coded for by genes that map between H2-D and the TL locus of the mouse. Studies of Ly1:Qa1$^+$ cells (which represent about 60% of Ly1 cells) have shown that these cells are responsible for induction of Ly123 cells to exert feedback inhibition, and that isolated Ly1:Qa1$^-$ cells do <u>not</u> induce detectable suppression.[7] In addition, these studies show that signals from both Ly1:Qa1$^+$ and Ly1:Qa1$^-$ cells are required for optimal formation of antibody by B cells. Thus, the ability of antigenic determinants to induce a detectable antibody response may depend largely on the ratio of Ly1:Qa1$^+$ AND Ly1:Qa1$^-$ T-cell clones that either bear receptors for that determinant or are preferentially stimulated by it.

In sum, the experiments discussed above have established several principles. First, the genetic program for a single differentiated set of cells, in this case immunologic cells, combines information coding for a unique pattern of cell-surface glycoproteins and a particular physiologic function. Second, the majority of immunologic cells are not effector cells poised to respond to foreign antigen, but regulatory cells that respond to signals or messages generated from within the immune system itself. Third, detectable immune responses reflect perturbations of a homeostatically balanced system, re-sulting from activation of cells of the inducer system by antigen.

There are, so far, several examples of disorders of this immunoregulatory circuit; NZB mice spontaneously develop an autoimmune disorder characterized by the production of a variety of autoantibodies and a clinical syndrome resembling human systemic lupus erythematosis. The major T-cell deficit of NZB mice is the absence of malfunction of an Ly123 T-cell set responsible for feedback regulation.[6]

Another recently described mutant mouse strain, MRL,[18] expresses an auto-immune disorder which is similar to, but more severe than, the one expressed in the NZB strain. In addition, MRL mice have a severe lymphoproliferative syndrome which principally affects Ly1 cells in peripheral lymph nodes. The immunoregulatory deficit in MRL mice maps to a completely different site in the suppressor circuit than does the one in NZB mice.[19] T cells from the MRL mouse exert <u>excessive</u> amounts of Ly123 dependent suppressor activity (after induction by Ly1 cells of the non-mutant congenic partner strain). However,

22

Ly1 cells from MRL mice <u>are</u> <u>not</u> <u>sensitive</u> to suppressor signals generated by
Ly123 feedback suppressor cells. Thus, although NZB and MRL mice have
different deficits in their immunoregulatory circuits, they have a common
immunologic disorder: inability to inhibit Ly1 inducer/helper cells, loss of
normal immunoregulation, and high levels of autoimmune antibodies.

We have not as yet determined the frequency of different T-cell sets in
autoimmune BXSB mouse strain, but initial experiments suggest that they have
a different immunoregulatory defect than the NZB and MRL. Their principle
lesion here appears to be a failure of Ly1 cells to <u>induce</u> Ly123 cells to
generate inhibitory activity. The three different lesions are illustrated
in Figure 1.

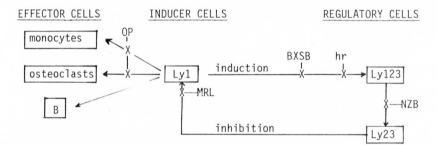

Fig. 1. Inbred and mutant mouse strains developing auto-immune disorders:
          Localization of lesion within an immunoregulatory circuit.

GENETIC BASIS OF COMMUNICATION WITHIN REGULATORY T-CELL CIRCUITS

How do Ly1:Qal$^+$ inducer cells communicate with "acceptor" regulatory
T cells? Limiting doses of inducer cells that have been stimulated by sheep
erythrocytes preferentially induce suppression of the in vitro response to
that antigen and do not induce suppression to a second (horse or chicken)
erythrocyte antigen, even when both antigens are present in cell culture (data
to be published).

These observations suggest that communication between Ly1:Qal$^+$ cells and
resting Ly123:Qal$^+$ T cells can be highly specific. One explanation for this
specificity is that both inducer and effector cells bear receptors specific
for the antigen and are brought into association by an "antigen bridge" (similar to the mechanism postulated for T-B interactions). Another possibility
which could account for both specificity and cross reactivity is that resting
T cells bear receptors specific for idiotypic (and/or "anti-idiotypic")
determinants carried on the Ly1 inducer population.

To determine whether Ly1:Qa1[+] induction of T-acceptor cells (phenotype Ly123[+]Qa1[+]) to exert substantial suppressive effects might be regulated by genes linked to the immunoglobulin heavy chain (Ig locus), Ly1 cells and non-immune T-acceptor cells were obtained from either BALB/c or CB-20 donors, a congenic pair of inbred mice differing only at a cluster of genes linked to the Ig locus.[20] We found that (Table I) (a) Ly1 cells induced suppression in cultures containing non-immune T + B cells from donors identical at the Ig locus and (b) Ly1 cells did <u>not</u> induce suppression in cultures containing T cells from donors that differed at the Ig locus and B cells from donors identical at the Ig locus. These results indicate that the two T-cell sets use gene products linked to the Ig locus to effectively interact with each other.

TABLE I

GENES LINKED TO Ig LOCUS CONTROL COMMUNICATION BETWEEN INDUCER AND ACCEPTOR T CELLS

Source of 10^5 SRBC-stimulated Ly1 cells	Source of non-immune T cells	Identity at Ig between Ly1 cells and T cells	Suppression (%)
a)* --	CB-20	yes	Standard*
CB-20	CB-20		92
--	BALB/c	no	Standard
CB-20	BALB/c		2
b)** --	BALB/c	yes	Standard**
BALB/c	BALB/c		98
--	CB-20	no	Standard
BALB/c	CB-20		0

*Source of B cells CB-20. Mean anti-SRBC PFC responses/10^6 cells of SRBC-stimulated cultures containing CB-20 or BALB/c T cells = 833±160; mean PFC responses of cultures containing purified B cells ± SRBC = 0.

**Source of B cells BALB/c. Mean anti-SRBC PFC response/10^6 cells of SRBC-stimulated cultures containing CB-20 or BALB/c T cells = 713±110; mean PFC responses of cultures containing purified B cells ± SRBC = 0.

The BAB.14 inbred congenic mouse strain, like the CB-20 congenic strain, expresses IgCH gene products of the C57BL/Ka (as defined by anti-allotypic antisera). However, unlike the CB-20 strain, BAB.14 expresses at least some V_H products of the BALB/c, and is thought to represent a recombinant carrying B6 C_H genes and (mainly) BALB/c V_H genes.[21] We therefore asked whether BAB.14

24

TABLE II

GENES CODING FOR THE CONSTANT PORTION OF THE Ig HEAVY CHAIN <u>DO</u> <u>NOT</u>
GOVERN REGULATORY T-T INTERACTIONS

Source of 10^5 SRBC-stimulated Lyl cells	Source of non-immune T cells in SRBC-stimulated cultures	Suppression* (%)
a) BALB/c	BALB/c	77
BALB/c	CB-20	0
BALB/c	BAB.14	98
b) CB-20	BALB/c	0
CB-20	CB-20	100
CB-20	BAB.14	14
c) BAB.14	BALB/c	68
BAB.14	CB-20	0
BAB.14	BAB.14	100

*
Source of B cells in all SRBC-stimulated cultures was BAB.14. Anti-SRBC
PFC/10^6 cells in cultures containing BALB/c T, CB-20 T or BAB.14 non-immune
T cells was 480±30, 460±40 and 570±60, respectively. Anti-SRBC PFC/10^6 cells
in cultures containing SRBC + BAB.14 purified B cells = 0.

For these and other reasons, we think that Ig-linked genes that govern
communication between inducer and acceptor regulatory T cells code for or control expression of V_H-like surface structures. If indeed these gene products
are responsible for accurate communication among cells that act to regulate
the production of autoantibody, it follows that accumulation of genetic
"mistakes" resulting in inappropriate expression of these V_H structures on
T-cell sets might lead to increasingly dangerous immunologic misunderstandings,
a loss of precise control over effector cell activity, and autoimmune reactions.
Moreover, since these products, as well as MHC-linked gene products ("Ir genes")
also influence communication among immunological cells, it is likely that
immunologic misunderstandings analogous to those that contribute to Ir gene
defects and immunologic diseases will also be associated with particular
Ig-linked polymorphic determinants. It is therefore essential to find out
whether inducer:acceptor communication governed by Ig-linked gene products is

T cells would interact with BALB/c T cells, CB-20 T cells or both. We found
that small numbers of SRBC-stimulated BALB/c Lyl cells induced substantial
(80-90%) suppression of the anti-SRBC response in cultures containing BALB/c
or BAB.14 non-immune T cells, but not in cultures containing CB-20 T cells.
These findings indicate that identity at Ig C_H locus, per se, does not allow
efficient T-T interactions. This is further shown by the finding that CB-20
Lyl cells induced high levels of suppression in cultures containing CB-20
non-immune T cells but not BALB/c or BAB.14 non-immune T cells. Taken together,
these findings indicate that identity at the Ig locus is required for efficient
inducer:acceptor T cell communication and this does not reflect Ig C_H genes
per se. In addition, it shows that this genetically restricted communication
between T-cell sets is independent of the Ig-phenotype of B cells in the assay
cultures. Thus, Ig restricted T-T communication reflects gene products
intrinsic to the relevant T-cell sets and cannot be accounted for by, for
example, passively acquired Ig-linked products produced by B cells in assay
cultures.

The experiments of Binz and Wigzell[22] and of Eichmann, Rajewsky and their
colleagues[23] have indicated that at least some sets of T cells carry at their
membrane surface products of Ig linked genes. These molecules resemble the
variable portion of immunoglobulin heavy (V_H) chains and may permit highly
specific cell interactions that regulate the production of antibodies carrying
well-defined idiotypic markers.[24,25] Possibly, Lyl-induction of resting
T cells to generate specific T suppression is governed by analogous or
identical Ig-linked gene products.

Genes coding for minor histocompatibility antigens may also be linked to
the Ig locus[26,27] and therefore represent additional candidates that may
participate in interactions between inducer and acceptor T cells. If so,
their influence cannot be attributed to standard "allogeneic effects"[28,29]
that might override suppression, since mixtures of T and B cells (Table I) or
immune Lyl cells and B cells (Table II) that differ at the Ig locus do not
stimulate positive allogeneic effects in vitro. Further, the results presented in Table II show that the structures that govern this interaction are
not expressed on B cells. One intriguing explanation for this observation
is that genes coding for V_H-like structures expressed on T cells are not
identical to those controlling expression of V_H structures on B lymphocytes.
However, there are other equally plausible explanations for this observation
and further analysis is necessary to address this point directly.

also influenced by MHC gene products. If so, the degree of correlation between some human "autoimmune" diseases and genetic polymorphisms might be improved considerably by <u>coordinate</u> analysis of both MHC and Ig haplotypes of relevant patient populations.

It is too early to say with any certainty whether these approaches will be fruitful. Speculations abound, but the delineation of the molecular basis of regulation by immunologic cell sets should allow answers to some of these questions within the next few years. We offer one prediction: with age there will be as much decline of T-cell function as there is in the decline of the second organ system that expresses the Thy1 antigen and is usually capable of complex interactions among component cells.

REFERENCES

1. Morse, H. C., III, Steinberg, A. D., Vchur, P. H. and Reed, N. D. (1974) J. Immunol. 113:688.
2. Cantor, H. and Boyse, E. A. (1975) J. Exp. Med. 141:1376.
3. Cantor, H. and Boyse, E. A. (1977) Cold Spring Harbor Symposium on Quantitative Biology 41:23.
4. Huber, B., Devinsky, O., Gershon, R. K. and Cantor, H. (1976) J. Exp. Med. 143:1534.
5. Eardley, D. D., Hugenberger, J., McVay-Boudreau, L., Shen, F. W., Gershon, R. K. and Cantor, H. (1978) J. Exp. Med. 147:1106.
6. Cantor, H., McVay-Boudreau, L., Hugenberger, J., Naidorf, K., Shen, F. W. and Gershon, R. K. (1978) J. Exp. Med. 147:1116.
7. Cantor, H., Hugenberger, J., McVay-Boudreau, L., Eardley, D. D., Kemp, J., Shen, F. W. and Gershon, R. K. (1978) J. Exp. Med. 148:871.
8. Cantor, H. and Asofsky, R. (1970) J. Exp. Med. 131:235.
9. Shen, F. W., Boyse, E. A. and Cantor, H. (1975) Immunogenetics 2:591.
10. Cantor, H., Shen, F. W. and Boyse, E. A. (1976) J. Exp. Med. 143:1391.
11. Jandinski, J., Cantor, H., Tadakuma, T., Peavy, D. L., and Pierce, C. W. (1976) J. Exp. Med. 143:1382.
12. Murphy, D. B. (1978) Springer Seminars in Immunopathology 1:111.
13. Gershon, R. K. (1974) Contemp. Topics Immunobiol. 3:1.
14. Finberg, R., Burakoff, S. J., Cantor, H. and Benacerraf, B. (1978) Proc. Natl. Acad. Sci. USA 75:5145.
15. Stutman, O. (1978) Immunol. Rev. 42:138.
16. Stanton, T. H. and Boyse, E. A. (1976) Immunogenetics 3:525.
17. Flaherty, L. (1976) Immunogenetics 3:533.
18. Murphy, E. D. and Roths, J. B. (1978) Proc. of 16th Internat. Cong. Hematol. Excerpta Medica, Amsterdam (in press).
19. Gershon, R. K., Horowitz, M., Kemp, J. D., Murphy, D. B. and Murphy, E. D. (1978) In: Genetic Control of Autoimmune Disease, N.R. Rose, P. E. Bigazzi and N. L. Warner, eds. Elsevier, North Holland.
20. Mage, R., Lieberman, R., Potter, M., and Terry, W. D. (1973) In: The Antigens 1, Academic Press, New York-London, p. 299.
21. Herzenberg, L. A. and Herzenberg, L. A. (1977) In: Handbook of Experimental Immunology, Oxford, Blackwell Scientific Pub.

22. Binz, H. and Wigzell, H.   (1977)   Cold Spring Harbor Symposia on Quant. Biol. Vol. 41, p. 275.
23. Karwinkel, U., Cramer, M., Berek, C., Hammerling, G., Black, S. J., Rajewsky, K. and Eichmann, K.   (1977)   Cold Spring Harbor Synposia on Quant. Biol. Vol. 41, p. 285.
24. Woodland, R. T. and Cantor, H.   (1978)   Eur. J. Immunol. 8:600.
25. Eichmann, K., Falk, I. and Rajewsky, K.   (1978)   Eur. J. Immunol. (in press).
26. Riblet, R. and Congleton, C.   (1977) Immunogenetics 5:511.
27. Rolink, T., Eichmann, K. and Simon, M. M.   (1979)   Immunogenetics (in press).
28. Katz, D. H. and Benacerraf, B.   (1975)   Transplant. Rev. 22:175.
29. Paul, W. E. and Benacerraf, B.   (1977)   Science 195:1293.

DISCUSSION

CUNNINGHAM: One thing that puzzles me is that I think of idiotype control
as being individual-specific even within the genetic identity of an inbred
strain.   I don't know if I fully understood the last part of your talk, but
you seemed to be saying there was control directed against V_H framework
regions that would be shared between individuals within one allotypically
marked strain.   What about the individuality of idiotype control?

CANTOR: It may be that there are indeed various limited numbers of V_H gene
products at the level of the T cell as opposed to B cell product and that the
interactions between these T cells may be controlled by certain immunodominant
determinants on, for example, framework specificities as well as "hypervariable"
specificities.   The other possibility is that we are dealing not with
idiotypes per se but perhaps of markers or interaction molecules - interaction
determinants that are associated with V_H structures and coded for by genes
which are linked to but not identical to the genes that code for the variable
portion of the heavy chain on immunoglobulin.   One thing that is becoming
more and more clear from the studies of Sercarz and others is that the net T
cell response to some rather complex antigens depends on a very few, perhaps
in some cases even one singular, determinant and that may account in part for
this particular observation.   We find for example that all the suppressive
T cells, and this is work done in collaboration with Diane Eardley and Dick
Gershon and part of it has been published, as judged by cell surface phenotype
and function will bind to sheep erythrocytes whereas helper cells will not.
All the binding can be inhibited by one of many of the sheep erythrocyte
proteins and so it may be for this particular system the dominant epitope
recognized on this very complex cell is in control of the immune system since
it may in turn control the generation of suppressor cells.

DELOVITCH: In autoimmune mice, in particular, the MRL mutants - do you
find normal numbers of Ly-1 positive cells and if so are they all I-J positive
or are they inducible by things like auto-anti-idiotype and so on?

CANTOR: Unfortunately, the question is a bit more complicated than it
seems on the face of it.   In the lymph nodes, where this lymphoproliferative
disorder occurs, virtually all the cells that we type as Thy-1 positive are
$Ly-1^+ 2^-$.   They cannot be typed by Qa-1.   I believe that Don Murphy is
typing them for I-J and I don't know the results.   I might mention that this
type of Ly-1 cell, that appears to be resistant to suppressive signals, is
also seen very frequently when one attempts to grow Ly-1 clones in culture.
Perhaps this sort of thing is selected for and one winds up with cells of
this phenotype and perhaps, in some respects, certain clones of Ly-1 cells
might lose susceptibility to suppression which seems to be a global thing in
the MRL mouse but in the normal course of immunologic events this might, if it
were done on a clonal basis, signify, for example, a very good memory response
which is difficult to suppress.

SPECULATION ON THE MECHANICS OF B CELL CLONAL DIVERSIFICATION

Alexander Lawton
Cellular Immunobiology Unit, Lurleen B. Wallace Tumor Institute, Departments
of Pediatrics and Microbiology, University of Alabama in Birmingham,
Birmingham, Alabama 35294

The recent development of techniques for identifying, isolating, and
cloning fragments of DNA containing specific structural genes has provided a
wealth of new information relevant to the problem of generation of B cell
clonal diversity. In this essay I will attempt to integrate some of this
biochemical information with aspects of the ontogenetic development of B
cells. Few questions will be answered; it is hoped that some issues for
future research may be raised.

CELLULAR LOCUS FOR GENERATION OF DIVERSITY

Debate on mechanisms of generation of diversity of antibodies has been
focussed almost exclusively on diversity of genes. The equally fascinating and
complex problem of the relationship of B-cell differentiation to expression of
diversity has received relatively little attention. The estimates of numbers
of inherited V genes made by the proponents of somatic mutation theories and of
the germ line theory have been steadily converging towards a figure of several
hundred for the kappa light chain family[1]. It has recently been directly
demonstrated that a mouse V_{κ} subgroup is represented by a family of closely
related germ line genes coding for positions 1-97, rather than a single germ
line gene per subgroup[2]. Moreover, the existence of additional genes (J
genes) coding the C-terminal segments of light chain V regions has been
discovered[3]. The possibility of individual V genes combining with any of
several J genes at the DNA level may substantially increase diversity. The
thrust of this new data is that antibody diversity may be accounted for on the
basis of inherited V and J genes. While somatic mutations or other types of
rearrangements may well contribute to diversity, there is currently no need to
postulate special rates or mechanisms for mutations.

It is reasonable to assume that the number of possible different antibody
specificities which may be generated from germ line genes is the product of the
number of V_L and of V_H genes. Each of these numbers may be further multiplied
by the number of J genes[3]. Utilization of this potential requires that each

combination of V_H and V_L comes to be expressed as the surface immunoglobulin receptor for a separate clone of lymphocytes. The question of how this
gene expression is regulated is at least as complex and challenging as was the
question of how the genetic diversity was initially created.

The ontogenetic expression of immunoglobulin diversity appears to be a
highly ordered process. The development of B lymphocytes in mammals and birds
begins at a precise time during gestation. The rate of increase in numbers of
B lymphocytes in mice is genetically regulated, such that variations between
individuals of the same inbred strain are very small, while significant differences exist between outbred individual mice or between different strains[4].
Consistent with genetic rather than environmental regulation of the ontogenetic
development of B cells is the lack of difference between germ free and conventional mice[5].

Klinman and his colleagues have used a type of limiting dilution assay to
study the development of individual precursor B lymphocytes. In BALB/c mice
they have observed a highly ordered developmental sequence of certain clonotypes. There are 3 distinct clonotypes, identified by their isoelectrofocusing
spectra, of precursors for the haptens DNP and TNP, respectively, which appear
in neonatal animals[6]. A temporal sequence exists in development of certain
clones[7]. The most striking example is the late development of the T15 clonotype of antibody to phosphorylcholine. While precursors of many specificities
can be detected well before birth, the T15 response does not appear until 5
days afterwards[8]. The T15 clonotype accounts for more than 70% of the
the response of BALB/c mice to phosphorylcholine, which argues strongly that it
contains a germ line V_H gene. Thus a particular germ line gene is expressed
in different neonates at the same developmental time.

In other studies of the ontogeny of B cells reactive with selected antigens
in mice, it has not been possible to distinguish individual clonotypes[9,10].
The results have nevertheless demonstrated: (1) the appearance of specific
precursors well before birth; (2) the rapid development of B cells reactive
with a variety of different antigens; and (3) an increase in the heterogeneity
of the response to a given antigen with increasing age. Several of these
points are discussed in more detail in Dr. Siskind's paper in this volume. It
is sufficient for my purposes to note that these results effectively eliminate
positive selection by environmental antigens as a major factor in initial
expression of diversity, and are consistent with the programmed expression of
germ line genes.

Studies on the development of antigen binding cells in the chicken bursa of Fabricius provided additional evidence for regulated sequential development of different clonotypes[11]. A particularly interesting observation derived from studies of the localization of antigen-binding cells within bursal follicles. Cells binding radiolabeled antigens were present in approximately 10% of follicles, as either single cells or small clusters of 2-4 cells; the great majority of sIgM+ cells in each follicle did not bind the test antigen. Since the lymphocytes of individual bursal follicles are derived from one or ony a few stem cells, these observations suggested that (1) a single stem cell gives rise to diverse clones of B lymphocytes within each follicle, and (2) different stem cells may generate progeny having similar or identical antigen binding specificity.

Regulation of expression of diversity must in some way be related to the most unique aspect of immunoglobulin genes - the fact that separate genes encode different segments of immunoglobulin polypeptide chains. Dreyer and Bennett proposed the two gene, one polypeptide hypothesis in 1965[12]. Tonegawa and colleagues recently confirmed this hypothesis by demonstrating that V and C genes which are separated in embryonic DNA become closely associated in the genome of mature plasma cells[13]. It is likely that the J genes mentioned earlier are also involved in this gene rearrangement[3]. The translocation event may provide a mechanism for another peculiarity of immunoglobulin gene expression: allelic exclusion. In contrast to the products of their co-dominant autosomal alleles which are expressed together in cells, individual B cells from heterozygotes express either the paternal or maternal Ig allele, but not both. It is logical to propose that allelic exclusion is the consequence of the mechanism which insures that each cell expresses only one set of V genes (V_H and V_L) and that both phenomena are in some way related to V gene translocation.

I now turn to a consideration of the cells in which expression of germ line antibody diversity almost certainly occurs. Pre-B cells, so-called because they are ontogenetically the first members of the B cell lineage[14], can be identified morphologically by unique phenotypic characteristics. These large-to medium-sized lymphocytes synthesize IgM within the cytoplasm as detected by immunofluorescence but do not express surface IgM receptors. The known properties of pre-B cells in mouse, rabbit and man are reviewed elsewhere[15]. I will discuss here only the characteristics of pre-B cells clearly important in understanding expression of immunolgobulin diversity.

Expression of potential immunoglobulin diversity, which probably exceeds 10^6 clonotypes[7], within a reasonable period of time clearly requires rapid cell division. There is evidence that sIg$^+$ B lymphocytes, which themselves divide relatively rarely, are derived from a population of sIg$^-$, rapidly dividing marrow precursors[16,17]. Pre-B cells in mice and in humans fall into two catogories with regard to growth kinetics. The larger cells label rapidly with DNA precursors, while small pre-B cells apparently divide at a much slower rate[18,19]. The rate at which the larger cells enter DNA synthesis (>80% labeled after 1 hour exposure to ^{3}H-thymidine) is consistent with a cell cycle time of less than 12 hours.

A second unique and perhaps important characteristic of pre-B cells is their lack of easily detectable cell surface Ig. This point has been a subject of debate, and is difficult to resolve because the results may be influenced by the methods used to detect sIgM. Whether any sIgM is expressed is probably not as important as the question of whether pre-B cells express functional immunoglobulin receptors. It has been clearly demonstrated that treatment with anti-μ antibodies under conditions which suppress development, or function of sIg$^+$ B lymphocytes in vivo or in vitro does not influence either number or function of pre-B cells[20,21]. Also, heterozygous rabbits suppressed for one kappa chain allotype maintain a normal population of pre-B cells expressing that allotype[22].

The absence of a functional antigen receptor on pre-B cells precludes a positive or negative role for antigen either during proliferation or in selecting useful somatic variants. For similar reasons, networks of anti-idiotypic antibodies would not be expected to influence these cells. This is not an argument against somatic mutations or other gene rearrangement mechanisms as contributors to antibody diversity, but rather for intrinsic regulation of the differentiation process by which this diversity becomes expressed.

Evidence for the ordered expression of particular clones during ontogeny has been mentioned earlier. Such observations may most easily be explained as resulting from sequential expression of germ line V genes. Since V and C genes for light and heavy chains, respectively are, linked in tandem, it seems logical that V gene linkage order may establish the order of expression. The same argument has been applied to the "switch" in expression of heavy chain class at a later stage of differentiation[23] and there is some evidence to support this idea[24].

Programmed sequential expression of V genes according to their linkage order creates a potential problem for combinational diversity. If the numbers of V_H and V_L genes are similar and both sets read out simultaneously, then certain V_H V_L combinations (i.e., V_{H1} $V_{\kappa 1}$)are more likely to be expressed than others (i.e., V_{H1} $V_{\kappa 200}$). If the translocation of V and C involves excision of genetic material[24], the potential diversity of germ line genes might be substantially limited.

This problem could be avoided by asynchronous onset of expression of heavy and light chain genes. It may therefore be very important that a substantial fraction of pre-B cells appears to synthesize μ heavy chains but no light chains. In mice and humans, preliminary investigations suggest that few of the large rapidly-dividing fraction of pre-B cells express light chains. The strongest evidence on this point comes from the recent work of Burrows et al.[25]. These investigators have fused murine fetal liver cells with a non-producer variant of a HAT-sensitive plasmacytoma cell line. All but one of the hybridomas produced synthesize intracytoplasmic μ chains without light chains, but neither secrete nor express μ chains on their surface. These observations not only confirm immunofluorescent data concerning the absence of light chain expression in murine pre-B cells, but provide a means of obtaining pre-B cell μ chains for immunochemical study.

The biologic characteristics of pre-B cells seem particularly well suited to the task of expression of the diversity of immunoglobulin genes present in the germ line. Study of these cells has been difficult because they are relatively rare and hard to purify. The ability to isolate the genome of these cells by formation of hybridomas offers particularly exciting potential for future research on regulation of the cellular expression of immunoglobulin diversity.

ACKNOWLEDGMENTS

These studies were supported in part by USPHS grants CA 16673, CA 13148, AI 11503, awarded by the National Institutes of Health, DHEW and 1-625 awarded by the National Foundation, March of Dimes. A. R. Lawton is the recipient of an NIH Research Career Development Award, AI 70780.

REFERENCES

1. Hood, L., Kronenberg, M., Early, P., and Johnson, N. (1977) in ICN-UCLA Symposia on Molecular and Cellular Biology, Vol. VI, Sercarz, E. E., Herzenberg, L. A. and Fox, C. F. eds., Academic Press, New York, pp. 1-27.

34

2. Seidman, J. G., Leder, A., Nau, M., Norman, B., and Leder, P. (1978) Science, 202, 11.
3. Weigert, M., Gatmaitan, L., Loh, E., Schilling, J., and Hood, L. (1978) Nature, 276, 785.
4. Cohen, J. E., D'Eustachio, P., and Edelman, G. M. (1977) J. Exp. Med. 146, 394.
5. Asofsky, R., personal communication.
6. Klinman, N. R. and Press, J. L. (1975) J. Exp. Med. 141, 113.
7. Klinman, N. R. Sigal, N. H., Metcalf, E. S., Pierce, S. K., and Gearhart, P. J. (1977) Cold Spring Harbor Symp. Quant. Biol. 41, 165.
8. Sigal, N. H., Gearhart, P. J., Press, J. L., and Klinman, N. R. (1976) Nature, 259, 57.
9. Goidl, E. A. and Siskind, G. W. (1974) J. Exp. Med. 140, 1285.
10. D'Eustachio, P. and Edelman, G. M. (1975) J. Exp. Med. 142, 1078.
11. Lydyard, P. M., Grossi, C. E., and Cooper, M. D. (1976) J. Exp. Med. 144, 79.
12. Dreyer, W. J. and Bennett, J. C. (1965) Proc. Natl. Acad. Sci. U.S.A. 54, 864.
13. Tonegawa, S., Hozumi, N. Mathyssens, G., and Schuller, R. (1977) Cold Spring Harbor Symp. Quant. Biol. 41, 877.
14. Raff, M. C., Megson, M., Owen, J. J. T., and Cooper, M. D. (1976) Nature, 259, 224.
15. Cooper, M. D., Lawton, A. R. (1979) in P and S Biomedical Sciences Symposia, Cells of Immunoglobulin Synthesis, Pernis, B. and Vogel, H. J. eds., Academic Press, New York, in press.
16. Osmond, D. G. and Nossal, G. J. V. (1974) Cell. Immunol. 13, 132.
17. Reyser, J-E and Vassalli, P. (1974) J. Immunol. 113, 719.
18. Okos, A. J. and Gathings, W. E. (1977) Fed. Proc. 36, 1294.
19. Owen, J. J. T., Wright, D. E., Habu, S., Raff, M. C., and Cooper, M. D. (1977) J. Immunol. 118, 2067.
20. Burrows, P. D., Kearney, J. F., Lawton, A. R., and Cooper, M. D. (1978) J. Immunol. 120, 1526.
21. Melchers, F., Andersson, J., and Phillips, R. A. (1977) Cold Spring Harbor Symp. Quant. Biol. 41, 147.
22. Hayward, A. R., Simons, M. A., Lawton, A. R., Mage, R. G., and Cooper, M. D. (1978) J. Exp. Med. 148, 1367.
23. Cooper, M. D. and Lawton, A. R. (1974) Sci. Am. 231, 58.
24. Honjo, T. and Kataoka, T. (1978) Proc. Natl. Acad. Sci. U.S.A. 75, 2140.
25. Burrows, P. B., LeJeune, M., and Kearney, J. F. Submitted.

Published 1979 by Elsevier North Holland, Inc.
Singhal, Sinclair, Stiller, eds. Aging and Immunity

ONTOGENY OF B-CELL FUNCTION: A ROLE FOR THE THYMUS IN REGULATING
THE MATURATION OF THE B-CELL POPULATION

GREGORY W. SISKIND.
Division of Allergy and Immunology, Department of Medicine, Cornell University
Medical College, New York, New York 10021.

INTRODUCTION.

It has been described by numerous laboratories that the immune system
matures during ontogeny in a discrete series of steps. A stepwise acquisition
of different cell surface markers has been described. The system acquires the
capacity to respond to different mitogens in a sequential manner. Finally, the
ability to respond to different antigens arises in a programmed, ordered
sequence. In general, immune function, in the mouse, is not mature at birth
but rather fully matures over the first few weeks of life. While details have
not been completely defined, it appears that the immaturity of immune function
in perinatal animals is mainly a reflection of an immaturity of helper T-cell
function and an increased suppressor cell activity.

It has become dogma that a step in the maturation of T cells occurs in the
thymus, or perhaps under thymic hormonal influence. B cells in avian species,
mature under the microenvironmental influence of the Bursa of Fabricius.
However, the mammalian equivalent of the avian bursa has not been identified
although several lymphoepithelial, gut-associated structures have been proposed as analogues. It is possible, although not proven, that in mammalian
species maturation of the B-cell population occurs totally within the bone
marrow.

In the present report I will summarize a series of studies dealing with the
maturation of B-cell function in the mouse. These studies were carried out in
a cell transfer system so designed that the function of the B-cell population
could be studied in an adult environment in the presence of adult helper cells.
In the course of this work we have identified four differentiation events in
the ontogeny of the function of the B-cell population, have shown that the B-
cell population of 14 day fetal LAF_1 mice contains all of the information
required to produce a heterogenous anti-dinitrophenyl (DNP) plaque forming cell
(PFC) response equivalent to that of adult mice, and have obtained evidence
that the thymus is involved in regulating one step in the differentiation of
the B-cell population.

Experimental Design (1, 2).

In most studies LAF$_1$ mice from Jackson Laboratories were employed. B cells from donors of known age are transferred into lethally irradiated recipients together with 3×10^7 to 10×10^7 thymus cells from young adult (6 to 8 week old) donors. The source of B cells was the fetal liver or neonatal (within 18 hours of birth) liver. When older donors were employed, the spleen or bone marrow was used as the source of B cells. In all cases, B cells from an individual donor were transferred into an individual recipient. In contrast, a pool of thymus cells from 5 to 15 donors was employed. Recipients were generally immunized one day after cell transfer with approximately 500 μg dinitrophenylated bovine gamma globulin (DNP-BGG), emulsified in complete Freund's adjuvants (CAF) and injected intraperitoneally.

The mice were generally sacrificed, for assay of splenic anti-DNP PFC two to three weeks after antigen injection. PFC were assayed by the Jerne technique. Affinity distributions were assayed by hapten (dinitorphenyl-ε-amino-n-caproic acid) inhibition of plaque formation as originally described by Andersson (3). Hapten concentrations ranging from 10^{-9} to 10^{-5} in half-log increments were used. Inhibition of plaque formation around high affinity antibody secreting cells occurs at low hapten concentration while inhibition of plaque formation around low affinity antibody secreting cells requires a high concentration of hapten.

Results and Discussion.

Irradiated mice reconstituted with B cells from adult donors (and adult thymus cells) produce a highly heterogeneous, high affinity, splenic PFC response to DNP-BGG. In contrast, when the source of B cells is fetal or neonatal donors the response was highly restricted in affinity, generally of low average affinity, lacking high affinity PFC. The B-cell population was found to acquire the ability to reconstitute irradiated mice to give a high affinity, heterogeneous, adult-like response relatively abruptly between 7 and 10 days of age (1).

Studies were carried out to determine if the B-cell population of fetal donors could be stimulated to produce high affinity PFC (2). Mice reconstituted with B-cells from fetal donors (plus adult thymus cells) were injected with 10 μg E coli lipopolysaccharide (LPS) at the same time as immunization with DNP-BGG. It was found that LPS treatment converts the response of mice reconstituted with B-cells from day 16 (or older) fetal donors to one of adult-like heterogeneity and affinity. In contrast, LPS had no effect on the response of mice reconstituted with B cells from 14 day fetal donors. Thus, the B-cell population acquires the capacity to respond to the polyclonal B-cell activator LPS (so as to produce a high affinity PFC response) between days 14 and 16 of fetal life (2).

The secondary response by mice reconstituted with fetal B cells was studied (2). It was found that mice reconstituted with day 14 fetal B cells produce a heterogeneous, high affinity, secondary PFC response following boosting with soluble DNP-BGG 3 week after primary immunization. The response is clearly of secondary character since high affinity PFC are already present in high incidence at 5 days after boosting. The results thus suggest that the day 14 fetal B-cell population already contains all of the information required to produce high affinity anti-DNP antibodies which are indistinguishable from those produced by the adult B-cell population. In addition, the results indicate that the fetal B-cell population is capable of being selectively stimulated, by antigen, such that there is a normal preferential expansion of high affinity memory cells. This suggests that the failure of mice reconstituted with fetal B cells to produce high affinity PFC during their primary response represents a failure to differentiate into antibody secreting cells. This implies that the differentiation event which occurs between 7 and 10 days of age represents the acquisition, by the B-cell population, of the ability to become antibody secreting cells.

Similar studies were carried out in six mouse strains (4) and with six T-dependent and three T-independent antigens (5). A similar general pattern of differentiation from the production of low affinity antibodies to the production of high affinity PFC was observed in every case. Several details should be noted. While each strain studied shows the same pattern of differentiation the age at which different strains acquire the capacity to produce a high affinity PFC response varies from day 18 of fetal life (e.g., AKR) to 21 days of age (C57BL/6). The responses to all of the T-dependent antigens studied mature, in the LAF_1 mouse, at the same time (between 7 and 10 days of age) with the exception of the response to the heterologous immunoglobulin BGG which matures just slightly later (between 10 and 14 days of age). In contrast, the responses to the three T-independent antigens studied all mature significantly later (between 21 and 28 days of age).

We sought to determine if the immature B-cell population would mature spontaneously within the cell transfer recipient (6). Irradiated mice were reconstituted with B cells from day 15 fetal donors or neonatal donors together with adult thymus cells. The recipients were challenged with DNP-BGG in CFA at various times thereafter. It was found that, in both cases, the immature B-cell population acquires the capacity to produce a high affinity, adult-like, PFC response with 3 days of residence within the adult cell transfer recipient. This suggests that the differentiation of the B-cell population is induced by some factor in the adult environment. In addition, the data suggest that the B-cell population of the day 15 fetal mouse is already capable of responding to the inducer.

In all studies described so far, the irradiated mice received thymus cells from adult donors in addition to the source of B cells. The effect of these "adult" thymus cells on the maturation of B-cell function was studied (7). Irradiated thymectomized mice were reconstituted with day 15 fetal B-cells. One to 3 weeks after cell transfer the animals received 10^8 adult thymus cells to provide helper activity and were immunized with DNP-BGG in CFA. In the absence of adult thymus cells, the fetal B-cell population remains immature in character during 3 weeks residence in the adult recipient. Thus, the results suggest that the adult thymus cell population is involved in regulating the differentiation of the B-cell population.

If the thymus is indeed involved in regulating the differentiation of the B-cell population, and the fetal B-cell population is already capable of responding to the inducer of differentiation, then it follows that the immaturity of function of the fetal B-cell population is due to an immaturity of the thymus cell population with respect to its ability to induce the maturation of the B-cell population. We therefore studied the ability of thymus cells from donors of various ages to mediate the differentiation of the B-cell population to be capable of producing a high affinity, adult-like, primary, PFC response (8). Irradiated thymectomized mice were reconstituted with B cells from 15 day fetal donors and 3×10^7 thymus cells from donors of various ages. The thymus cell population acquires the capacity to induce the differentiation of the B-cell population between 7 and 10 days of age. The results are thus consistent with the hypothesis that the differentiation of the B-cell population to be able to generate high affinity antibody secreting cells in the primary response is regulated by some cell in the thymus or by a factor produced by it.

Conclusions.

1. Four differentiation events in the ontogeny of the function of the B-cell population have been identified. In the LAF_1 mouse they are as follows:

a. Between days 14 and 16 of fetal life the B-cell population acquires the capacity to respond to LPS so that when LPS is administered together with antigen a high affinity, primary PFC response to the antigen occurs.

b. Between days 16 and 17 of fetal life the B-cell population acquires the capacity to produce indirect (IgG) PFC in the primary response. Prior to day 16 of fetal life the B-cell population produces only direct (IgM) PFC.

c. Between 7 and 10 days after birth the B-cell population acquires the capacity to produce high affinity antibody secreting cells in the primary response to a T-dependent antigen.

d. Between days 21 and 28 after birth the B-cell population acquires the capacity to produce relatively high affinity antibody secreting cells in the primary response to a T-independent antigen.

2. The differentiation event reflected in the acquisition of the capacity to produce high affinity antibody secreting cells in the primary response is a general characteristic of the maturation of the B-cell population, in that it has been observed in six mouse strains and with nine antigens.

3. The B-cell population of day 14 fetal LAF_1 mice contains all of the information required to produce the entire spectrum of affinitites of anti-DNP antibodies such as is characteristic of the response of the B-cell population of normal adult mice.

4. The differentiation event which occurs, in LAF_1 mice, between 7 and 10 days of age and permits their B-cell population to produce high affinity antibody secreting cells in the primary response to a T-dependent antigen is induced or facilitated by some cell in the adult thymus or a factor produced by it.

5. Between 7 and 10 days of age the thymus cell population acquires the capacity to induce the differentiation of the immature B-cell population.

6. The thymus is involved in at least one step in the differentiation of the B-cell population.

Acknowledgements.

Supported in past by grants from the National Institutes of Health numbers AI-11694, and CA-20075.

REFERENCES

1. Goidl, E.A., and G.W. Siskind. 1974. Ontogeny of B-lymphocyte function. I. Restricted heterogeneity of the antibody response of B lymphocytes from neonatal and fetal mice. J. Exp. Med. 140:1285.

2. Goidl, E.A., J. Klass, and G.W. Siskind. 1976. Ontogeny of B-lymphocyte function. II. Ability of endotoxin to increase the heterogeneity of affinity of the immune response of B lymphocytes from fetal mice. J. Exp. Med. 143:1503.

3. Andersson, B. 1970. Studies on the regulation of avidity at the level of the single antibody-forming cell. J. Exp. Med. 132:77.

4. Sherr, D., M.R. Szewczuk, and G.W. Siskind. Unpublished observation.

5. Sherr, D.H., M.R. Szewczuk, A. Cusano, W. Rappaport, and G.W. Siskind. 1979. Ontogeny of B-lymphocyte function. IX. Differences in the time of maturation of the capacity of B lymphocytes from fetal and neonatal mice to produce a heterogeneous antibody response to the thymic-independent antigens. Immunology. 36:891.

6. Sherr, D., M.R. Szewczuk, and G.W. Siskind. 1977. Ontogeny of B-lymphocyte function. IV. Kinetics of maturation of B lymphocytes from fetal and neonatal mice when transferred into adult irradiated hosts. J. Immunol. 119:1674.

7. Sherr, D.H., M.R. Szewczuk, and G.W. Siskind. 1978. Ontogeny of B-lymphocyte function. V. Thymus cell involvement in the functional maturation of B-lymphocytes from fetal mice transferred into adult irradiated hosts. J. Exp. Med. 147:196.

8. Szewczuk, M.R., D.H. Sherr, and G.W. Siskind. 1978. Ontogeny of B-lymphocyte function. VI. Ontogeny of thymus cell capacity to facilitate the functional maturation of B lymphocytes. Europ. J. Immunol. 8:370.

DISCUSSION

DELOVITCH: Since the last two talks were quite related – I would welcome questions directed to both speakers.

CHILLER: Would adult "nude" mice have undifferentiated B cells or would you predict that they would all give you low affinity B cell types?

SISKIND: I would predict that they would not have absolutely normally functioning B cells. I think that several reports recently suggest that "nude" mice do not make normal responses to even T independent antigens, quite completely comparable to those of "hairy" controls. I think that the prediction is that "nude" mice would not have absolutely normal B cells and I think there is some evidence for it.

PAUL: Firstly, just to elaborate on Jacques Chiller's point. I recall certain instances in which deprivation of the thymus has remarkable affects on the B cell system. One comes from the study recently done in Irwin Scher's lab where they found much more profound defects in B cell function of "nude" mice than in CBA/N themselves which are also defective. So this suggests that the observation that you spoke of is probably very general.
The question really is in what way does the thymic change that occurs between days 7 and 10 promote the expression of cells with relatively high affinity? Now, I would assume and I don't know if you would agree – that the role of the thymus is not so much in generation of precursors which would express high affinity receptors on their membrane – although I guess that is a formal possibility but more likely it is somehow encouraging a set of cells which is probably present in relatively low numbers to expand much more vigorously than the low affinity partners.

SISKIND: I don't quite agree with that.

PAUL: What I was getting to, which comes from some information out of Cantor's lab, was the question that whether or not one might propose that the idiotype/allotype restricted helper system might first develop between 7 and 10 days of age and whether the utilization of this system might give particular advantage to high affinity precursors so that they then came to dominate the population. It might be interesting to search for those phenomena at that particular time.

SISKIND: I think that is a formal possibility. I have a feeling some differentiation step is involved to give antibody secretors and if that is true, low affinity cells are seen early because of a slight leakiness of this system combined with the fact that low affinity antibody-producing clones are far more common than high affinity clones, assuming totally random events. I think that it is the appearance of some low affinity responsive cells which would (themselves) secrete in this case. Low affinity clones you would see – so I think you could handle it without bringing in any more specific regulation than that. Purely by the operation of Occam's razor I would say you could explain this without going further on a statistical level.

CINADER: Could you describe how you eliminate the possibility that the low affinity producers may in fact be low quantity producers?

SISKIND: I would just shift all of this by saying we have a differentiation event from a low secretor to a high rate secretor. In most circumstances where you are not markedly skewing the population to be extraordinarily homogeneous with respect to one clone, the distributions you get probably reflect affinity.

CUNNINGHAM: I think you know what I am going to say. If we want to apply Occam's razor, the simplest explanation for your results, as with many of ours, is that high affinity antibody is not produced in early ontogeny because the cells aren't there. My explanation of your experiments would be that it takes antigen and/or T cells to stimulate the production of variant B cells with high affinity. In that connection, I would mention an experiment that we did a few years ago which is very similar to yours in design. It was simply to park fetal liver in irradiated animals and to sample the spleens of these animals at intervals to see if cells able to make plaques to sheep red cells in culture would come up. To our surprise nothing would emerge for weeks unless you added antigen. Immediately after you put antigen in, within 2 or 3 days lots of B cells able to respond to sheep red cells appeared. My interpretation again is that the antigen created those cells with that potential ability.

SISKIND: I am becoming progressively more impressed by some of the data which suggests that, indeed,more and more of the information for the diversity in the immune response is encoded in the genome and less and less in somatic generation of diversity.

LEON: I just wanted to comment on your statement that there seem to be B cell defects in response to T independent antigens in "nude" mice. I can only speak for the dextran system and say that BALB/c "nude" mice respond as well if not better to dextran in terms of number of plaques and the distribution of affinities is essentially the same as one finds in normal mice. If one believes with Goran Möller that these T independent antigens are indeed polyclonal activators then by analogy with your dextran sulphate and LPS experiments that is exactly what you would expect.

SISKIND: Yes, in other words, that would be consistent with the idea that the response to one that was not a non-specific activator would be aberrant and the one that is a nonspecific activator of the type would turn on a very early cell in the series.

AGING AND IMMUNE FUNCTION IN MAN: INFLUENCE OF SEX AND GENETIC BACKGROUND

LEONARD J. GREENBERG
Department of Laboratory Medicine and Pathology, Box 198 Mayo Bldg.,
University of Minnesota Medical School, Minneapolis, Minnesota 55455

INTRODUCTION

In spite of our limited capacity to significantly increase longevity as indicated by present day survival data, all through history there have been many documented examples of individuals, who before the advent of vaccination and antibiotics, managed to live beyond the age of 75 years and be functionally effective. Were these individuals merely the upper part of a normal distribution curve describing longevity or do they represent a group of people that is specially endowed for long life? The answer to this question is by no means clear since we have a rather limited understanding of both the etiology and pathogenesis of aging. Nevertheless, studies in man and animals indicate that both sex and genetic background play important roles in determining the life span of the species. Life insurance statistics show quite clearly that the progeny of long-lived parents live significantly longer than those of short lived parents. [1] Furthermore in man and most animal species the female of the species lives longer than the male. [2] At the mechanistic level the study of the differential proliferative capacity of cell types from birth to death suggests that cells and organs are programmed in a precise manner for specific functions in a finite lifetime. In this context Burnet [3] has suggested that the thymus may act as a biological clock that is genetically programmed to operate at a rate consistent with the lifetime of the species. More recently, Burnet[4] has modified his theory of aging in a way that combines the stochastic random error theory with genetic programming. The random accumulation of errors in most cell types results from genetically determined degrees of error-proneness in DNA polymerases and other enzymes that are responsible for the fidelity with which the macromolecular pattern, primarily of DNA, is replicated or reconstructed after damage and repair. The presence of these error-prone polymerases in immunocytes, in particular in thymus derived lymphocytes, could result in the age-dependent loss of T cell function with the subsequent development of auto-immune phenomena, manifestations of aging and age-related diseases. In view of the fact, however, that autoantibody in older individuals is a very common event [5] and would be difficult to explain on the basis of mutation, Adler[6] has proposed that the unifying event or events which could account for these phenomena could be the consequence of a series of virus infections. Since under normal conditions the principal function of the T effector lymphocyte is the elimination of virus infected cells,[7] a T cell immunodeficiency, either present prior to virus infection or as a consequence of virus infection, could not only render the individual susceptible to severe or fatal consequences of the infection, but could also promote and perpetuate a state of immunological imbalance favoring the development of autoimmune disease.

In the sections that follow I shall review the evidence for the concept of an autoimmune basis of aging in the light of our current understanding of the regulation of immune function by genes of the major histocompatibility complex (MHC) of the species. Furthermore, I shall introduce new data, derived from human studies, which clearly demonstrate that both sex and histocompatibility background influence immune function in an age-dependent fashion.

AGE ASSOCIATED CHANGES IN LYMPHOCYTE FUNCTION

Studies from many laboratories have demonstrated that both humoral [8-12] and cell-mediated immune function [13-17] decrease with age while the percentage of lymphocytes bearing T cell markers does not appear to decline significantly with age in either mouse[18] or man.[19] Although humoral immunity declines with age the situation is more complex. Since the ability to mount a humoral immune response is for the most part dependent upon the interaction or collaboration of T lymphocytes (both helper and suppressor), macrophages and B lymphocytes, the decreased antibody-forming capacity that occurs with aging could be due to an alteration in the number or function of any of these cell populations. The fact that the humoral response to T-dependent antigens appears to decline to a greater degree and at an earlier age than response to T-independent antigens, suggests that the decline in antibody-forming capacity is primarily a result of a decrease in T helper cell activity with age. Moreover, the relative preservation of B cell function with aging is supported by studies evaluating the mitogenic response of murine spleen cells.[18] As in the case of antibody production B cell activity appears to decline to a lesser extent and at a later age than does T cell activity. The ability of macrophages to collaborate with T and B cells in antibody production does not appear to decline with age. [20,21] These observations suggest that the primary age-related effect on the immune system is a decrease in T cell functional capacity resulting in

45

impaired cooperative interactions and regulatory functions. The resulting
imbalanced immune system appears to have an important pathogenetic influence
on the production of autoantibodies and diseases of aging in both humans and
mice. [5,17,22]

IMMUNE FUNCTION DISEASES OF AGING AND LONGEVITY

Studies with different strains of inbred mice have demonstrated a marked
variation in longevity which appears to be related to their genetic background
and to the integrity and level of activity of their immune systems. Short-
lived strains of mice are generally more susceptible to autoimmune disease and
the earlier development of malignancy than are long-lived strains.[11,23]
Shortened survival is often associated with an earlier decline in cell-mediated
immunity.[11] The observation of an earlier decline of suppressor cells in NZB
mice [24,25] might provide a basis for the expression and expansion of autoimmune
clones resulting in the loss of self tolerance for both tissue cells and
lymphocytes. In the latter case the development of anti-T cell antibodies
could lead to a more pronounced T cell immunodeficiency resulting in more
severe autoimmune disease and increased susceptibility to other diseases of
aging. In man, circumstantial evidence linking immune dysfunction with both
oncogenicity and autoimmunity derives from experience with patients suffering
from various immunodeficiency diseases. Patients with sex-linked agamma-
globulinemia have a high incidence of leukemia and lymphoma.[26] Patients with
congenital thymic aplasia (DiGeorge's Syndrome) are thought to represent the
human analog of the nude mouse. In its complete form the DiGeorge syndrome is
characterized by the absence of the thymus and parathyroids.[27] Children with
this disease have no detectable cell-mediated immunity [28] and although they
have adequate levels of immunoglobulin, there is a striking deficiency in
antibody production. Such patients often experience recurrent infections and
have a greatly shortened life span. In the adult population old people with
defective cell-mediated immunity have a decreased life expectancy when compared
to those with normal T cell function.[29]

VIRUS INFECTION, THE MHC AND AUTOIMMUNITY

As was alluded to previously the principal function of the T effector
lymphocyte is the elimination of virus infected cells.[7] Individuals with
decreased ability to make antibody but with normal cell-mediated immune function

have a normal clinical relationship to virus infection [6] whereas humans or animals with defective cellular immunity may have severe or even fatal consequences of virus infection.[30] Aside from the tissue specific pathological effects of virus infection, periodic infection with virus may also bring about a deterioration of cellular immunity and the development of autoantibodies.[6] Such virus mediated effects may come about in several ways. Studies in mice have shown that shortly after virus infection, viral antigens appear on the cell surface in association with H-2K and H-2D gene products. [31] This phenomenon was demonstrated serologically, by virtue of the fact that anti-H-2 or anti-virus sera produced simultaneous capping of both antigens, and functionally, by the generation of cytotoxic T lymphocytes subsequent to co-culture with mouse spleen cells that were exposed to inactivated virus for a short period of time. [32] Although association of viral antigen and H-2 was not demonstrated directly in the latter case, it can be inferred from the fact that lysis of target cells showed H-2 restriction and lysis could be blocked by anti-H-2 serum. [33] Although these studies indicate an association between non MHC and MHC antigens, the precise structural manifestation of this membrane association is still unclear. Current thinking has T responder lymphocytes reacting to both non MHC and MHC antigens of the stimulating and target cells. However, it is not known whether or not T cells recognize both types of antigen (dual recognition) or some type of interaction product (altered self). In the latter case virus infected cells, under normal conditions, could be eliminated in an autoimmune rejection phenomenon. [34] However, if cell-mediated were defective, virus production and infection might be expected to continue with extensive tissue damage and development of antibodies against both viral and host tissue antigens. Furthermore, although normal, non-stimulated lymphocytes are very difficult to infect, stimulated lymphocytes can be infected with virus. [35] Consequently a deficit in cell-mediated immunity could develop if antigen sensitive lymphocytes, which attack virus infected tissues, become infected themselves and are ultimately destroyed. Finally, virus infected lymphoid tissue can acquire the capacity to destroy normal lymphoid cells. [36] The aforementioned studies are compatible with a theory of aging proposed by Walford [37] in that they provide a possible mechanism for an age-dependent deterioration of lymphoid cells that determine self-recognition. Progressive breakdown of this recognition system results in the onset of autoimmune phenomena and age-associated diseases. This notion takes on added significance when considered in terms of the role of the MHC in the regulation of immune responsiveness and disease susceptibility. [38,39]

HLA, DISEASE SUSCEPTIBILITY AND IMMUNE FUNCTION

Numerous studies over the past decade have demonstrated association between a variety of disease states and specific HLA antigens, a subject which has been extensively reviewed. [40-42] Although a number of diseases show definite association with an HLA-B allele, some show even stronger association with HLA-D suggesting that some disease associations are due to the effect of genes in the HLA-D region or to genes in strong linkage disequilibrium with HLA-D genes. Of particular relevance are the B8-Dw3 associated autoimmune type disorders which include juvenile onset diabetes, myasthenia gravis, celiac disease, dermatitis herpetiformis and Addison's and Graves' diseases. [43-49] Although the precise mechanism by which histocompatibility antigens influence disease susceptibility is not known, the current thinking that HLA-D genes and I region genes are analogous, raises the possibility that at least some disease associations could be due to aberrant regulation, by Ir or IS genes, of immune responses to specific disease inducing antigens. In this regard we might consider some aspects of the development of autoimmune disease, which is both a disease of aging and which also occurs in early life in some individuals. In addition to an age-associated deficit in T cell function susceptibility, in some instances, is influenced by both sex and genetic background with a higher incidence of certain diseases in women. In the B8-Dw3 associated disorders individuals that are B8 display hyperhumoral immunity as compared to patients that are not B8. Diabetics that are B8 produce higher antibody titers against insulin and pancreatic islets[50,51] while in Addison's disease they elaborate higher titers of anti-adrenal antibodies. [52] These observations prompted us to examine the influence of histocompatibility background, sex and age on immune function. Toward this end we assessed immune function in vitro of old and young men and women of the B8 and non-B8 background.[53] It can be seen from Fig.1 that there is a marked age-associated decrease in T cell function in both men and women as indicated by a decreased response to both Con A and PHA stimulation in vitro. However, when the data are analysed in terms of the genetic background (Fig.2), the presence of B8 in both young and old women is associated with a decreased response to PHA whereas there was no apparent B8 effect in men. Furthermore, both young and old men that are B8 have significantly higher responses to PHA

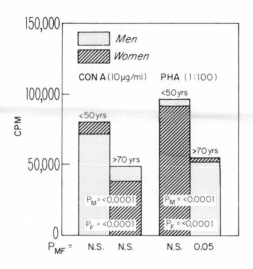

Fig.1. Effect of age and sex on the response to Con A and PHA.

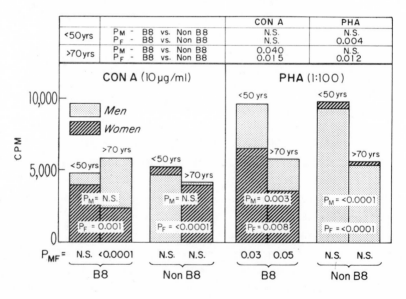

Fig.2. Effect of age, sex and genetic background on the response to Con A and PHA.

than their female counterparts. This effect was not observed in the case of
non-B8's. With respect to Con A the B8 effect is absent in young individuals
but present in old women and to some extent in old men. Another measure of T
cell function that was examined was the response to allogeneic stimulation.
Mixed lymphocyte culture reactivity was normalized to the 75th percentile,
typing responses were eliminated and the data analyzed in terms of age, sex and
the influence of B8. It can be seen from Table 1 that young women have a

TABLE 1

EFFECT OF AGE, SEX AND GENETIC BACKGROUND ON MIXED LYMPHOCYTE CULTURE REACTIVITY

		MEN				WOMEN		
	AGE[a]	N	REACTIVITY		AGE	N	REACTIVITY	P
	Y	158	77		Y	358	90	.0001
	O	59	84		O	56	81	NS
	P		.07		p		.01	
B8	Y	17	87		Y	109	88	NS
N B8	Y	141	76		Y	249	91	.0001
	P		.08		P		NS	
B8	O	16	92		O	9	82	NS
N B8	O	43	81		O	47	81	NS
	P		NS		P		NS	

[a] Y and O refer to the age groups < 50 yrs and > 70 yrs respectively whenever
they appear.

significantly higher MLC reactivity than young men and old women. This effect
is only prevalent, however, in the non-B8 group. Neither sex nor B8 appear to
influence MLC reactivity in the old age group. Analysis of the effects of age,
sex and genetic background on complement levels is presented in Tables 2 and 3.
Alternate pathway components C3, C5, C6 and C7 (Table 2) are elevated in the old
age group; C3 and C7 in both men and women, C5 in women and C6 in men. In
addition C4 is elevated in old women, an effect which is present only in the
non-B8 population (Table 3). Total complement and C1 are both significantly
higher in old women that are B8 as compared to non-B8's (Table 3). The

50

influence of B7,which is thought by some to be associated with hypohumoral
immunity, is only manifest in old women and is associated with a decrease in
total complement, C1, C2 and C5 as compared to non-B7's. Since a similar
type of analysis with other B locus antigens did not reveal any significant
influence on immune function, we examined the effect of age and sex on HLA
antigen frequency distribution and phenotype composition.

TABLE 2
EFFECT OF AGE AND SEX ON COMPLEMENT LEVELS

AGE GROUP	N	TOTAL C^a	$C1^a$	$C4^a$	C2	C3	C5	C6	C7	$C8^a$	$C9^a$
Total Y	90	77	312	421	3163	2083	4780	5202	4712	191	68
Total O	137	79	327	560	3100	2534	7176	6340	6645	223	74
P		NS	NS	NS	NS	.001	.015	.038	.002	NS	NS
Y	33	73	305	461	2796	2174	5010	5000	4775	192	75
MEN											
O	71	78	342	492	3046	2570	7640	6521	7001	219	75
P		NS	NS	NS	NS	.05	NS	.06	.04	NS	NS
Y	57	79	316	397	3436	2011	4596	5404	4650	189	64
WOMEN											
O	66	81	310	608	3156	2486	6573	6235	6437	241	67
P		NS	NS	.04	NS	.01	.001	NS	.03	NS	NS

TABLE 3
EFFECT OF AGE, SEX AND GENETIC BACKGROUND ON COMPLEMENT LEVELS

AGE GROUP	N	TOTAL C^a	$C1^a$	$C4^a$	C2	C3	C5	C6	C7	$C8^a$	$C9^a$
B8 O	13	99	365	425	3281	2123	8030	5270	6127	348	71
Women											
N-B8 O	53	76	290	720	3117	2641	5949	6717	6592	206	65
P		.003	.04	.03	NS	NS	NS	NS	NS	NS	NS
B7 O	20	72	263	465	2798	2552	5360	5950	5743	142	55
Women											
N-B7 O	46	84	325	632	3313	2464	6978	6330	6668	274	73
P		.03	.01	NS	.08	NS	.01	NS	NS	NS	NS

a X 1000 in both Tables 2 and 3

HLA FREQUENCY, HETEROZYGOSITY AND LONGEVITY

The MHC of higher animals shows a considerable amount of genetic polymorphism. The maintenance of such a polymorphic state implies evolutionary advantage for HLA heterozygotes in man and H-2 heterozygotes in mice. [54,55] Although the availability of inbred strains of laboratory animals has been of considerable value in the establishment of uniformity for selected genetic attributes, some good and some bad, the effects of inbreeding, in general, have been invariably deleterious. Breeders of livestock have long been aware of the superior fitness conferred by the heterozygous constitution which is known as heterosis or hybrid vigor. In the laboratory dramatic results have been achieved through hybridization of NZB mice with other strains including CBA/H mice. In all cases the hybrids lived longer than the NZB mice but not as long as CBA/H mice. [11,56] Hybridization not only resulted in increased survival but also in a delay in the appearance of autoimmune symptoms implying that the defects are polygenic in nature and that heterozygosis at many loci may be involved. In this context Doherty and Zinkernagel[57] have concluded from in vitro and in vivo experiments in mice, infected with LCM virus, that both immune responsiveness and immune surveillance are considerably enhanced in mice that are heterozygous at the H-2 gene complex. In the case of man we are already dealing with an extremely outbred population which displays considerable genetic variability and is more or less adapted to its environment. However, the finding of Doherty and Zinkernagel,[57] with its implications for survival, has prompted investigators from several laboratories to analyze the degree of HLA heterozygosity with age. Although these studies are not in complete agreement, there appears to be some tendency toward increased heterozygosity, at least at the B locus, with age. These studies do, however, agree that there are no significant changes in the frequency of any particular HLA antigen with age. [58-62] An analysis of almost 1000 normal caucasoids in Minnesota (Table 4), however, revealed no significant changes in the percentage of presumptive HLA homozygotes in either sex or in any of the three age groups studied. In general the appearance of homozygotes followed the frequency distribution of the HLA antigens themselves; ie the highest frequency homozygote involved HLA-A2, an antigen which occurs most frequently in caucasoids. A comparison of the presumptive haplotype frequencies between age classes revealed only one significant difference. A marked enrichment of the A2-B12 haplotype was observed in the old age group when compared to young individuals (p=0.001). A highly significant sex difference was observed in the prevalence of HLA-A1 and B8. It can be seen from Table 5 that the frequencies of both A1 and B8 are significantly higher in old men

52

than in women of a comparable age whereas young women have a higher frequency
of A1 than young men. The increased frequency of both A1 and B8 is not

TABLE 4
EFFECT OF SEX AND AGE ON HLA HOMOZYGOSITY

| AGE GROUP | N | PERCENTAGE OF PRESUMPTIVE HLA HOMOZYGOTES[a] | | |
		A Locus	B Locus	Both Loci
> 70 yrs				
Men	128	17	17.9	7
Women	202	16.3	14.8	7.9
Total	330	16.6	16	7.6
51-69 yrs				
Men	196	12.8	18.9	4.1
Women	210	17.1	20	8.6
Total	406	15	19.5	6.4
< 50 yrs				
Men	89	13.5	13.5	5.6
Women	158	12.6	16.4	5
Total	247	12.9	17.8	5.3

[a]Chi^2 analysis reveals no significant differences

surprising inasmuch as these two antigens are normally in strong linkage disequilibrium. The phenomenon of linkage disequilibrium not only occurs between
selected alleles of the AB, BC,BD,BDR, and DDR loci but is thought to provide
the basis for HLA and disease association by virtue of linkage between disease
susceptibility genes and HLA genes. In certain instances disease states have
been shown to manifest strong association with both HLA-B and D alleles
suggesting but not proving the existence of more extensive HLA-disease linkage
group. The influence of both sex and histocompatibility background on immune
function and susceptibility to certain disease states, described in a previous
section, prompted us to examine the influence of sex and age on the degree of
linkage disequilibrium between three pairs of HLA-A and B alleles, A2-B12,
A3-B7 and A1-B8, all known to display significant linkage. It can be seen from

TABLE 5

EFFECT OF AGE AND SEX ON HLA ANTIGEN FREQUENCY DISTRIBUTION

HLA	>70yrs Total (330)	Men (128)	Women (202)	Chi²	51-69 yrs Total (406)	Men (196)	Women (210)	<50 yrs Total (247)	Men (89)	Women (158)	Chi²
A Locus											
1	.3592	.4929*	.2888*	13.3	.2864	.3179	.2571	.3401	.3258*	.3481	10
2	.5060	.4844	.5198		.5210	.5333	.5095	.4980	.5393	.4747	
3	.2454	.2812	.2228		.2228	.2820	.2667	.2510	.2135	.2721	
9	.1939	.1874	.1980		.1901	.1641	.2143	.2024	.1236	.2468	
10	.1364	.1250	.1436		.1284	.1641	.0952	.1296	.1460	.1203	
11	.1121	.1016	.1188		.1136	.1077	.1191	.1134	.1236	.1076	
19	.1575	.1327	.1733		.2173	.2256	.2095	.1943	.2247	.1772	
28	.0485	.0469	.0495		.0469	.0359	.0571	.0891	.1124	.0760	
B Locus											
5	.1303	.1094	.1436		.1358	.1385	.1333	.1660	.2359	.1266	
7	.2849	.2266*	.3218*	13.9	.2840	.2359	.3286	.2632	.1910	.3038	
8	.2184	.3380*	.1555*		.2049	.2103	.2000	.2348	.2247	.2405	
12	.2333	.2969	.1931		.2815	.2667	.2952	.2227	.2247	.2215	
13	.0576	.0547	.0594		.0617	.0615	.0619	.0364	.0449	.0317	
14	.0576	.0625	.0545		.0396	.0513	.0286	.0850	.0899	.0823	
15	.1273	.1172	.1337		.1309	.1539	.1095	.1012	.1011	.1013	
16	.0545	.0312	.0693		.0691	.0769	.0619	.0688	.1011	.0633	
17	.0727	.0781	.0693		.0815	.0821	.0810	.0769	.0787	.0760	
18	.0364	.0391	.0347		.0395	.0410	.0381	.0567	.0337	.0692	
21	.0091	.0000	.0148		.0000	.0000	.0000	.0162	.0337	.0063	
22	.0303	.0313	.0297		.0296	.0256	.0333	.0486	.0225	.0633	
27	.1061	.1016	.1089		.0420	.0564	.0286	.0769	.0899	.0696	
35	.1424	.1406	.1436		.1506	.1949	.1095	.1296	.1011	.1456	
40	.1697	.1641	.1733		.1803	.1641	.1952	.1700	.1798	.1646	

Table 6 that linkage between A2 and B12 in the total population derives
primarily from women. The maximum linkage effect can be seen in individuals
over 70 yrs of age indicating an enrichment of this haplotype with age and
implying survival advantage. In the case of A3 and B7 (Table 7) an analysis of

TABLE 6

EFFECT OF AGE AND SEX ON LINKAGE BETWEEN HLA-A2 AND HLA-B12

AGE GROUP	N	ANTIGEN FREQUENCY		D	CHI^2	HAPLOTYPE FREQUENCY
		A2	B12			
> 70 yrs						
Total	330	.5060	.2333	.0336	12	.0706
Men	128	.4844	.2969	.0414	5.6	.0869
Women	202	.5198	.1931	.0300	6.6	.0612
< 50 yrs						
Total	247	.4980	.2267	.0148	NS	.0499
Men	89	.5393	.2267	.0113	NS	.0497
Women	158	.4747	.2215	.0165	NS	.0489
TOTAL[a]	983	.5097	.2502	.0179	9.7	.0581
MEN	413	.5181	.2663	.0121	NS	.0594
WOMEN	570	.5035	.2386	.0218	8.7	.0594

[a]Includes individuals between 51-69 yrs in Tables 6-8

the total population reveals significant linkage in men and women.This linkage
effect is quite prominant in young women but appears to decay with age
suggesting a possible survival disadvantage in women bearing this haplotype.
Finally, as can be seen from Table 8, very strong linkage exists between A1
and B8. This linkage effect is greatly enriched in men over 70 yrs as
compared to young men. Women, on the other hand, show a marked decrease in
the A1 and B8 linkage with age. As might be expected from the observed increase in the frequencies of both A1 and B8 in old men as compared to women
of the same age (Table 5) there is also a marked increase in the A1-B8 haplotype frequency of these men (Table 8) when compared to women of the same age

group and to young individuals of both sexes. Women, however, manifest a decrease in the A1-B8 haplotype frequency with age.

TABLE 7

EFFECT OF AGE AND SEX ON LINKAGE BETWEEN HLA-A3 AND HLA-B7

AGE GROUP	N	ANTIGEN FREQUENCY		D	CHI^2	HAPLOTYPE FREQUENCY
		A3	B7			
> 70 yrs						
Total	330	.2454	.2848	.0182	5.7	.0384
Men	128	.2812	.2266	.0300	6.3	.0483
Women	202	.2228	.3218	.0199	1.2	.0328
< 50 yrs						
Total	247	.2510	.2631	.0416	26	.0606
Men	89	.2135	.1910	.0233	3.6	.0347
Women	158	.2721	.3038	.0512	19.8	.0755
TOTAL	983	.2584	.2787	.0280	44	.0489
MEN	413	.2663	.2228	.0245	16	.0415
WOMEN	570	.2526	.3193	.0312	28	.0549

CONCLUDING THOUGHTS

In this chapter we have examined the influence of sex and genetic background on age-associated changes in immune function in man. The data shows that both young and old women expressing B8 have lower responses to T cell mitogens than do men of comparable age and women that are non-B8's suggesting a deficit in T cell function. The way in which B8 influences T cell reactivity in women is not clear. However it is possible that the T cell deficit is related to the marked age-associated decrease in the A1-B8 haplotype frequency in women. Whether the A1-B8 background is already programmed for a deficit in T cell function or it predisposes women to T cell destruction is not known. Either situation, however, could account for the autoimmune type disorders, some of which have higher incidence in women, that are associated with this haplotype. It appears that neither the A1-B8 nor A3-B7 haplotypes have survival advantage in women whereas at least in the case of A1-B8 there is a strong

56

TABLE 8
EFFECT OF AGE AND SEX ON LINKAGE BETWEEN HLA-A1 AND HLA-B8

AGE GROUP	N	ANTIGEN FREQUENCY		D	CHI^2	HAPLOTYPE FREQUENCY
		A1	B8			
>70 yrs						
Total	330	.3592	.2184	.0775	67	.1006
Men	128	.4929	.3380	.1228	29	.1764
Women	202	.2888	.1555	.0506	30	.0633
<50 yrs						
Total	247	.3401	.2348	.0764	77	.0999
Men	89	.3258	.2247	.0632	18	.0845
Women	158	.3481	.2405	.0839	57	.1087
TOTAL	983	.3177	.2240	.0709	307	.0917
MEN	413	.3422	.2403	.0752	123	.0994
WOMEN	570	.3000	.2123	.0685	181	.0869

indication of survival advantage in men. Although A2-B12 does not manifest any apparent influence on immune function, it appears to have survival advantage in both men and women. Finally,with respect to heterozygosis it is not necessarily true that this constitution in inherently laudable. If indeed heterozygotes are more fit, in a particular environment, it is only because their genetic system has become adjusted to that environment, a situation which is subject to change with time.

ACKNOWLEDGMENTS
    This work has been supported by funds from the JACOB M. GREENBERG memorial fund.

REFERENCES
1. Rockstein, M. (1974) in Theoretical Aspects of Aging, Rockstein, M. ed., Academic press, New York, pp.1-10.
2. Rockstein, M. (1958) J. Gerontol., 13,7.
3. Burnet, F.M. (1970) Immunological Surveillance, Pergamon Press, New York.

4. Burnet, F.M. (1970) Lancet, 2, 480.
5. Hallgren, H.M., Buckley, C.E. III, Gilbertsen, V.A. and yunis, E.J. (1973)
   J. Immunol., 111, 1101.
6. Adler, W.H. (1974) in Theoretical Aspects of Aging, Rockstein, M., ed.,
   Academic Press, New York, pp. 32-42.
7. Snell, G.D. (1978) in Immunological Reviews, Moller, G., ed., Munksgaard,
   Copenhagen, pp.3-69.
8. Paul, J.R. and Bunnell, W.W. (1932) Am. J. Med. Sci., 183, 90.
9. Rowley, M.J., Buchanan, H. and MacKay, I.R. (1968) Lancet, 2, 24.
10. Thomson, O. and Kettel, K. (1929) Z. Immunitaetsforsch., 63, 67.
11. Yunis, E.J., Fernandes, G. and Greenberg, L.J. (1975) in Birth Defects,
    Orig. Artic. Ser. 11, Bergsma, D., ed., Sinauer Assoc. Inc., Sunderland,
    Mass.,pp.185-192.
12. Yunis, E.J. and Greenberg, L.J. (1974) Fed. Proc., 33, 2017.
13. Gervais, P., Gervais, A., Morault, S. and Damon, H. (1967) Rev. Fr. Allerg.,
    7, 161.
14. Giannini, D. and Sloan, R.S. (1957) Lancet, 1, 525.
15. Greenberg, L.J. and Yunis, E.J. (1972) Gerontologia, 18, 247.
16. Tuft, L., Hock, V.M. and Gregory, D.C. (1955) J. Allergy, 26, 359.
17. Walford, R.L. (1970) The Immunologic Theory of Aging, Munksgaard,Copenhagen.
18. Makinodan, T. and Adler, W.H. (1975) Fed. Proc., 34. 153.
19. Hallgren, H.M., Kersey, J.H., Gajl-Peczalska, K.J., Greenberg, L.J. and
    Yunis, E.J. (1974) Fed. Proc., 33, 646.
20. Konen, T.G., Smith, G.S. and Walford, R.L. (1973) J. Immunol., 110, 1216.
21. Price, G.B. and Makinodan, T. (1972) J. Immunol., 108, 403.
22. Yunis, E.J., Fernandes, G. and Greenberg, L.J. (1976) J.Am. Geriatr. Soc.,
    24, 285.
23. Yunis, E.J., Stutman, O. and Good, R.A. (1971) Proc. Natl. Acad. Sci.,4, 111.
24. Chused, J.M., Steinberg, A.D. and Parker, L.M. (1973) J. Immunol., 3, 52.
25. Ha, T-Y., Waksman, B.H. and Treffers, H.P. (1974) J. Exp. Med., 139, 13.
26. Peterson, R.D.A., Kelly, W.D. and Good, R.A. (1964) Lancet, 1, 1189.
27. DiGeorge, A.M. (1968) in Birth Defects, Orig. Artic. Ser.4, 116.
28. Lischner, H.W. and Huff, D.S. (1975) in Birth Defects, Orig. Artic. Ser. 11,
    Bergsma, D., ed., Sinauer Assoc. Inc., Sunderland, Mass., pp.16-29.
29. Roberts-Thomsen, I.C., Whittingham, S., Youngchaiyud, U. and MacKay,I.R.
    (1974) Lancet, 2,368.
30. Allison, A.C. and Burns, W.H.(1971) in Immunogenicity, Borek, F., ed.,
    North Holland Publ. Co., Amsterdam, Ch. 6.
31. Schrader, J.W., Cunningham, B.A. and Edelman, G.M. (1975) Proc. Natl. Acad.
    Sci.,72, 5066.
32. Schrader, J.W. and Edelman, G.M. (1977) J. Exp. Med., 145, 523.
33. Koszinoski, U. and Ertl, H. (1975) Nature, 267, 160.
34. Liburd, E.M., Russell, A.S. and Dossetor, J.B. (1973) J. Immunol.,111, 1288.
35. Jimenez, J., Bloom, B.R., Blume, M.R. and Oettgen, H.F. (1971) J. Exp.
    Med., 133, 470.
36. Profitt, M.R., Hirsch, M.S. and Black, P.H. (1973) Science, 182, 821.
37. Walford, R.L. (1976) Lancet, 12, 1226.
38. Katz, D.H. and Benacerraf, B. (1976) The Role of Products of the Histo-
    compatibility Gene Complex in Immune Responses, Academic Press., New York.
39. McDevitt, H.O. (1978) Ir Genes and Ia Antigens, Academic Press., New York.
40. Dausset, J. and Hors, J. (1975) Transplant. Rev., 22, 45.
41. van Rood, J.J., van Hooff, J.P. and Keuning, J.J. (1975) Transplant. Rev.,
    22, 75.
42. Svejgaard, A., Platz, P., Ryder, L.P. Nielsen, L.S. and Thomsen, M., (1975)
    Transplant. Rev., 22, 3.
43. Barbosa, J., Noreen, H., Emme, L., Goetz, F., Simmons, R., Najarian, J. and

Yunis, E.J. (1976) Tiss. Agns., 7, 233.

44. Fritze, D., Herrman, Jr. C., Naeim, F., Smith, G.S. and Walford, R.L. (1974) Lancet, 1, 240.

45. Grumet, F.C., Payne, R.O., Konishi, J. and Kriss, J.P. (1974) J. Clin. Endocrinol. Metab., 39, 115.

46. Nerup, J., Platz,P., Anderson, O.O., Christy, M, Lyngsoe, J., Poulsen, J.E., Ryder, L.P., Nielsen, L.S., Thomsen, M. and Svejgaard, A. (1974) Lancet, 2, 864.

47. Solheim, B.G., Ek, J., Thune, P.O., Baklien, K., Brattie, A. Rankin, B., Thorsen, A.B. and Thorsby, E. (1976) Tiss. Agns. 7, 57.

48. Stokes, P.L., Asquith, P., Holmes, G.K.T., Mackintosh, P. and Cooke, W.T. (1972) Lancet, 2, 162.

49. Thomsen, M., Platz, P., Anderson, O., Christy, M., Lyngsoe, J., Nerup, I., Rasmussen, K., Ryder, L. Nielsen, L. and Svejgaard, A. (1975) Transplant. Rev., 22, 126.

50. Morris, P.J., Vaughn, H., Irvine, W.J., McCallum, F.J., Gray, R.S., Campbell, C.J., Duncan, L.P.J. and Farquhar, J.W. (1976) Lancet, 2, 652.

51. Schernthaner, G., Ludwig, H., Mayr, W.R. and Willvonseder, R. (1976) First Internat. Symp. on HLA and Disease, Munksgaard, Copenhagen.

52. Schernthaner, G., Mayr, W.R. and Ludwig, H. (1976) First Internat. Symp. on HLA and Disease, Munksgaard, Copenhagen.

53. Greenberg, L.J. and Yunis, E.J. (1978) Fed. Proc. 37, 1258.

54. Bodmer, W.F. (1972) Nature, 237, 139.

55. Burnet, F.M. (1973) Nature, 245, 359.

56. Yunis, E.J., Fernandes, G. and Greenberg, L.J. (1973) 2nd Internat. Workshop on Primary Immunodeficiency Disease in Man, St. Petersburg, Fla.

57. Doherty, P.C. and Zinkernagel, R.M. (1975) Nature, 256, 50.

58. Bender, K.,Ruter, G., Mayerova, A. and Hiller, Ch. (1973) Sympos. Ser. Immunol. Stand., 18, 287.

59. Gerkins, V.R., Ting, A., Menck, H.T., Casagrande,J.T., Terasaki, P.I., Pike, M.C. and Henderson, B.E. (1974) J. Nat. Cancer Instit., 52, 1909.

60. Magurova, H., Ivanyi, P., Sajdlova, H. and Trojan, J. (1975) Tiss. Agns., 6, 269.

61. Bender, K., Mayerova, A., Klotzbucher, B., Burckhardt, K. and Hiller, Ch. (1976) Tiss. Agns., 7, 118.

62. Converse, P.J. and Williams, D.R.R. (1978) Tiss. Agns., 12, 275.

DISCUSSION

TALAL: I would like to ask you two questions. Some years ago, we showed in Sjogren's Syndrome that the presence of B8-DW3 predisposes to a low response to PHA particularly with suboptimal PHA concentrations and also to a greater severity of autoimmune attack as judged by the extent of lymphocytic infiltration in the salivary glands, which I think fits in very beautifully with what you said. My question deals specifically with the PHA and Con A differences in the female compared to male. Have you looked at autoantibodies of any sort in those individuals?

GREENBERG: We did look at autoantibodies but not autoantibodies that relate directly to the thymus. We looked at anti-nuclear constituents as a function of age and sex. They reach a maximum at 30 years of age in women. They both start out at the same point, the men decay towards the middle years and the women reach a first peak at 30 years of age. That decays and then anti-nuclear antibodies increase in both sexes. Now with respect to macrophage function, we have done reconstruction studies in which we are hard pressed to see the macrophage effect on T cells. The antigen effect is quite easy but if we eliminate macrophages by nylon wool and by adherence and look at the populations that remain, both with respect to markers and response to antigens and mitogens, the mitogen response is intact while the antigen response is gone.

WISNIEWSKI: Do you have any information about Progeria, Down's syndrome or Senile dementia; these are examples of premature aging.

GREENBERG: No I don't. The incidence of progerics is so low that they are difficult to find.

MAKINODAN: In your population sampling did they come all from Minnesota?

GREENBERG: I'm sorry I didn't mention that and I should have because I have been talking about ethnic compartments. This is 1,000 people, both men and women, from the Minnesota population which is predominantly of middle European extraction, all caucasoids.

GENERAL DISCUSSION: SESSION I

REGULATION AND GENETICS OF IMMUNE RESPONSE

TALAL: I'd like to ask either Harvey (Cantor) or Hans (Wigzell) if you
have any information about the qualitative or quantitative characteristics of
idiotype networks either on a cell surface or in the humoral response as a
function of aging. At a meeting that was just held dealing with the subject at
NIH we heard some evidence that there might be an increased idiotypic response in
aged animals. I wonder if you have any information on it?

WIGZELL: No information available from either Harvey or me. We don't
know anything - about this at least.

DELOVITCH: Would Hans like to tell us more about induction of idiotype
positive cells in a general sense or perhaps their general feelings upon
what could induce idiotype specific cells and how they perhaps can regulate
either T-macrophage or T-B interaction?

WIGZELL: This would correspond to an increased level of augmentation. I
will not answer your question, but I would just like to bring forward something
which I think is of interest and which has to do with idiotypes and allo-
antigeneic variability. That is, in the sense of T cells being obsessed for
MHC structures and the like, and defining auto anti-idiotypic antibodies
which can seemingly functionally replace MHC components. That, in conjunction
with the finding that the polymorphism in the MHC and binding ability of the
MHC, K and D components may be Ia components for certain fragments of the
antigen, makes it of course very crucial to ask things like we have
done in the idiotypic work. We have found that you can induce immuno-
activation of these by idiotype positive blasts. We can induce killer T cells,
the specificity of which is seemingly the idiotype on another T cell. At the
same time we have no evidence whatsoever that this is MHC restricted. One of
the things I think will become very important in the future is trying to
link, let's say, asking the question whether immunoglobulin-like determinants
can fully replace the MHC determinant in the regulation. In other words, if
they not only can function from the point of view of communication but also
can function as very select targets which would not necessarily implicate
an MHC structure interaction. With regards to the MHC components whether they
would induce idiotypes, let's say, in the thymic epithelium selection process-
I have no evidence.

CANTOR: Perhaps the most potent activating signal for Ly-1 induced
suppression is the B cell blast. At least one molecular component on the
surface of the B cell blast that is involved is surface Ig as judged by the
inability of B cell blasts to activate Ly-1 stimulated suppression if they
are capped with anti-Ig. I think it is important to realize that although the
regulatory network can be dissected out with respect to sets of T cells there
is also what one might call product feedback where the product is the activated
B cell or some component on the activated B cell which seems to have what one
might call an antigen presenting or a stimulus presenting function analogous
to the macrophage in other systems. The other point I would like to make is
much more speculative, but one I am wondering about because it would make some
of the phenomenology of the T cell specificity a bit more easy to understand.
There is no doubt that the T cells are preoccupied with MHC products and
seemingly with immunoglobulin products. There is evidence that some of the

preoccupation of T cells for MHC products may begin during their differentiation in the thymus. One wonders whether this is associated directly with their selection of immunospecificity for immunoglobulin determinants or whether this represents a completely different type of maturation process. One solution which would make things a lot easier in envisioning a structural model to explain both would be if when further sequence work were done on the structure of Ig and HLA that there were obvious sequence homologies, so that, in the process of acquiring or selecting for T cells that have a certain spectrum of reactivity to MHC products, one was coselecting reactivity for structurally related Ig associated determinants.

GOOD: I would like to ask Dr. Cantor whether or not the regulatory circuits in these NZB and MRL$_a$ mice, and the other autoimmune strains he has been working with, are altered by any of the procedures that very much change the clinical situation in these animals, that is, prolong their survival. There are many means now by which the NZB mice have had their life prolonged from endocrinological manipulations to actinomycin D to hypertransfusion to diets. Do any of these alter the regulatory circuit?

CANTOR: We have looked at only one of those techniques in collaboration with Norm Talal, that is, the effects of treating NZB mice, males and females, with different hormones - testosterone or estrogen. At the outset the results were rather confusing primarily because I think we were looking exclusively at the regulatory interactions that resulted in a response specifically to sheep erythrocytes, particularly as the animal ages and certainly if it is being treated by surgery and possibly nonphysiologic amounts of hormones. It may be more fruitful to look at these regulatory interactions using as a read-out system at total immunoglobulin production - or more specifically perhaps using an auto-antigen such as DNA of the sort that Dr. Talal has been using. The answer to your question in short is we are just starting to look at those sorts of mice using these sorts of assays.

GOOD: Have you looked in ontogenetic perspective at the time of appearance of these defects that you have pinpointed? Are they present from the earliest stages that you can measure them, or do they come on? The reason I ask this is that working with Kincaid we have found that, even in the fetal liver, there is a hematopoeitic abnormality in these animals that can be clearly defined.

CANTOR: Yes, I think that is a very important point. We have looked most extensively at the NZB and there is no doubt, from criteria of phenotypic characterization of the different T cells, that from square one - that is, from birth - they have a different pattern of T cell sets than do the BALB/c mice. We have not done as much in studying their function because at that age we have a difficult time looking at their ability to produce antibody responses. Although these mice do have clearcut defects in regulation at the T cell level, this of course does not rule out the possibility that in addition they may have defects at the B cell level. If one wanted to put an X somewhere in the differentiative tree of the lymphoid system, the lesion could be at the stem cell level. If one has several different interactions that seem to be required for normal regulation, then it is likely that the different inbred strains and different types of autoimmune diseases may turn out to be one or a combination of these lesions. One of them might be an apparent overactivity of B cells but that may not be intrinsic to the B cells but rather that these B cells may not signal regulatory T cells, for example. The most important point that analysis of the different inbred mutant strains has told us is that the immunoregulatory defects are heterogeneous and that if one had similar sorts of in vitro assays for measuring immune function in man and separating the defects one might come up with a more useful definition of these diseases from the point of view of etiology and perhaps treatment.

SISKIND: I wanted to make a comment about the thing that Talal brought up with regard to anti-idiotype responses in aging. We have been looking at a model in which we can see an auto-anti-idiotype response taking place during a normal immune response to T-independent or to T-dependent antigens and this is assayed by the fact that idiotype (PFC response by these animals) can be augmented by having a very low concentration of hapten in the assay system. In other words, we have a variety of evidence which establishes that hapten augmentation of plaque formation in the assay system is an assay for idiotype blocked PFC. If one looks at mice of different ages with this type of an assay, one finds that the incidence of hapten augmentable plaque-forming cells increases in older animals implying that these animals produce more auto-anti-idiotype antibody.

SESSION 11

Aging and Immune Regulation

Chairman: A.J. Cunningham
Ontario Cancer Institute, Toronto

Published 1979 by Elsevier North Holland, Inc.
Singhal, Sinclair, Stiller, eds. Aging and Immunity

NATURALLY OCCURRING SUPPRESSOR CELLS IN THE BONE MARROW AND SPLEEN OF
AGING MICE

R.C. McGARRY AND S.K. SINGHAL
Department of Microbiology and Immunology, University of Western Ontario,
London, Ontario, Canada N6A 5C1.

Many aspects of both humoral and cell-mediated immune function are known to
decline with age (21). These diminished responses could conceivably result
from a decline in numbers or intrinsic function of any of the components
involved in immune responses. However, among those functions which appear
normal in aged mice include numbers of stem cells, antigen-sensitive cells and
the accessory cell components (15, 16). Our earlier studies showed B cells
from aged mice could form both antibody producing cells (27) and normal
numbers of colonies in agar (12). Furthermore, in aged spleens the B cell
response to mitogens was found to decline more slowly than that of T cells (12).
The major intrinsic defect noted in aging mice involves an age-dependent loss
of T cell function both in vivo and in vitro. Most measurable T cell responses
have been found to be deficient in aging mice including numbers of thymocyte
precursors (34), mixed lymphocyte culture reactivity (14, 20), GVH responses
(17), T cell mitogen responses (2, 12, 21) and impairment of suppressor T
cells (15) and helper activity in both primary and secondary antibody responses
(3). While it has been suggested that these defects may involve functions such
as differentiation, division potential or ability to synergize with other cell
types (21), it has not been clear whether these defects reside within the cells
or are due to the effects of other cell types capable of actually suppressing
their function. Suppressor cells have, in fact, been shown to develop in old
animals. These cells are capable of inhibiting responses to mitogens (18), MLC
reactivity (14) and antibody responses to SRBC or DNP (15).

In previous studies from our laboratory, we showed that there resides in
mouse BM, a naturally occurring, radiosensitive, Fc positive cell capable of
suppressing primary in vitro responses to T-dependent and T-independent
antigens (10, 27, 30). Suppression resulted from the release of a low
molecular weight ($<$10,000) factor which, like the cells, suppressed early
events in antibody formation (11, 27, 32). Studies dealing with the generation
of suppressor cells in aging mice showed that the decline of humoral antibody
response with age was accompanied by: (a) an increase in the suppressive

activity of cells in the bone marrow, (b) the appearance of splenic suppressor
cells which released soluble mediators and acted early in the immune response
when added to young syngeneic spleen cells, and (c) an increase in the suppressive activity in the serum (27, 32). Both BM and splenic suppressor could not
be removed with carbonyl iron (27). The non-T nature of both these suppressor
cells was indicated by (i) the failure of anti-theta and anti-T cell serum plus
complement to abrogate suppression (9); (ii) their presence in nude mice (9);
(iii) the retention of these cells on polyvalent anti-Ig columns (27); and (iv)
the enrichment of cells bearing surface Ig in the purified suppressor spleen
cell population obtained by velocity sedimentation (27).

These results suggested that a rise in the activity of non-T and non-
macrophage suppressor cells may be responsible for the depression in humoral
immunity seen in aging mice (19, 20). In this report, we shall extend our
observations on the nature of the suppressor cell and mediator and speculate
on their significance on immunologic aging.

Suppression by bone marrow and spleen cells of aged mice.

In vitro suppression by old spleen and bone marrow cells was dose-dependent
with no effect on cell viability. The possibility that the BM suppressor could
be a stem cell was suggested by a significant loss of suppressor activity
following treatment with anti-stem cell antiserum (Fig. 1).

In addition, a significant loss of suppressor activity was observed following
treatment of BMC with anti-H2 antibody plus complement (Fig. 2).

Furthermore, unlike pre-T cells (7), the bone marrow suppressor cell could
be precultured for 1-4 days with no loss of activity. Preculture of bone
marrow suppressor cells with Con A which is known to induce theta positive
blasts in the BM (6) followed by anti-T serum, had no effect on the suppressor
(9). However, spleen cells from lethally-irradiated, BM reconstituted mice,
which have been shown to suppress the in vitro PFC response of syngeneic spleen
cells were sensitive to anti-T cell serum and complement (Fig. 3). This is in
agreement with a recent report by Dauphinee and Talal who were able to abrogate
the BM suppressor of NZB mice with the thymosin treatment followed by anti-
theta and complement, suggesting that the BM suppressor to be a pre-T cell.
This study further confirmed our finding that the BM suppressor cell could not
suppress the increased autoimmune responses against DNA in these mice (28, 29).

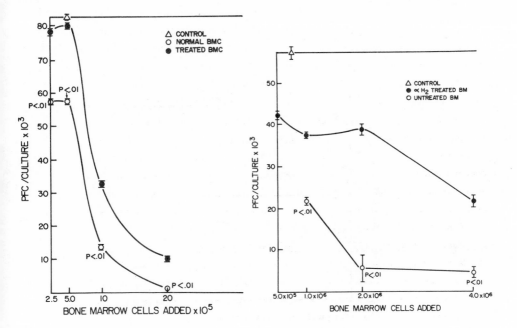

Fig. 1   Effect of anti-stem cell Ab on the suppressor cell in the bone marrow.
          20 x 10^6 BMC/ml were incubated with 1:50 dilution of anti-stem Ab
          (supplied by Dr. E. Golub) for 1 hr followed by C' treatment for 1 hr
          at room temperature. 15 x 10^6 spleen cells plus SRBC were then
          cultured with normal or treated BMC for 5 days. Vertical bars
          represent SE.

Fig. 2   Effect of anti-H₂ antibody on the suppressor cell in the bone marrow.
          20 x 10^6 BMC/ml were incubated with 1:5 dilution of anti-H₂ antibody
          (Dr. T. Delovitch) for 1 hr followed by C' treatment for 1 hr at room
          temperature. 15 x 10^6 normal spleen cells plus SRBC were then
          cultured with normal or treated BMC for 5 days. Vertical bars
          represent S.E.

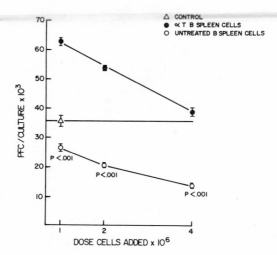

Fig. 3   Effect of anti-T cell Ab on splenic suppressor cells in lethally
          irradiated bone marrow reconstituted mice. Mice were reconstituted
          with 10^7 BMC. 6 days later 20 x 10^6 spleen cells/ml were incubated
          with anti-T cell antiserum (Cedarlane) for 1 hr followed by C' for
          1 hr at room temperature. 15 x 10^6 normal spleen cells plus SRBC
          were then cultured with varying numbers of normal or treated B-spleen
          cells for 5 days. Vertical bars represent S.E.

Suppression by Soluble Mediator

Fractionation of BMC supernatants by column chromatography and ultra-filtration revealed the presence of a suppressor factor. Bone marrow suppressor factor (B-SF) was produced by non-adherent BMC, had a molecular weight 1000 to 10,000, suppressed the antibody response in vivo and in vitro, and stimulated DNA synthesis in BMC but not thymocytes. The kinetics of suppression by BSF was similar to the BM suppressor cell. In addition, the suppressor activity of BSF could be absorbed by normal spleen cells and a minimum of 6-8 hrs preincubation with BSF was required for their response to be suppressed in vitro (Table I) or upon their adoptive transfer into lethally irradiated recipients (Figs. 4, 5) B-SF suppressed across strain barriers and was produced by all strains of mice including DBA, CBA, $C_{57}Bl$, NZB, B/W and BDF_1.

TABLE I

KINETICS OF IN VITRO SUPPRESSION BY B-SF

ADDITION TO CULTURE	PFC/CULTURE $\pm$ SE	% SUPPRESSION	P VALUE
Ag only	1804 ± 115		
B-SF	320.8 ± 28.02	82.2%	0.01
B-SF WASH 2 hrs	1535.4 ± 255.06	14.9%	NS
B-SF " 4 hrs	1439.6 ± 169.80	20.2%	NS
B-SF " 6 hrs	1616.6 ± 209.45	10.4%	NS
B-SF " 8 hrs	932.5 ± 196.21	48.3%	0.05
B-SF " 12 hrs	237 ± 54.49	86.8%	0.01

15×10^6 spleen cells were cultured with 0.1 ml of BSF added at time 0 following which cells were washed at different intervals and recultured for 5 days with SRBC.

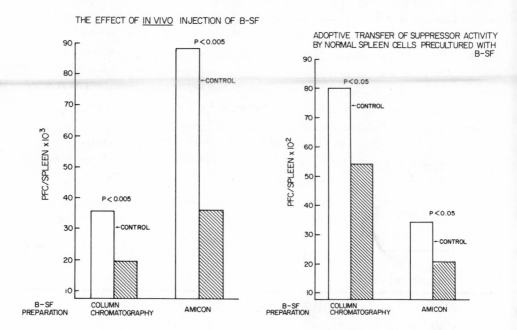

THE EFFECT OF IN VIVO INJECTION OF B-SF

ADOPTIVE TRANSFER OF SUPPRESSOR ACTIVITY
BY NORMAL SPLEEN CELLS PRECULTURED WITH
B-SF

Fig. 4   Mice were injected IP with 0.1 ml 10% SRBC plus 0.3 ml of control
buffer or suppressor factor obtained by column chromatography.
Spleens were assayed 6 days later.

Fig. 5   20 - 30 x 10^6 spleen cells/ml were cultured for 6 hours with 0.1 ml
of control buffer or suppressor factor obtained by column
chromatography or Amicon ultrafiltration. Cells were then harvested
and 50 x 10^6 spleen cells were injected i.v. into lethally
irradiated recepients with 0.1 ml 10% SRBC and assayed 6 days later.

Physical chemical characterization of B-SF revealed its heat stability up to 100° and indicated the presence of carbohydrate with little or no protein The active factor could be extracted in chloroform-methanol. Thin layer chromatography revealed significant amounts of polar glycolipids, possibly gangliosides. Suppressive supernatants, obtained from aged spleen cells showed similar kinetics and characteristics. Some of the characteristics of B-SF, including its molecular weight, heat stability and characteristics on TLC plates resemble the properties of a ganglioside which has recently been shown to participate in transmission of membrane mediated information and in regulation of immune responses (13, 31).

The striking similarities in physical characteristics of BM and aged spleen suppressor cells and soluble mediators, in addition to the similarities of their kinetics of action, suggests them to be the same cell. We have shown that BM increases its ability to suppress with age, possibly reaching a critical level before migrating to the spleen. Recently, Bennett et al. (1) have described a cell capable of suppressing the development of in vitro cell mediated immunity. This suppressor activity from BCG injected, T cell deprived mice migrated from the bone marrow to the spleen in a fashion that may be analogous to the situation in normal aging.

It has also been shown that normal mouse serum is suppressive in vitro (35) and we found that this suppressive activity increases with age (27). This increase in activity may reflect the increasing numbers or activity of suppressor cells in the spleens and bone marrow of aging mice. That this may be the case was indicated by our studies showing serum from thymectomized, lethally irradiated, bone marrow reconstituted mice to be more suppressive in vitro than serum from mice receiving T cells (9). Experiments are currently underway to further characterize and analyse the mechanism of suppression by BSF and serum factor.

REFERENCES

1. Bennett, J.A., Rao, V.S. and Mitchell, M.S. (1978) Proc. Nat. Acad. Sci. USA 75, 5142.
2. Callard, R.E. and Basten, A. (1977) Cell. Immunol. 31, 13.
3. Callard, R.E. and Basten, A. (1978) Eur. J. Immunol. 8, 552.
4. Chen, M.G. (1971) J. Cell Physiol. 78, 225.
5. Cinader, B., Paraskevas, F. and Koh, S. (1978) Cell Immunol. 40, 445.
6. Cohen, J.J. and Patterson, C.K. (1975) J. Immunol. 114, 374.
7. Cohen, J.J. and Fairchild, S.S. (1976) J. Exp. Med. 144, 456.

8.   Dauphinee, M.J. and Talal, N.   (1979)   J. Immunol. 122, 936.

9.   Duwe, A.K. and Singhal, S.K.   (1979)   Cell. Immunol. 43, 363.

10. Duwe, A.K. and Singhal, S.K.   (1979)   Cell. Immunol. 43, 372.

11. Duwe, A.K. and Singhal, S.K.   (1978)   Cell. Immunol. 39, 79.

12. Duwe, A.K., Roder, J.C. and Singhal, S.K.   (1979)   Immunology 37, 293.

13. Esselman, W.J. and Miller, H.C.   (1977)   J. Immunol. 119, 1994.

14. Gerbase-De Lima, A., Meredith, P. and Walford, R.L.   (1975)   Fed. Proc. 34, 159.

15. Doidl, E.A., Innes, J.B. and Weksler, M.E.   (1976)   J. Exp. Med. 146, 1037.

16. Goldstein, G., Scheid, M., Boyse, E.A., Schlesinger, D.H. and van Wauwe, J.   (1979)   Science 204, 1309.

17. Goodman, S.A. and Makinodan, T.   (1975)   Clin. Exp. Immunol. 19, 533.

18. Halsall, M.H., Heichick, M.L., Deitchman, J.W. and Makinodan, T.   (1973)   Gerontologist 13, 46.

19. Heidrick, M.L. and Makinodan, T.   (1973)   J. Immunol. 111, 1502.

20. Konen, T.G., Smith, G.S. and Walford, R.L.   (1973)   J. Immunol. 110, 1216.

21. Makinodan, T. and Adler, W.H.   (1975)   Fed. Proc. 35, 153.

22. Makinodan, T., Albright, J.W., Good, P.I., Peter, C.P. and Heidrick, M.L.   (1976)   Immunology 31, 903.

23. Mosier, D.E., Cohen, P.L. and Johnson, B.M.   (1975)   In Suppressor Cells in Immunity eds. S.K. Singhal and N.R. Sinclair, pp 28.

24. Mosier, D.E. and Johnson, B.M.   (1975)   J. Exp. Med. 141, 216.

25. Peter, C.P.   (1971)   Fed. Proc. 30, 526.

26. Price, G.B. and Makinodan, T.   (1972)   J. Immunol. 108, 402.

27. Roder, J.C., Duwe, A.K., Bell, D.A. and Singhal, S.K.   (1978)   Immunology 35, 837.

28. Roder, J.C., Bell, D.A. and Singhal, S.K.   (1978)   J. Immunol. 121, 29.

29. Roder, J.C., Bell, D.A. and Singhal, S.K.   (1978)   J. Immunol. 121, 38.

30. Roder, J.C., Bell, D.A. and Singhal, S.K.   (1977)   Cell. Immunol. 29, 272.

31. Ryan, J.J. and Shinitzky, M.   (1979)   Eur. J. Immunol. 9, 171.

32. Singhal, S.K., Roder, J.C. and Duwe, A.   (1978)   Proc. Fed. Am. Soc. Exp. Biol. 37, 55.

33. Smith, A.M.   (1976)   J. Immunol. 116, 469.

34. Tyan, M.L.   (1977)   J. Immunol. 118, 846.

35. Veit, B. and Michael, S.G.   (1973)   J. Immunol. 111, 341.

DISCUSSION

TALAL: I'd like to support your idea that this cell works on a B cell because we have, as you know, found probably the same cell in the bone marrow and have compared its properties in DBA/2 and NZB mice. The bone marrow suppressor cell of NZB mice is perfectly able to suppress the DBA/2 plaque forming cell response in the spleen, so the NZB has this cell and it is functional. However, the NZB spleen cannot respond either to its own bone marrow suppressor or to the bone marrow suppressor from the DBA/2. So, the spleen is refractory to the signalling from this cell. When we fractionate spleen cells into T and B cell subpopulations, the refractory cell is the B cell. So that would support the idea that it is working on a B cell. Now we differ in that our bone marrow suppressor cell is inducible by Goldstein's thymus fraction-5 and, when induced, does express Theta and then can be killed by anti-theta and complement. So we think of it as a pre-T cell. What we would like to know, maybe you can tell us about this, is what is the cell recognizing? What is the nature of this signalling network? Is it in anyway restricted by H-2 or by Ig?

SINGHAL: Our attempts to suppress anti-DNA antibodies by this suppressor cell entirely failed. It would not touch antibodies directed against DNA. Of course, it is present in the NZB and BW animals. I cannot say anything about whether it would suppress its own response or not, but it is present.
Con A treatment which turns on T cells in the marrow, followed by incubation with anti-theta and complement does not eliminate this suppressor cell. We have tested only one preparation of thymosin like-material supplied to us by Ed Potworowski. Anti-theta treatment killed a certain percentage of cells, but it had no effect on suppression.

BASH: I wonder if your data exclude a third possibility - namely that your cell may be a macrophage precursor?

SINGHAL: This cell does not appear to be a promonocyte, monocyte, or a macrophage. It is non-adherent, relatively radio-sensitive and cannot be eliminated by carbonyl iron and/or anti-macrophage serum and complement treatments. Furthermore, the kinetics of suppression by phagocytic cells is quite different. This cell has to be present during the first 24 hrs at the induction phase of the response, whereas phagocytic cells can suppress when added as late as 3 or 4 days after initiation of the IgM response.

BASH: Some of these properties appear to be of precursor cells.

SINGHAL: Yes. We have considered this cell to be a pre-B cell because of its sensitivity to dextran sulfate which is a known pre-B cell mitogen. Preincubation of these cells with dextran sulfate for 24 hrs in serum free medium results in an increased release of the suppressor factor which I described in my presentation.

Published 1979 by Elsevier North Holland, Inc.
Singhal, Sinclair, Stiller, eds. Aging and Immunity

SEX HORMONES, DISORDERED IMMUNOLOGIC REGULATION AND AUTOIMMUNITY

N. TALAL, J.R. ROUBINIAN AND S. SAWADA
Department of Medicine, University of California, San Francisco
and Section of Arthritis/Clinical Immunology, Veterans
Administration Medical Center, San Francisco, California

Our laboratory has been investigating the relationship between
the immunologic and endocrine systems. The major studies have involved the NZB/NZW F_1 (B/W) mouse model for systemic lupus erythe-
matosus (SLE). This animal spontaneously develops LE cells, antibodies to nucleic acids, and immune complex glomerulonephritis.
The disease occurs earlier and with greater severity in female
mice who have a 50% mortality by seven months of age. Mortality
in males does not reach this point until well after one year of
life. We found that sex hormones significantly modulate autoimmunity and survival in this strain. Androgens suppress and
estrogens accelerate disease. These results may help explain
the marked female predominance of lupus in the human population.
SLE is ten times more common in females compared to males if one
considers women during the years of active reproductive capability.
This ratio falls to three to one when one compares premenopausal
and postmenopausal females to males.

Before discussing the murine disorder, let us briefly consider
a clinical experience that concerns a pair of monozygotic twins
with Klinefelter's syndrome.[1] Males with Klinefelter's syndrome
have an extra X chromosome (XXY) and develop gynecomastia and
sparse bodily hair. They are prone to autoantibodies and autoimmune disease.[2] We recently studied monozygotic twins with
Klinefelter's syndrome (TABLE 1); both had features of

78

autoimmunity, but one twin had clinical SLE, and the other had myasthenia gravis. The twin with SLE had high-titered antibodies to nucleic acids and to lymphocyte surface antigens which were lacking in the twin with myasthenia gravis. Both had significant levels of antibodies to the acetylcholine receptor. These observations demonstrate that genetic and hormonal influences are important in the pathogenesis of human autoimmune disease. They also suggest that environmental factors play a role in determining which autoimmune disease develops in a given patient.

Let us now turn to a consideration of autoimmunity in B/W mice. As already mentioned, female B/W mice have a much earlier onset of disease. Prepubertal castration of male B/W mice, performed at two weeks of age, resulted in an essentially female pattern of disease expression.[3] Castrated males developed high-titered antibodies to DNA and died prematurely of an accelerated glomerulonephritis. Prepubertal castration of female B/W mice failed to improve survival, although some subtle immunologic improvements were observed.

The administration of 5-α-dihydrotestosterone to castrated female B/W mice resulted in a highly significant amelioration of disease.[4] Androgen-treated mice had reduced levels of antibodies to DNA, less deposition of immune complexes in the renal glomeruli, and greatly prolonged survival. By contrast, mice treated with 17-β-estradiol had exactly opposite effects. The estrogen-treated mice developed more autoantibodies, more severe immune complex renal deposits, and had markedly decreased survival. The ability of androgen and estrogen to modulate one important parameter of autoimmunity, the levels of IgG antibodies to DNA, is shown in FIGURE 1.

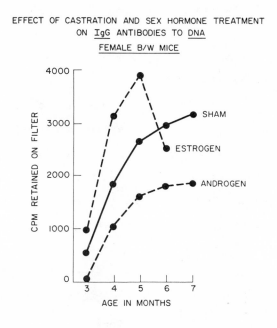

EFFECT OF CASTRATION AND SEX HORMONE TREATMENT
ON IgG ANTIBODIES TO DNA
FEMALE B/W MICE

Fig. 1. The effect of androgen and estrogen on IgG antibodies to DNA in female B/W mice. Animals were castrated prepubertally and received hormone-containing capsules subcutaneously at the time of surgery.

In these experiments, the presence of the thymus was required
to observe some of these hormone-dependent changes.[4] For example,
the accelerated development of IgG antibodies to polyadenylic acid
that appeared in castrated B/W male mice was not seen in animals
also subjected to neonatal thymectomy. Experiments underway are
investigating more precisely what aspects of T cell function and
which T cell subpopulations are influenced by sex hormones.

The experiments presented up to now can be considered prophylactic in that the administration of androgen was initiated
at an age prior to the development of clinical autoimmune disease.
To more closely approximate the situation in patients with SLE,
androgen administration was delayed until an age when disease was
already established. Three and six-month old female B/W mice
were chosen for these therapeutic experiments.[5] The administration of 5-α-dihydrotestotestrone at these ages still resulted in
a marked prolongation of survival accompanied by less evidence
of immune complex deposition in the kidneys. However, in contrast
to the prophylactic experiments, there was no significant reduction in anti-DNA antibody concentrations in these mice undergoing
delayed androgen treatment. Androgen-induced changes in the complement system and/or immune complexes may explain this result.
Androgen is known to induce several complement components in mice,
and complement is important in the clearance of circulating immune
complexes. Abnormalities in the immune complex clearance are
present in many patients with SLE. The possible influence of
androgen on immune complex metabolism in B/W mice is currently
under investigation.

For over two decades, NZB and B/W mice have been the classical
animal models for studying SLE. Recently, another murine strain

which spontaneously develops a lupus-like syndrome has been developed by Dr. E. D. Murphy and his colleagues at the Jackson Laboratories.[6] This strain, called MRL/lpr, is genetically predisposed to the formation of LE cells, antibodies to DNA, and immune complex glomerulonephritis. It is analagous to the B/W mouse in these respects. In addition, this new strain develops massive generalized lymph node enlargement due to the presence of a θ-positive population.[7] The related strain, MRL/++, lacks the autosomal recessive gene lpr and develops neither autoimmunity nor lymphoproliferation. These two strains are over 90% genetically identical. We have recently found that T cells in MRL/lpr mice stimulate spleen cells from MRL/++ mice to produce antibodies to DNA. Using an in vitro culture system and a radioimmunoprecipitation assay to measure antibodies to DNA,[8] we found that θ-positive cells from MRL/lpr spleen or lymph node produce a significant ($p < 0.005$) increase in anti-DNA antibody production (TABLE 2). Thus, in this new model, SLE is associated with the presence of helper T cells which specifically promote autoantibody production. This model contrasts with the NZB mouse in which a deficiency of suppressor T cells is associated with autoimmunity.[9-11]

Human SLE probably represents a common clinical pathway that develops from more than one immunopathogenic mechanism. Some lupus patients may have abnormalities of suppressor cells whereas others may demonstrate overactivity of helper cells. Because of the interlocking nature of the immune system and the importance of T cell circuits and idiotype networks, abnormalities of both suppression and help may exist together or at different times in a single patient. The availability of more than one animal model

for lupus should aid in unraveling the complexities of disordered
immunologic regulation which underlie the autoimmune diseases.

TABLE 1

MONOZYGOTIC TWINS WITH KLINEFELTER'S SYNDROME DISCORDANT FOR
AUTOIMMUNE DISEASE

Autoantibody	Twin One	Twin Two
Antinuclear Factor	1:160	Absent
LE Cell	Present	Absent
Anti-DNA	Present	Absent
Anti-Poly A	Present	Absent
Anti-Lymphocyte	Present	Absent
Anti-Acetylcholine Receptor	Present	Present
Diagnosis	SLE	Myasthenia Gravis

TABLE 2

ENHANCEMENT OF ANTI-DNA ANTIBODY PRODUCTION BY MRL/++ SPLEEN CELLS
AFTER THE ADDITION OF MRL/lpr T CELLS

Cell Source	ng DNA Bound/Culture
MRL/++ Spleen	110 ± 33
MRL/++ Spleen plus MRL/lpr Spleen T Cells (C' Treated)	442 ± 68
MRL/++ spleen plus MRL/lpr Spleen T Cells (anti-θ and C' Treated)	61 ± 15

83

ACKNOWLEDGMENTS

Our research was supported by the Medical Research Service of
the Veterans Administration, by U.S. Public Health Service Grant
(AM-16140), by a Grant from the Kroc Foundation, and a Contract
from the State of California.

REFERENCES

1. Michalski, J.P., Synder, S.M., McLeod, R.L. and Talal N. (1978)
   Arthritis Rheum., 21, 306-309.
2. Stern, R., Fishman, J., Brusman H. and Kunkel, H.G. (1977)
   Arthritis Rheum., 20, 18-22.
3. Roubinian, J.R. Papoian, R. and Talal, N. (1977) J. Clin.
   Invest., 59, 1066-1070.
4. Roubinian, J.R., Talal, N., Greenspan, J.S., Goodman, J.R.
   and Siiteri, P.K. (1978) J. Exp. Med., 147, 1568-1583.
5. Roubinian, J.R., Talal, N., Greenspan, J.S., Goodman, J.R.
   and Siiteri, P.K. (1979) J. Clin. Invest., 63, 902-911.
6. Murphy, E.D. and Roths, J.B. (1978) in Genetic Control of
   Autoimmune Disease. N.R. Rose, P.E. Bigazzi and N.L. Warner,
   ed., Elsevier, N. Holland/New York, pp. 207-219.
7. Andrews, B.S., Eisenberg, R.A., Theofilopoulos, A.N., Isui, S.,
   Wilson, C.B., McConahey, P.J., Murphy, E.D., Roths, J.B. and
   Dixon, J.F. (1978) J. Exp. Med., 148, 1198-1215.
8. Sawada, S. and Talal, N. (1979) J. Immunol., 122,
9. Shirai, T., Hayakawa, K., Okumura, K. and Tada T. (1978)
10.Barthold, D.R., Kysela, S. and Steinberg, A.D. (1974)
   J. Immunol., 112, 9-16.
11.Krakauer, R.S., Waldmann, T.A. and Strober, W. (1976)
   J. Exp. Med., 144, 662-673.

DISCUSSION

PAUL: Does the female that has successive implantations with androgen live longer than a BW male? It would appear that way from your work.

TALAL: The answer is yes. The male develops accelerated disease at about 9 or 10 months of age. We found that there is a spontaneous reduction in the amount of androgen that those male animals make at that age. So if at 8 months of age we implant the male with an androgen containing capsule then it lives significantly longer than it would if it didn't get implanted. Possibly it has an autoimmune testicular involvement of some sort.

ABDOU: I would like to know your thoughts about two things. If you extrapolate this to a human situation, I am sure you are aware that there is no hormonal abnormality in a male lupus patient. Secondly, how could sex hormonal abnormality induce a supposed suppressor dysfunction in an NZB model?

TALAL: I think as one looks more carefully, not at simply metabolites, but at balances and activities between non-major metabolites, that abnormalities are going to appear. So I think the question of whether there is a hyperestrogenic influence in human lupus is a very active question. I believe that we are going to see abnormalities of sex hormones that could be influenced. I am saying it is playing modulating influences in the expression of disease. The Klinefelter patients have been shown to be hyperestrogenic. Your second question has to do with suppressor cells and the influence of hormones. We have tried to look at the question of where androgen and estrogen may be acting. I am not a strong proponent of the idea that lupus is simply due to a suppressor problem and I think one of the things that the MRL strain illustrates beautifully is that we may have a model of lupus due to an over-active helper cell. So I would not want to say that androgen restores suppressive function, rather I would hope that it is acting more to appropriately adjust T cell circuits. Also, I would not rule out the fact that it is going to have effects on other cell populations like B cells and macrophages.

CANTOR: The androgen treated females, which have a strikingly lengthened life span, seem to produce relatively large amounts of anti-DNA antibody. You raised the intriguing possibility that the androgen might, for example, act via inducing a gene which might increase complement levels and deal with complexes differently so that they don't reach the kidneys. This does fit with some of our preliminary experiments indicating that the androgen-treated females did not seem to have the sorts of restored T cell regulation that we were looking for. So my question is – you may be ameliorating the disease by increasing the handling and breakdown of complexes before they reach the kidney. Is this borne out by studies of radiolabelled DNA anti-DNA complexes in the two strains of mice?

TALAL: We are doing those studies now, we don't have any information.

Published 1979 by Elsevier North Holland, Inc.
Singhal, Sinclair, Stiller, eds. Aging and Immunity

LYMPHOCYTE REACTIVITY TO PROTEIN ANTIGENS: IN VIVO CONSEQUENCES OF ORAL
EXPOSURE TO PROTEINS AND IN VITRO PROPAGATION OF ANTIGEN SPECIFIC T CELLS.

J.M. CHILLER, R.G. TITUS, R.D. SCHRIER, B.J. KURNICK, J.T. KURNICK, AND
E. DEFREITAS
National Jewish Hospital and Research Center, Denver, Colorado 80206, U.S.A.

A. Orally Induced Specific Tolerance: Cellular Dissection

Immune anergy resulting from the introduction of antigen via the gastrointestinal tract represents the earliest described example of the phenomenon of
experimentally induced immunologic tolerance (1-3). More recently, there has
been renewed interest in the phenomenon, more specifically with regard to the
cellular level affected and the basis by which it is induced and maintained.
Our laboratory has pursued the model of oral tolerance induced in mice to protein antigens originally described by Hanson et al. (4) wherein mice administered protein antigens via the intragastric (IG) route exhibit a profound state
of immune anergy to subsequent parenteral parental immunogenic challenges. The
following characteristics have been delineated:

1. IG treatment with such T-dependent antigens as ovalbumin (OVA), human
gamma globulin (HGG) and keyhole limpet hemocyanin (KLH) induces specific
carrier tolerance to subsequent challenges with the protein or haptenated
protein conjugates. Such a tolerant state is long lasting (2-4 months following
a single IG treatment), affects IgM, IgG and IgE specific responses and is
maintained when spleen cells from animals IG treated with protein are adoptively transferred to lethally irradiated syngeneic recipient mice.

2. IG administration of large amounts of T-independent antigens such as
bacterial lipopolysaccharide (LPS), polyvinyl pirrolidone (PVP) or dinitrophenylated ficoll (DNP-F) does not lead to an anergic state.

3. T-dependent antigens administered to specifically primed animals do not
convey specific anergy. On the contrary, primed mice exposed to antigen via
the intragastric route respond vigorously to the antigen. The basis for this
conclusion can be seen in Table I, which depicts an experiment in which the
following protocol was utilized. Groups of mice were primed to OVA by IP
injection with OVA in complete Freund's adjuvant. Control animals were injected with saline in CFA. Four weeks later, an equal number of mice in each
group received either 20 mg OVA or saline IG. Those mice which had been
initially primed with OVA in CFA were analyzed 5 days after feeding for splenic
IgG PFC specific to OVA. Those mice initially primed with saline in CFA were

subsequently challenged with OVA in CFA IP and assessed individually for PFC specific to OVA. The results of this experiment (Table I) show that mice parentally primed to OVA in CFA exhibited a marked anamnestic response to OVA given intragastrically (compare group B with group A). However, the identical oral regimen of OVA which led to immunity to OVA primed mice (group B) led to tolerance in the CFA primed control animals (compare group D with group E). Furthermore, no response was observed in mice initially primed with saline in CFA and then exposed to OVA IG (group C). Thus, the ability to induce oral tolerance was dependent upon the immune state of the animal: non-primed mice exposed to OVA IG were tolerized whereas specifically primed mice exposed to OVA IG were immunized.

Table I   Effect of Administering Antigen Orally in Primed Mice

Treatment		Challenge Group		Response $\pm$ SE
				(Ind. PFC/10^6 spleen cells)
Days: 0	28	35 & 49		
OVA/CFA	saline	none	A	5 ± 3
OVA/CFA	OVA	none	B	291 ± 78
Sal/CFA	OVA	none	C	2 ± 1
Sal/CFA	saline	OVA/CFA	D	183 ± 54
SAl/CFA	OVA	OVA/CFA	E	11 ± 3

Response of mice in groups A, B and C were assayed 5 days after the IG treatment (20 mg OVA) given on day 28. Response of mice in groups D and E were assayed 5 days after the second of identical challenge regiment (400 μg OVA in CFA IP) given on days 35 and 49.

4.   Dissection of the cellular level affected by the oral administration of T-dependent antigens into normal mice reveals that while T cell function is specifically silenced, B cell activity can be recovered. T cell function affected includes T helper activity, antigen induced T cell proliferation and delayed type hypersensitivity (DTH) to protein measured by footpad swelling (Table II). T helper cell function in orally-tolerant mice was assessed by

challenging mice administered OVA IG with a haptenated form of the antigen, namely, DNP-OVA injected IP with CFA. Eight days after challenge, OVA fed mice showed a markedly depressed response to DNP-OVA as compared to mice initially treated IG with saline. Furthermore, OVA fed mice were able to respond in a normal fashion to DNP coupled onto a heterologous carrier, namely DNP-KLH.

T cell proliferative capacity was assessed in HGG tolerant mice, although it should be stressed that the identical conclusion was reached in the situation where OVA was used as the tolerizing antigen. Mice fed HGG or saline were injected one week later at the base of the tail with either HGG or OVA in CFA. Eight days later, a suspension of T cells from the draining lymph nodes of each group of mice was cultured in vitro in the presence of either HGG or OVA in an assay system previously described (5). The results of such an experimental protocol show that whereas HGG fed mice immunized with HGG were unable to proliferate in vitro to HGG as compared to control animals administered saline IG, HGG fed mice immunized with OVA provided T cells capable of proliferating to OVA to an extent similar as that of T cells derived from mice IG treated with saline and subsequently challenged in the tail with OVA.

Finally, T cell function inherent in delayed type hypersensitivity was assayed by the means outlined in the legend to Table III. The results of this experimental approach show that compared to saline treated controls, OVA fed mice were unable to mount a DTH response to OVA but were unhindered in their capacity to demonstrate a DTH reaction to the control antigen HGG.

Thus, the induction of oral tolerance to protein antigens in mice resulted in the specific abrogation of three T cell functions, namely T cell helper activity, T cell proliferative capacity and the ability to mediate DTH.

In marked contrast to the anergy of T cell function exhibited by mice orally tolerized to proteins, specific B cell function in such animals appears to be unaltered. This conclusion is based on 2 different experimental approaches aimed at rescuing B cell activity inherent in mice demonstrating phenotypic tolerance to T dependent antigens. In the first case, specific B cell function was determined by the ability to obtain an anti-OV response in mice IG pretreated with OVA coupled to a carrier such as horse erythrocytes (HE). The design of this approach was predicated on the assumption that, lacking T helper activity, OVA fed mice would be unable to be challenged with OVA alone. However, if such animals possessed OVA responsive B cells, they should be able to respond to OVA presented on a recognizable carrier i.e., on HE. Table III shows that this indeed appears to be the case, namely, that OVA fed mice respond to OVA-HE as well as do animals pretreated with saline.

Table II.   Status of T cell functions in orally-tolerant mice

T Cell Functions studied	Intragastric treatment[a]	Challenge antigen[b]	Response in relevant assay[c]	
T helper activity			PFC/10^6 spleen cells $\pm$ (SE) x 10^{-2}	
	Saline	DNP–OVA	34.6	(1.6)
	OVA	DNP–OVA	0.6	(1.6)
	OVA	DNP–KLH	10.2	(1.7)
	Saline	DNP–KLH	9.2	(2.2)
T cell proliferative capacity			Uptake of ^{3}HRdR, cpm $\pm$ (SE) x 10^{-3}	
	Saline	HGG	163	(5)
	HGG	HGG	8	(4)
	HGG	OVA	124	(8)
	Saline	OVA	139	(5)
Mediation of DTH			Increase in footpad thickness, mm $\pm$ (SE)	
	Saline	OVA	0.95	(0.07)
	OVA	OVA	- 0.03	(0.05)
	OVA	HGG	1.00	(0.11)
	Saline	HGG	1.13	(0.11)

[a] Groups of BDF_1 mice were administered 20 mg OVA or groups of A/J mice received 3 doses of 8 mg each of HGG by stomach intubation. Control animals were given saline alone.

[b] Challenge occurred 7 days after either the single or initial intragastric treatment. Either 200 μg of DNP-OVA or DNP-KLH were emulsified in CFA and injected i.p. Either 100 μg of HGG or OVA incorporated in CFA was injected at the base of the tail.

[c] The revelant assay was performed 8 days after challenge. The splenic PFC response represents the IgG PFC response to DNP measured in individual mice of groups ranging from 4 to 8 in number. Proliferative responses shown are those obtained after 5 days of culture at the optimal antigen concentration. Background (saline) proliferation values were subtracted; they ranged between 0.7 and 3.8 x 10^{-3} cpm. Delayed type hypersensitivity reactions were elicited according to the following protocol. Mice were sensitized by injecting 50 μg of antigen emulsified in 20 μl CFA subcutaneously into each side of the base of the tail. Eight days later, delayed type hypersensitivity (DTH) was elicited by challenging the animals in the footpad with 30 μl of a 2% suspension of heat-aggregated antigen in saline. The contralateral footpad, serving as a control, was injected with saline alone. Twenty-four hours post-challenge, footpad thickness was measured with calipers and the extent of swelling was calculated by subtracting the thickness of the saline-injected footpad from that of the antigen-challenged footpad. Groups of mice consisted of 5 to 10 animals each. The values given signify the arithmetic mean of the response + the standard error of the mean.

Furthermore, the response so elicited is specific to OVA in that the plaque forming cells (PFC) revealed are specifically inhibited by OVA. A second approach to the same question involved the use of LPS with the rationale that it may act as a surrogate helper activity in the demonstration of B cell capacity. Using the approach whose experimental details are outlined in the legend to Table III, it was seen that whereas mice tolerant to OVA did not respond to a challenge with OVA or with LPS alone, such animals did form OVA specific PFC following treatment with OVA and LPS to an extent equivalent to that seen in control groups of mice. Further preliminary experiments support the notion that LPS in the latter instance may be acting as a T cell surrogate rather than ablating specific T cell suppression since animals rescued from tolerance by the dual LPS/OVA regimen neither displayed DTH to OVA nor had cells which could provide specific help in a secondary in vitro response.

5. Spleen cells from mice administered antigen IG were capable of adoptively transferring suppression to syngeneic normal recipients (6,7). This specific effect was abrogated when spleen cells were treated with anti Thy1.2 and complement and evident when spleen cells were enriched to T lymphocytes by nylon wool fractionation.

The observations outlined above provide some insight into the cellular parameters associated with tolerance which can be induced to various antigens via the oral route. The findings that the phenomenon maybe restricted to certain classes of antigen (T dependent) and associated with loss of T cell but not B cell functions may be related to the presence of suppressor T lymphocytes if it is assumed that such cells may be preferentially induced by T dependent antigens and mediate their mode of action by regulating T cell rather than B cell function. However, a final scheme inherent in this state of tolerance must await further details of the mechanism by which it is induced and maintained. At present, the system is of potential interest from the standpoint that it represents a biological means by which the immune system is exposed to the world of foreign antigens. The fact that anergy as well as immunity can be derived from the introduction of antigens by such a route raises the fundamental issue of the fate of antigen in the gastrointestinal tract and how these products can lead to divergent stimulation of the immune network.

B. Propagation of Specific T Cells

The capacity to propagate T lymphocytes in vitro has received the recent attention of many laboratories (8-14) where it has been shown in both murine

Table III   Status of B cell Function in Orally-tolerant Mice

Intragastric Treatment[a]	Challenge antigen	Response[d] Indirect PFC/10^6 spleen cells $\pm$ (SE)	
Saline	OVA[b]	283	(90)
OVA	OVA	23	(4)
OVA	OVA-HE	201	(75)
Saline	OVA-HE	267	(129)
Saline	OVA[c]	145	(48)
OVA	OVA	1	(0.4)
OVA	LPS	2	(1.0)
OVA	OVA/LPS	429	(147)
Saline	OVA/LPS	356	(78)

[a] Groups of BDF$_1$ mice were administered 20 mg OVA by stomach intubation. Control animals were given saline alone.

[b] Seven days after intragastric treatment, the groups of mice indicated received 2×10^8 OVA-HE in CFA delivered i.p. Controls were challenged with 400 μg OVA in CFA. Three weeks later all mice were challenged with 200 μg OVA in CFA.

[c] Seven days after intragastric treatment, the groups of mice indicated were treated with 500 μg OVA injected i.p. followed at 3 hr with 50 μg LPS injected i.v. Control groups of animals received OVA but no LPS. Two weeks later, all animals were challenged i.p. with 400 μg OVA in CFA, and 2 weeks thereafter, the control mice only were challenged with 200 μg OVA in CFA given i.p.

[d] Seven days after the last challenge with antigen, mice were evaluated individually for splenic IgG PFC to OVA. Each group represents the arithmetic mean of the response of 5 to 8 animals $\pm$ standard error of the mean.

and human systems that it is possible to perpetuate if not immortalize T cells which show specific functional properties such as cytotoxicity mixed lymphocyte reactivity and helper function in antibody formation. The experiments to be described below represent a summary of the efforts of our laboratory in applying the methodology used by others to propagate T cells with the purpose of enriching T cells specific to protein antigens as measured either by their capacity to proliferate or to provide specific helper function.

The starting point of these experiments derives from a method which we have utilized to measure specific T cell proliferation wherein T cells obtained from lymph node (LN) of mice primed with antigen in CFA at the base of the tail respond vigorously in vitro when exposed to the homologous antigen (5). Utilizing this means of priming, BDF_1 mice were immunized with 100 ug OVA in CFA and lymph nodes removed 7 days later. One portion of the lymph node cells was tested for antigen specific proliferation and a second portion was cultured with B cells and antigen to assess helper capacity. The remaining OVA primed lymph node cells were stimulated in culture with antigen and four days later, a time when the number of blast cells was at a peak, the cultures were harvested and cells placed on Ficoll Hypaque to enrich for blast and viable cells. Aliquots of such cells were as before tested for helper and proliferation capacity while the remainder were cultured at a density of $1x10^5$ cells/ml in the supernatant fluid (SUP) obtained 24 hours after incubating normal syngeneic spleen cells with Con A. Four days after growth in the SUP from which Con A was either removed or neutralized, blast cells were again assessed for either helper or antigen induced proliferative capacity. Thus, 3 types of cells, primed lymph node cells, antigen induced blast cells and SUP propagated blast cells were tested for two activities, namely capacity to undergo antigen induced proliferation and ability to provide antigen specific help in a secondary hapten carrier system.

The results presented in Table IV reveal data obtained from one of several such experiments. In this case, varying concentrations of T cells obtained at each step, ie., OVA primed lymph node cells, antigen induced blast cells and SUP propagated blast cells, were tested for their capacity to cooperate with B cells, the latter obtained as anti Thy 1.2 and complement treated spleen cells from DNP-KLH primed syngeneic mice. It can be seen that each step of the procedure yielded increasing helper activity, an effect most noticeable when lower number of cells were tested. For example, whereas $2x10^3$ lymph node cells from primed animals failed to provide helper function, $2x10^3$ Ag propagated blast cells provided some cooperation, while the same

Table IV   Comparative Helper Capacity of Lymph Node Cells,
AG Induced Blasts and SUP Propagated Blasts[a]

| Helper Cells | Response ($PFC/10^6$)[b] | | | | | | | | |
| | LNC | | | AG Blasts | | | Sup Blasts | | |
# X 10^{-4}	Med.	DNP-O	DNP-K	Med.	DNP-O	DNP-K	Med.	DNP-O	DNP-K
25	4	3300	275	–	–	–	–	–	–
5	4	400	60	49	2100	10	0	1467	4
1	12	113	56	40	2000	25	15	4000	3
0.2	4	10	8	7	380	51	0	1157	1
0.1	3	0	4	1	0	15	0	219	0
0.1 (NMS + C)							–	1067	–
0.2 (NMS + C)							–	1328	–
0.1 (Thy 1.2 + C)							–	19	–
0.2 (Thy 1.2 + C)							–	3	–

[a] Comparative helper activity of BDF_1 primed lymph node cells, antigen activated blast cells and SUP propagated blast cells as a function of decreasing number of helper cells/well. DNP-KLH primed BDF_1 spleen cells treated with anti Thy 1.2 + C were used as a source of B cells (5×10^5 cells/well).

[b] Indirect plaque-forming cells (PFC) from triplicate cultures expressed as $PFC/10^6$ spleen cells. The data presented are day 6 responses; similar trends were obtained on days 5 and 8. DNP-OVA (DNP-O), DNP-KLH (DNP-K) or medium (Med.) was added to each source of helper cells evaluated. The anti Thy 1 + C treatment of the B cell source allowed DNP-KLH to be used as a specificity control (PFC response of spleen cells to DNP-KLH was 3933 before and 87 after removal of Thy 1^+ cells). Non-conjugated SRBC were tested in each group and few if any plaques to SRBC were observed. Lymph node cells, antigen induced or supernatant grown blast cells cultured without hapten primed spleen cells did not produce PFC even in the presence of specific antigen.

[c] SUP propagated blast cells were treated with either normal mouse serum (NMS) + C or anti-Thy 1.2 + C before assessing for helper function.

number of SUP propagated blast cells provided significantly more helper function. The helper capacity seen in all cases was OVA specific since cultures responded to challenge with DNP-OVA but not with DNP-KLH. A point of further significance shown in Table IV is that the helper effect generated at each step was totally abrogated by treating the cultured cells with anti Thy 1.2 serum and complement.

The stepwise functional enrichment which was evident for specific helper activity was also apparent when the 3 sources of cells were tested for antigen induced proliferation. In this case, each source of cells was cultured at a concentration of 1×10^4 cells per well in the presence or absence of 5×10^5 irradiated filler cells obtained from spleens of normal syngeneic mice. The response to specific antigen (OVA) or nonspecific antigen (HGG) was monitored on days 2-4 of culture. The data presented in Table V which reveals the results obtained on day 3 of culture, serve to emphasize several points. First, as was the case for helper function, there was a stepwise enrichment of proliferative capacity at each step of the protocol. Thus, whereas 10^4 primed lymph node cells responded minimally, if at all to specific antigen even in the presence of filler cells, antigen induced blast cells responded to a small but highly significant degree while SUP propagated blast cells responded in a more pronounced fashion. Second, the antigen induced response was specific in that no proliferation was apparent with HGG. Third, the OVA induced response was totally dependent on the presence of irradiated filler cells. Finally, other data not presented show that each of the 3 sources of cells respond to an equivalent degree to the nonspecific mitogen Con A and that the inability of 10^4 primed lymph node cells to respond to antigen appears to be a reflection of specific cell frequency, since 4×10^5 cells from the same source responded vigorously to the antigen.

The finding that filler cells are necessary in order to demonstrate proliferation of the enriched population of antigen reactive T cells is itself of interest and has been further pursued. The following points summarize the findings relevant to this question. First, effective "filler effect" can be provided by irradiated spleen cells which have been depleted of T cells, but not by spleen cells treated so as to deplete adherent or accessory cells. Second, in the case where spleen cells are depleted of adherent cells by passage through G-10 Sephadex, supplementation with small numbers of peritoneal cells replenishes the capacity to support T cell proliferation. Third, either syngeneic or semisyngeneic cells are required for effective filler function, more specifically cells which demonstrate syngeny restricted

Table V   Enrichment of Antigen Specific Proliferation Capacity

	Net Response − CPM ± (SE) x 10^{-3}			
	+ Filler Cells		− Filler Cells	
	OVA	HGG	OVA	HGG
LN Cells	0.2 (0.1)	0.2 (0.1)	0.3 (0.2)	0.1 (0.1)
AG Blast	4.6 (0.8)	0.2 (0.1)	0.4 (0.2)	0.1 (0.1)
SUP Blast	14.8 (2.1)	0.2 (0.1)	0.2 (0.1)	0.2 (0.1)

$1x10^{4}$ of each cell source were placed in culture with saline OVA (100 µg/ml) or HGG (100 µg/ml) in the absence (− filler cells) or the presence (+ filler cells) of $5x10^{5}$ irradiated (3000 r) syngeneic spleen cells. Triplicate samples of each experimental point were harvested following a 24 hr pulse with ^{3}HTdR on day 3. Responses are expressed as the average value from which background (saline) responses were subtracted.

to the Ia region of the major histocompatibility complex. Fourth, the protocol which yields enrichment of T cells vis-a-vis specific helper and proliferative function also results in the apparent depletion of alloreactive cells. And finally, it is possible to select from BDG_{1} primed lymph node cells, cells which can preferentially react to the antigen in the context of either one of the parental haplotypes.

The foregoing brief compilation of findings regarding the propagation of antigen reactive helper cells to proteins represents the beginning of efforts whose final aim will be to obtain clones of specific helper cell populations, a feat which has recently been accomplished by others using erythrocyte antigens (15,16). Ideally, such methodology coupled to the observations made above, should permit a more detailed analysis into the problem of lymphocyte interaction and the restriction imposed by products of the major histocompatibility complex.

REFERENCES

1. Besredka, A. (1909) Ann. Dist. Pasteur Lille 23, 166.
2. Wells, H.G. and Osborne, T.B. (1911) J. Infect. Dis. 8, 66.
3. Chase, M.W. (1946) Pro. Soc. Exp. Biol. Med. 61, 257.
4. Hanson, D.G., Vaz, N.M., Maia, L.C.S., Hornbrock, M.M., Lynch, J.M. and Roy, C.A. (1977) Int. Arch. Allergy Appl. Immunol. 55, 526.
5. Corradin, G., Etlinger, H.M. and Chiller, J.M. (1977) J. Immunol. 119, 1048.
6. Ngan, J. and Kind, L.S. (1978) J. Immunol. 120, 861.
7. Richman, L.K., Chiller, J.M., Brown, W.R., Hanson, D.G. and Vaz, N.M. (1978) J. Immunol. 121, 2429.
8. Ruscetti, R.W., Morgan, D.A. and Gallo, R.C. (1977) J. Immunol. 119, 131.
9. Gillis, S. and Smith, K.A. (1977) Nature 268, 254.
10. Nabholz, M., Engers, H.D., Collavo, D. and North, M. (1978) Current Topics Micro. Immunol. 81, 176.
11. Fathman, C.G. and Hengartner, H. (1978) Nature 272, 617.
12. Baker, P.E., Gillis, S. and Smith, K.A. (1978) J. Exp. Med. 149, 273.
13. Glasebrook, A.L. and Fitch, F.W. (1979) Nature 278, 171.
14. Kurnick, J.T., Gronvik, K., Kimura, A.K., Lindblom, J.B., Skoog, V.T., Sjoberg, O. and Wigzell, H. (1979) J. Immunol. 122, 1255.
15. Schreier, M. and Tees, R. Int. Arch. Allerg. Immunol., in press.
16. Watson, J.D. J. Exp. Med., in press.

This work was supported by USPHS Grant Al 13131 and CA 21825.

DISCUSSION

TANNER: Is there a change with age in tolerization produced by feeding, and secondly, is there a dose effect such that over-feeding produces one thing and under-feeding produces another?

CHILLER: I hate to think that the latter were true. For the first question, our data is rather preliminary in terms of old mice being fed. They certainly are harder to tolerize but why becomes the problem. Are they harder to tolerize, for example, because they have been exposed environmentally to antigens which crossreact with ovalbumin and now, rather than looking at an aged animal, we are actually looking at a primed animal. Although the answer is that it is harder to tolerize them, I am not sure why. Insofar as a dose, you can certainly get the effect with smaller doses given at repeated times.

Published 1979 by Elsevier North Holland, Inc.
Singhal, Sinclair, Stiller, eds. Aging and Immunity

THE CELLULAR BASIS AND POLYMORPHISM OF AGE DEPENDENT CHANGES IN THE IMMUNE
SYSTEM

BERNHARD CINADER AND KATSUJI NAKANO

Institute of Immunology, University of Toronto, Toronto, Ontario, Canada
M5S 1A8

INTRODUCTION

Age dependent changes include a relative decline of synthetic capacity in
the response to a newly encountered antigen.[1-4] It was our goal to examine the
underlying cellular changes of the immune system and the polymorphism of these
changes. To this end, we used acquired immunological tolerance, as a probe,
and reconstitution of lethally irradiated animals, as a principal tool for the
identification of cellular changes.[5,6] We obtained further insight into these
processes by modifying immune responsiveness with various antimitotic drugs.
Conclusions, deduced from these experiments on tolerance induction, were tested
in terms of antibody response: we measured plaque-forming cells (PFC) to sheep
erythrocytes (SRBC) of lethally irradiated animals, reconstituted with lymph
node cells and thymus cells; the latter being of varying ages. In addition, we
determined age dependent changes in factors [7,8], which appear in the serum after
immunization.[9,10]

MATERIALS AND METHODS have been described elsewhere.[9,11-19]

RESULTS AND DISCUSSION

Age dependent resistance to tolerance induction was examined in terms of a
regime by which 8 week old mice could be rendered tolerant. SJL/J mice of this
age became only partially tolerant, while mice of strains BALB/cJ, C3H/HeJ,
CBA/J,A/J, and C57BL/10J became profoundly unresponsive.[13] If animals of
various strains were tested in the same way, at a more advanced age, it became
apparent that additional strains developed resistance to tolerance-induction.
The changes are virtually imperceptible in strains, for which the A/J mouse is
a prototype (Fig. 1). Resistance to tolerance-induction of SJL/J mice is
found not only with aggregate freed rabbit (RGG) and human gamma globulin (HGG),
but also with serum albumin.[13] Macrophages or, more precisely, adherent or
accessory cells, are somehow involved in the resistance to tolerance induction,
developed by SJL/J mice after the age of six weeks. Even at this age,

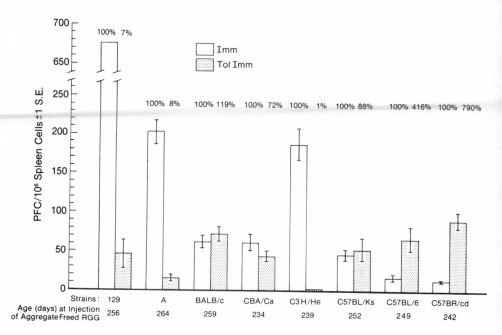

Fig. 1. Tolerizability of various strains of old (215-259 days old) mice.[19]
Various strains of mice of ages (in days) indicated in Figure, were injected
i.p. with aggregate-freed RGG (0.2 mg/g body weight) or left uninjected. Seven
days later, all the animals received an i.v. injection of 0.5 mg heat aggregated
RGG: after a further 10 days, they were given i.p. 0.5 mg heat aggregated
RGG. Indirect plaque forming cells (PFC) were determined 5 days after the last
immunization. The heights of vertical bars give the mean numbers of PFC in
animals immunized (☐) and in animals tolerized and immunized (▨). The
heights of vertical lines give two standard errors of the means.

tolerance could be induced in these mice, if macrophage function was diminished,
be it by blockage of phagocytic capacity or by circumvention of phagocyte-
involvement by a tolerogen, freed of aggregates by biofiltration.[13] We have
examined this further by reconstitution of lethally irradiated recipients. A
double cell transfer experiment was carried out and the number of plaque forming cells was determined when tolerance-inducing antigen had been given to
primary recipients, irradiated immediately before or 3 days before they received
thymus and bone marrow cells and aggregate freed antigen (Fig. 2). The ratio
of plaque forming cells (irradiation Day 0/irradiation Day -3) was 1.3, if
tolerance-inducing antigen was not given to the primary recipient and was 9.7
if a tolerance-inducing antigen had been given. There was a ten-fold decrease

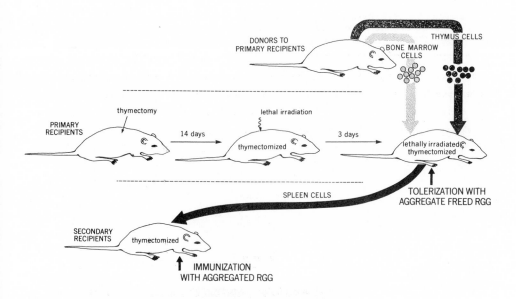

Fig. 2. Protocol designed to examine the role of accessory cells in the resistance to tolerance induction.[6,14]

in plaque number, if primary recipients were irradiated 3 days before the cell transfer, rather than on the day of cell transfer (Table 1).

TABLE 1

THE EFFECT OF ACCESSORY CELLS ON TOLERANCE INDUCTION[14]

Primary recipients were irradiated (950 rad) 3 days before or on the day of cell transfer when they received i.v. 1×10^8 thymus and 2×10^7 bone marrow cells. Some groups of animals were also given, at the same time, aggregate freed RGG (5 mg i.p.). Seven days later, the primary recipients became spleen cell donors (5×10^7 cells/recipient) for lethally irradiated (850 rad) secondary recipients which were immunized at the same time and again 10 days later (0.5 mg heat aggregated RGG first i.v., then i.p.) and were sacrificed 2 weeks after the cell transfer.

Group	Time of Irradiation[a] in Days	Dose of Aggregate Freed RGG in mg	Number of Recipients	PFC/10^6 Spleen Cells[b]
1	0	0	3	143.5 ± 12.5
2	0	5	3	11.6 ± 1.9
3	-3	0	4	107.0 ± 9.6
4	-3	5	5	1.2 ± 0.8

100

TABLE 1 (cont.)
a Zero time is the time of cell transfer.
b The plaque number of animals in Group 1 was compared with that in Group 3
   (p<0.005). PFC from Group 2 were compared with Group 4 (p<0.005).

It appears as if a relatively radiation-resistant cell was involved in the
resistance to tolerance induction. A somewhat different strategy was employed
to confirm this conclusion. The accessory cell content of primary recipients
was reduced maximally by preirradiation of the recipients and by their reconstitution with thymus and bone marrow cells which had been passed over glass
wool (Fig. 3).

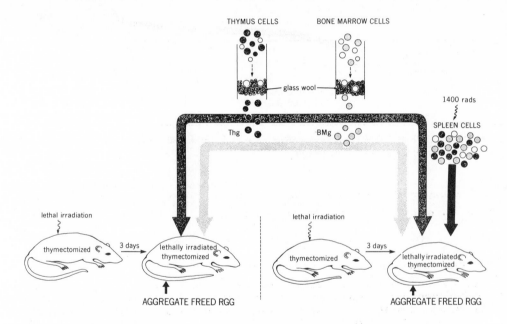

Fig. 3. Protocol for experiments designed to determine the role of adherent
and radiation-resistant cells in resistance to tolerance.[6,14]

Under these circumstances, a virtually complete state of tolerance was induced.
The role of adherent cells, in the resistance to tolerance induction, was
further examined by giving irradiated spleen cells to mice which were otherwise treated, as indicated above; this resulted in a significant increase in
plaque number (Table 2). Thus, using two somewhat different strategies, we
have demonstrated the involvement of a radiation-resistant cell in resistance
to tolerance induction. We could, however, show that the age dependent changes
were not due to changes in this radiation-resistant cell, but due to changes

TABLE 2

THE EFFECT OF ACCESSORY CELLS (OPERATIONALLY DEFINED BY RADIATION RESISTANCE
AND ADHERENCE TO GLASS) ON TOLERANCE INDUCTION IN THYMECTOMIZED MICE[14]

Female 5-week-old SJL mice were thymectomized and were lethally irradiated
(950 rad) when they were 7.5 weeks old. Three days after the irradiation, all
animals were injected i.v. with thymus cells and bone marrow cells which had
been passed through glasswool (1 x 10^8 Thg and 2 x 10^7 BMg). Animals in Groups
2 and 4 were given (i.v.), in addition, 5 x 10^7 irradiated (1300 rad) spleen
cells. At the same time, animals in Groups 3 and 4 received 5 mg aggregate
freed RGG (i.p.). All animals were injected with 0.5 mg heat aggregated RGG
i.v. on the 7th day, i.p. on the 17th day, and were sacrificed on the 21st day
after cell transfer (i.e., on the 24th day after whole body irradiation).

Group	Aggregate Freed RGG (mg)	Irradiated Spleen Cells	No. of Mice	PFC/10^6 Spleen Cells[a]
1	0	−	3	26.6 ± 5.7
2	0	+	4	190.7 ±36.1
3	5	−	2	0
4	5	+	4	34.8 ± 5.0

[a] A comparison was made between plaque forming cell numbers.
Groups 1 and 2: $p<0.005$; Groups 3 and 4: $p<0.005$.

in T cells. To this end, we employed for reconstitution, cell preparations
from which we had removed adherent cells which ingested magnetic particles or
adhered to them.[20] Thymectomized, 3-day preirradiated, 8 week old female SJL/J
were reconstituted with 2.5 x 10^7 adherent cell (Ad)-deprived bone marrow cells
and 10^8 Ad-deprived thymus cells. The donors of the bone marrow cells were 8
weeks old and the donors of the thymus cells were 3 or 12 weeks old. In addition to the thymus and bone marrow cells, the animals received radiation-·
resistant spleen cells (5 x 10^7; 1300 rad) from either 3 or 12 week old donors
and were given i.p., immediately afterwards, 2.5 mg aggregate freed RGG; 7 days
later, the animals received (i.v.) 0.5 mg aggregated RGG, mixed with 5 x 10^7
irradiated spleen cells from 8 week old donors. After a further 10 days, 0.5 mg
aggregated RGG was injected i.p. and 4 days thereafter, the animals were sacrificed and plaque forming cells were determined. It will be seen from Table 3
that animals tolerized in the presence of 3 or 12 week old irradiated spleen
cells gave similar responses. On the other hand, the age of the thymus cells
affected responsiveness and the responsiveness of tolerized animals was lower
when the thymus cell donors were 3 rather than 12 weeks old. It was thus con-
clusively demonstrated that age dependent change in resistance of SJL/J mice to

TABLE 3

THE EFFECT OF THE AGE OF RADIATION-RESISTANT SPLEEN CELLS AND THYMUS CELLS ON TOLERANCE INDUCTION[17]

Thymectomized, 3-day preirradiated, 8 week-old SJL mice were reconstituted with 2.5×10^7 adherent cell (Ad)-deprived bone marrow cells and 10^8 Ad-deprived thymus cells. The donors of bone marrow cells were 8 weeks old and the donors of thymus cells were 3 or 12 weeks old. In addition to thymus and bone marrow cells, animals received radiation-resistant spleen cells (5×10^7; 1300 rad) from 3 or 12 week old donors; immediately after transfer, they were given 2.5 mg aggregate freed RGG. Seven days later, the animals received i.v. 0.5 mg aggregated RGG mixed with 5×10^7 irradiated spleen cells from 8 week old donors. After a further 10 days, 0.5 mg aggregated RGG was injected i.p. and 4 days thereafter, the animals were sacrificed and number of plaque forming cells (PFC) was determined.

Age (Weeks) of T Cell Donors	Ad 3w[a] 5×10^7	Ad 12w[a] 5×10^7	PFC/Spleen; $\log_{10}$(Mean)± 1SD[b]
3	+	-	3.1 ± 0.6
	-	+	3.2 ± 1.0
12	+	-	4.2 ± 0.6
	-	+	4.0 ± 0.4

[a]Ad 3w and Ad 12w signify the injections with irradiated spleen cells; number indicating age in weeks of the donors.
[b]Comparison of log PFC; line 1 versus 2: p>0.9; line 3 versus 4: p=0.5-0.6. Comparison in terms of T cell age: p=0.001-0.01.

tolerance induction was due to changes in T cell-properties and that these changes manifested themselves as a consequence of an interaction with radiation-resistant adherent cells. These adherent cells did not undergo a demonstrable age dependent change.

The role of the radiation-resistant adherent cell became also apparent in another situation: we encountered differences, dependent on the identity of the tolerogen, in the ages at which tolerance resistance could be detected. In this context, human myeloma protein IgG3 proved to be a particularly ineffective tolerogen, in that 3 week old SJL/J mice which could be easily tolerized with RGG, resisted tolerance induction with IgG3. Several other strains developed resistance to tolerance induction, at an age at which they could become tolerant to other heterologous immunoglobulins. For instance, A/J mice which, as mentioned, retained the ability to become tolerant to RGG at a relatively advanced age, developed resistance to tolerance induction with IgG3 at the age of 28-34 weeks. This difference in the age at which tolerance

resistance to different antigens is manifested, may be connected with the
tendency of IgG3 to polymerize. In our experiments,[18] great care was taken to
inject molecules immediately after they had been carefully freed of polymers.
However, it is probable that IgG3 would polymerize in vivo and that, as a consequence, a radiation-resistant adherent cell would be activated. This activation might reveal incipient changes in T cell sub-populations, which would
otherwise remain undetected.

Analysis of the nature of the previously mentioned T cell changes was our
next objective. To this end, we studied in parallel SJL/J mice, which became
resistant at a relatively young age and A/J mice which retain the capacity for
tolerance to RGG for the entire period of our test, i.e. up to 55 weeks of age.
In A/J mice, suppressor cells could not be shown (by test for infectious
tolerance) if tolerance was induced neonatally, but could be shown at the age
of 11 days or later (Table 4).

TABLE 4

APPEARANCE OF SUPPRESSOR CELLS DURING EARLY LIFE OF A/J MICE[10,19]

Tolerance was induced with aggregate freed rabbit gamma globulin (sRGG; 2.5 mg)
in A/J mice at the age of 2-5, 11-16, 29-34 or 50-52 days. These animals
became, 10 days later, donors of thymus cells for lethally irradiated (900 rad),
57-71 day old recipients who were also given 2×10^7 bone marrow cells from
57-74 day old normal donors. Groups of animals received either 4×10^7 thymus
cells from normal (n) or 10^8 thymus cells from tolerant donors (t) or a mixture
of 10^8 thymus cells from tolerant donors and 4×10^7 thymus cells from normal
donors (t+n). Animals were given 2 injections with 0.4 mg of heat aggregated
rabbit gamma globulin (aRGG); the first, i.v. 7 days, the second, i.p. 17 days
after cell transfer. The indirect PFC in the spleens were determined 14 days after
the last injection. The indirect plaque forming cell (PFC) ratio for animals
receiving mixture of tolerant and normal (t+n) over animals receiving normal
cells (n) is given as a function of age.

Age (Days) at Injection of sRGG (2.5 mg)	Type of Reconstituted Recipient	PFC/10^6 Spleen Cells ± 1S.E.	Ratio (t+n)/n
2-5	n	70.8 ± 10.6	
	t	11.3 ± 1.3	
	t+n	73.7 ± 11.8	1.0
11-16	n	22.7 ± 4.2	
	t	2.6 ± 0.6	
	t+n	11.4 ± 2.6	0.5
29-34	n	37.3 ± 5.6	
	t	1.8 ± 0.5	
	t+n	3.8 ± 1.1	0.1
50-52	n	30.7 ± 9.6	
	t	0.5 ± 0.2	
	t+n	6.4 ± 2.2	0.2

It will be seen from Table 5 that we have not found suppressor cells among thymus cells of SJL/J mice, tolerized at a very early age. A fairly profound loss of T cell-cooperative capacity occurred when 11-12 day old mice became T cell donors at the age of 21-22 days, but there was no evidence for the appearance of suppressor cells. Age dependent resistance to tolerance induction is not confined to the SJL/J mice. It can also be observed in C57BL/6J mice; the onset of the resistance is seen later in life; the cellular origin of the change is attributable to loss of suppressor cells. By tests for infectious tolerance, we could show that there was an age dependent decline in suppressor activity.[19]

TABLE 5

AGE DEPENDENT CHANGE IN SJL/L MICE; A SEARCH FOR SUPPRESSOR CELLS AND COOPERATIVE CAPACITY OF HELPER CELLS[10,19]

Tolerance to RGG was induced (0.2 mg/g body weight) in SJL/J mice when they were 1-4, 11-12 or 77-81 days old; 10 days later, these animals became donors of thymus cells for lethally irradiated, 56-65 day old recipients, who were also given 1.5×10^7 bone marrow cells from 18-24 day old normal donors. Three groups of animals received either 4×10^7 thymus cells from normal donors or 10^8 thymus cells from tolerant donors (t) or 4×10^7 thymus cells from normal and 10^8 thymus cells from tolerant donors (t+n). Animals were given 2 injections with 0.4 mg aRGG: the first, i.v. 7 days after cell transfer; the second, i.p. 17 days after cell transfer. Indirect PFC in the spleens were determined, 5 days after the last injection. The indirect plaque forming cell (PFC) ratio for animals receiving mixtures of tolerant and normal (t+n) over animals receiving normal cells (n) is given as a function of age.

Age (Days) at Injection	Type of Reconstituted Recipient	PFC/10^6 Spleen Cells $\pm$ 1 S.E.	Ratio (t+n) / n
1-4	n	557 $\pm$ 84	
	t	168 $\pm$ 23	
	t+n	1010 $\pm$ 295	1.8
11-12	n	443 $\pm$ 92	
	t	58 $\pm$ 20	
	t+n	296 $\pm$ 110	0.7
77-81	n	913 $\pm$ 159	
	t	392 $\pm$ 57	
	t+n	667 $\pm$ 116	0.7

Our conclusion, as to the lesion which leads to tolerance-resistance, was further tested in terms of the antibody-response, elicited by sheep erythrocytes.[9] Lethally irradiated animals were reconstituted with a mixture of lymph node cells and thymus cells or with lymph node cells alone. The age of

the lymph node cell donors was kept constant and the age of the thymus cell
donors was varied. Reconstituted animals were immunized with sheep red cells
and plaque forming cells were counted in cell suspensions from pooled lymph
nodes. A suppressive action of thymus cells was identified if animals, reconstituted with thymus cells and lymph node cells, made a lower response to SRBC
than did animals reconstituted with lymph node cells, alone. Thymus cells of
young mice of all tested strains, between the ages of 3.5-8 weeks, significantly
reduced the plaque numbers found in lymph nodes of reconstituted animals.
Thymus cells from SJL/J donors older than 13 weeks, did not inhibit, but on
the contrary, augmented the response of lymph node reconstituted animals. We
detected a loss of suppressive capacity in SJL/J mice by two different probes,
one dependent on drug-effects on tolerance induction to heterologous Ig, the
other on the plaque forming antibody response to SRBC. If loss of suppressor
capacity was, in fact, the cause for the changes in tolerance inducibility,
it should be possible to demonstrate loss of suppressor factor. Such a factor
has been described as small molecular weight (SMW) suppressive factor and
isolated by diaflo filtration from sera of animals during the primary response[7];
its presence has been detected in BALB/cJ and AKR/J mice.[8] We conducted experiments to determine whether the concentration of SMW factor differed as a
function of age.[9] SJL/J mice of varying ages were injected with SRBC or were
left uninjected and sera were collected, 7 days later. Different volumes of
UM-10 ultra-filtrates from sera collected from SJL/J mice, at three different
ages (3, 13, and 26 weeks), were injected i.p. in SJL/J mice, 6-8 weeks of age.
The animals were challenged with 5×10^8 SRBC, i.p., 45 minutes later. The
number of 19S and 7S plaque forming cells was determined, 5 days later, by a
plaque forming test. Control groups received an equal amount of UM-10 filtrate
from normal mouse serum, collected from mice of the same age as the immunized
animals. The number of PFC of test animals was expressed as a percent of that
of the controls. The UM-10 filtrates, collected from 7 day sera of animals,
immunized at the age of 3 weeks, suppressed both the 19S and 7S anti-SRBC PFC,
at all doses examined. With 0.4 ml of UM-10 filtrate the 19S response was
suppressed by 70% and the 7S response by 60%, which are levels comparable to
those of other strains.[8] UM-10 filtrates from SJL/J mice, at the age of 13
and 26 weeks, were not suppressive, at any dose. In fact, a dose of 0.4 ml
was enhancing for both 19S and 7S responses. It thus appears that suppressor
factors were produced in lower quantities or that factors which promote the
immune response were produced in increased quantities, so that the suppressive
effect could no longer be demonstrated. Thus, we have found age dependent

change in the activity of suppressor cell, in terms of tolerance, antibody
formation or release of soluble suppressor factor.

We shall next turn to a consideration of the relation between thymus progenitors and peripheral progenitors of the suppressor function. In this context,
we examined the effect of thymectomy, as a function of age and of the interval
between thymectomy and exposure to tolerogen. Seventeen days after thymectomy,
there was no change in tolerance level. A profound change was noticeable 33
days after thymectomy. The response of thymectomized, immunized animals was
lower than that of non-thymectomized, immunized animals. In contrast, the
response of thymectomized, tolerized-immunized animals was either the same as
that of non-thymectomized animals, or in the oldest animals, was even greater.
If the response of tolerized-immunized animals is expressed as a fraction of
the response of the corresponding immunized animals, it becomes apparent that
resistance to tolerizability increases, as a consequence of thymectomy. As
the supply of the suppressor-progenitor cells from the thymus ceases, the
peripheral precursors are the only source of cells which participate in tolerance induction and maintenance. This peripheral cell compartment decreases
with increasing age, so that animals, 67 days old when tolerized, show 16% of
the immune response of non-tolerized animals, but 45% when a similar comparison
is made between thymectomized animals. At the age of 140 days, the corresponding values are 39% and 115% (Table 6).

TABLE 6
THE EFFECT OF THYMECTOMY ON THE LEVEL OF TOLERANCE[19]
a)   TOLERIZABILITY OF NORMAL SJL/J MICE

SJL/J mice were either injected i.p. with aggregate freed RGG (0.2 mg/g body
weight) at the ages indicated in the Table, or left uninjected. Seven days
later, the animals received an i.v. injection of 0.5 mg heat aggregated RGG;
after a further 10 days, they were injected i.p. with 0.5 mg of heat aggregated
RGG. Indirect plaque forming cells were determined 5 days after the last
immunization.

Treatment with Antigen	PFC/10^6 Spleen Cells ± 1SE		
	Age at Injection of Aggregate Freed RGG:		
	67 days	105 days	140 days
Immunized	267±16	657±60	408±22
Tolerized-Immunized	42±11	223±26	158±43
Ratio: Tolerized-Immunized / Immunized	0.16	0.34	0.39

TABLE 6 (cont.)

b) TOLERIZABILITY OF THYMECTOMIZED SJL/J MICE

SJL/J mice were thymectomized; 33 days later, they were either injected i.p.
with aggregate freed RGG (0.2 mg/g body weight) at the ages indicated in the
Table or left uninjected. Seven days later, the animals received an i.v.
injection of 0.5 mg heat aggregated RGG; after a further 10 days, they were
given an i.p. injection of 0.5 mg heat aggregated RGG. Indirect plaque forming
cells were determined, 5 days after the last immunization.

	PFC/10^6 Spleen Cells ± 1SE		
Treatment with Antigen	Age at Injection of Aggregate Freed RGG:		
	67 days	105 days	140 days
Immunized	173±42	259±37	308±30
Tolerized-Immunized	77±13	238±35	355±34
Ratio: $\dfrac{\text{Tolerized-Immunized}}{\text{Immunized}}$	0.45	0.92	1.15

c) INDIRECT PLAQUE FORMING CELLS OF IMMUNIZED OR TOLERIZED-IMMUNIZED
THYMECTOMIZED SJL/J MICE AS A FRACTION OF THE RESPONSE OF INTACT SJL/J MICE

	Age at Injection of Aggregate Freed RGG:		
Treatment with Antigen	67 days	105 days	140 days
Immunized	0.65	0.39	0.75
Tolerized-Immunized	1.83	1.07	2.25

Thus, in the 140 day old SJL/J mice, there is practically no stock of peripheral precursor cells and what was a tolerizing encounter for younger animals, has become a sensitizing experience.

The cell, involved in the polymorphism of declining tolerance inducibility, appears to be the first cell type to be activated, when an antigen or tolerogen is encountered by the immune system. The evidence for this contention is obtained from drug-induced changes which will be described next. Colchicine is a drug which appears to bind to and disrupt microtubules.[21,22] It enhances the immune response when given simultaneously with antigen.[23] If SJL/J mice are treated with colchicine, simultaneously with the administration of a tolerogen (Fig. 4), their ability to become tolerant is reduced.

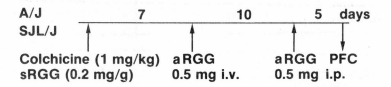

Fig. 4. Scheme for injections with colchicine, aggregate freed RGG (sRGG) and aggregated RGG (aRGG).[19] Numbers above the line show intervals (in days) between injections and between the last injection and the PFC assay.

The extent of this reduction increases with age, until ultimately the administration of tolerogen appears to sensitize rather than to tolerize (Fig. 5). Thus, it appears as if the activation of suppressor cells was prevented by colchicine and this may allow some degree of unresponsiveness to be established in younger animals; with increasing age, this source of suppressor cells decreases dramatically. A/J mice are able to replace the inactivated suppressor cells (Fig. 6), young SJL/J mice can also do so, but not as efficiently as A/J mice (Fig. 5); older SJL/J mice are very deficient in this respect. If this mechanism operates, a combination of thymectomy and colchicine should have a more profound effect than either treatment, alone, in preventing tolerance, even in A/J mice and of course also in SJL/J mice; Figure 7 shows this to be the case. In short, colchicine affects activation of the suppressor system, possibly controlling amplifier cells or feedback suppressors. The capacity for replacement of these cells depends on the thymus. In A/J mice the capacity for regeneration of the involved cells is much greater than in SJL/J mice of any age. In older SJL/J mice, this capacity is even lower than in younger mice.

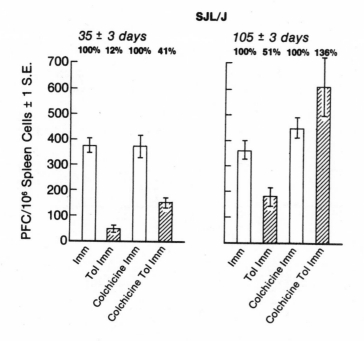

Fig. 5. The effect of colchicine, aggregate freed and aggregated RGG administered as shown in Fig. 4 on the immune response of SJL/J mice.[19] Age at
injection with aggregate freed RGG and responses as percentage of that corresponding animals are shown in the two lines at the top of the graph.

When given two days before tolerance induction, cyclophosphamide also
reduces tolerance inducibility. This was shown by an experiment that was
carried out as follows: SJL/J mice were injected with cyclophosphamide (200 mg/
kg body weight) or left untreated; 2 days later, they were given aggregate
freed RGG and, 10 days thereafter, they were sacrificed. The properties of
thymus cells from tolerized and normal animals were evaluated after transfer
to lethally irradiated recipients which, in addition, received bone marrow
cells from normal donors and were finally immunized. We shall first consider
SJL/J mice, tolerized when 30-36 days old. Tolerized-immunized animals show
17% of the response, made by immunized animals. If donors were treated with
cyclophosphamide, tolerized-immunized animals showed 51% of the response,
made by immunized animals. With older donors, 83-89 days of age when given
tolerogen, the change was from 34% to 66% of the corresponding plaque forming
response. It can be concluded that cyclophosphamide, given two days before

110

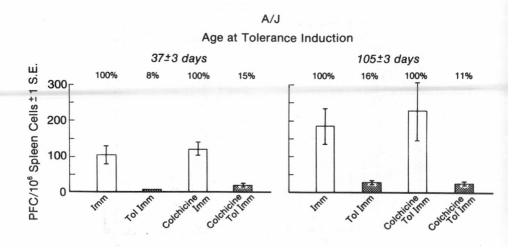

Fig. 6. The effect of colchicine, aggregate freed and aggregated RGG administered as shown in Fig. 4 on the immune response of A/J mice.[19] Age at injection with aggregate freed RGG and responses as percentage of that corresponding animals are shown in the two lines at the top of the graph.

tolerance induction, has a preferential effect on the suppressor circuits which, therefore, must contain one of the first cells to be activated in an encounter between a foreign macromolecule and the immune system.

We shall turn to some consideration of the inheritance of accelerated age dependent resistance to tolerance induction to aggregate freed RGG. To this end, we compared tolerance induction in parental animals and in their hybrids (A/J x SJL/J, SJL/J x A/J, BALB/cJ x SJL/J, SJL/J x NZB/BINJ and NZB/BINJ x SJL/J).[16] Hybrids between A/J and SJL/J and between BALB/cJ and SJL/J and mice of the parental strains were rendered tolerant, were immunized, and were tested, at a constant time after tolerance induction. Among young animals, the mean half-life in hybrids was similar to that of the parental A/J or BALB/cJ mice; in older animals it was similar to that of the parental SJL/J mice. Since the normal half-life of antigen-elimination varied with strain and age, half-life of elimination from tolerant animals was normalized to the half-life in corresponding normal animals. It remained apparent that 3 week old hybrids eliminated ^{131}I-RGG like their A/J or BALB/cJ parents, while the 8 week old and 12 week old hybrids resembled their SJL/J parents: the resistance to tolerance induction was an age dependent phenomenon, not only in

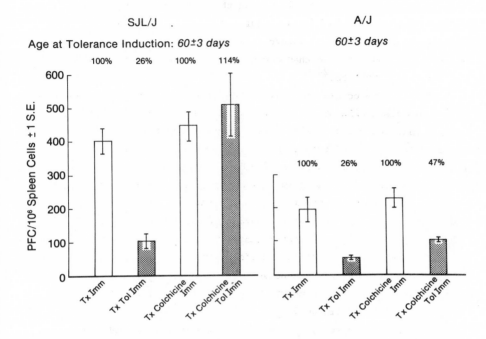

Fig. 7. Effect of colchicine on tolerance induction in thymectomized SJL/J and A/J mice.[19] SJL/J mice and A/J mice, 43 days old, were thymectomized (Tx). These animals were, 17 days later, given i.p. aggregate freed RGG (0.2 mg/g body weight) or colchicine (1 mg/kg body weight) or both aggregate freed RGG and colchicine. One group was left uninjected. Seven and 17 days later, all the animals were immunized with 0.5 mg heat aggregated RGG; 5 days after the last immunization, they were sacrificed and indirect plaque forming cells were counted. Heights of bars indicate PFC/10^6 spleen cells. Vertical lines indicate 2 standard errors of the mean.

SJL/J mice but also in its hybrid of offspring. If the inheritance was examined in terms of 8 week old F_1 hybrids, it appeared that the inheritance of the SJL mode was dominant. The differences in progression between SJL/J and F_1 hybrids indicated that more than one gene was involved. It had become apparent from preceding data that some hybrids, tolerized at the age of 8 weeks, eliminated antigen with a half-life that could not be classified as being that of either the maternal or the paternal animal. It seemed possible that this reflected the rate at which tolerant hybrids shifted to the responsiveness of the SJL/J parent. We, therefore, examined half-life distribution in various types of hybrid and back-cross offspring, as a function of age. Even among hybrids tolerized at the age of 12 weeks, there were always some individuals with a half-life that was considerably longer than that of the SJL/J parent.[16] This was more marked in A/J x SJL/J than in SJL/J x A/J hybrids. It was most striking in hybrid offspring of BALB/cJ x SJL/J matings. Clearly, this was a further indication that more than one gene was involved, a conclusion that has recently been confirmed.[24]

The extent and time course of tolerance-resistance in hybrids and NZB/BINJ parental animals is similar (Fig. 8). It would, therefore, appear that SJL/J and NZB/BINJ mice undergo similar T cell changes, which are responsible for resistance to tolerance induction. Were it otherwise, resistance to tolerance in hybrids between SJL/J and NZB/BINJ would be more severe than in their parents, since resistance is dominantly inherited, as we know from studies of hybrids between SJL/J and normal mice, such as A/J mice.

It has been suggested that an early defect of NZB mice is $Ly-1^+2^+3^+Qa-1^+$ feedback suppressor cells, so that resistance to tolerance induction in NZB/BINJ may be connected with a defect in the differentiation and/or function of T cells, expressing the $Ly-1^+2^+3^+$ phenotype.[25] The genetic experiments furnish some reason to believe that one common gene may be involved in the SJL/J and NZB/BINJ resistance to tolerance induction - it may control cells of $Ly-1^+2^+3^+$ phenotype. This is made even more likely by the report that C57BL, BALB/c and CBA mice which show late resistance to tolerance inducibility (Fig. 1), also show a reduced proportion of $Ly-1^+2^+3^+$ cells, in later life.[25] We have seen, from our genetic experiments, that at least two genes are involved in resistance to tolerance induction. We have little information on a product of a second gene which is involved.

SUMMARY

Resistance against tolerance induction has been used in our laboratory as a probe for the rate at which aging of the immune system occurs. We have found vast strain differences in this respect. SJL/J mice have served as a proto-type of accelerated senescence and A/J as a prototype of delayed senescence. We have identified BALB/cJ, C57BR/cdJ, C57BL/6J, C57BL/KsJ and CBA/CaJ, as strains which show resistance to tolerance induction, when they are 34-37 weeks old.

The mainfestation of resistance to tolerance induction is dependent on a radiation resistant, adherent cell, but this cell itself does not undergo age dependent changes. Changes do occur in the suppressor component of the T cells. A cell is involved, which appears to be among the first components of

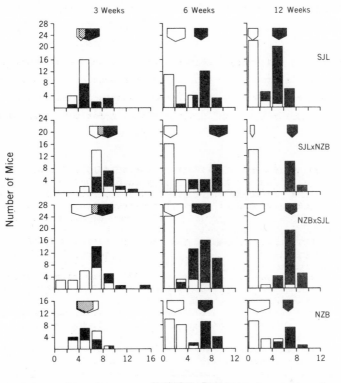

Fig. 8. Tolerance induction in hybrids between SJL/J and NZB/BINJ and in the inbred parental animals.[18] Animals of different ages were divided into two groups. Animals in one group were not given a tolerizing injection, animals in the second group were injected i.p. with aggregate freed RGG (0.2 mg/g body weight) and 2 weeks later, animals in the second group were given s.c. 0.25 mg heat aggregated RGG in IFA. After a further week, animals in both groups were injected i.p. with 10μg aggregate freed ^{125}I-RGG. Antigen elimination was observed for 8 days. Half-life is plotted as a function of the number of animals which eliminate antigen with a given half-life. Black blocks show antigen elimination in animals not pretreated with antigen (first group). Open blocks show elimination in tolerized and immunized groups (second group). Arrows show the mean for each subgroup and the width of the arrow is 2 standard deviations.

the immune system to proliferate upon encounter with a tolerogenic macro-molecule, since drugs which affect cell division such as colchicine and cyclophosphamide, interfere with tolerance induction. Genetic experiments have led to the conclusion that the early immune defect of SJL/J and NZB/BINJ mice may be identical and that more than one gene is involved in resistance to tolerance induction. The product of one of these genes may affect the differentiation and/or function of T cells expressing the $Ly-1^+2^+3^+$ phenotype.

ACKNOWLEDGMENTS

We are indebted to the Medical Research Council and the National Cancer Institute for financial support, to Dr. Austin Sargent of the University of Saskatchewan for a generous gift of the serum Laventure IgG3 and last, but not least, to Mrs. Sui Koh and Mr. Ladislav Horvath for technical assistance.

REFERENCES

1. Price, G.B. and Makinodan, T. (1972) J. Immunol. 108, 403-412.
2. Price, G.B. and Makinodan, T. (1972) J. Immunol. 108, 413-417.
3. Makinodan, T. and Peterson, W. (1966) Dev. Biol. 14, 96-111.
4. Peterson, W. and Makinodan, T. (1972) Clin. Exp. Immunol. 12, 273-290.
5. Cinader, B. (1977) in Allergy and Clinical Immunology, Mathov, E., Sindo, T., and Naranjo, P. ed., Excepta Medica, Amsterdam, pp. 19-27.
6. Cinader, B. (1977) Ann. Immunol. (Inst. Pasteur), 128C, 415-425.
7. Lee, S.T. and Paraskevas, F. (1976) Clin. Exp. Immunol. 24, 177-184.
8. Lee, S.T. and Paraskevas, F. (1977) Cell Immunol. 32, 171-182.
9. Cinader, B., Paraskevas, F. and Koh, S. (1978) Cell. Immunol. 40, 445-450.
10. Cinader, B. and Nakano, K. (1978) in Immunology 1978, Gergely, Medhyesi, Hollán, ed., Akadémiai Kiadó, Budapest, pp. 17-31.
11. Kaplan, A.M. and Cinader, B. (1973) Cell. Immunol. 6, 429-441.
12. Kaplan, A.M. and Cinader, B. (1973) Cell. Immunol. 6, 442-456.
13. Fujiwara, M. and Cinader, B. (1974) Cell. Immunol. 12, 11-29.
14. Fujiwara, M. and Cinader, B. (1974) Cell. Immunol. 12, 194-204.
15. Fujiwara, M. and Cinader, B. (1974) Cell. Immunol. 12, 205-213.
16. Fujiwara, M. and Cinader, B. (1974) Cell. Immunol. 12, 214-229.
17. Hosono, M. and Cinader, B. (1977) Int. Archs Allergy appl. Immunol. 54, 289-299.
18. Hosono, M., Cinader, B. and Ellerson, J. (1977) Immunological Communication, 6, 239-257.
19. Nakano, K. and Cinader, B. (1979) in preparation.
20. Shek, P.N., Chou, C.T., Dubiski, S., and Cinader, B. (1976) Immunology, 30, 549-558.
21. Edelman, G.M., Yahara, I. and Wang, J.L. (1973) Proc. Natl. Acad. Sci. 70, 1442-1446.
22. Sherline, P. and Mundy, G.R. (1977) J. Cell. Biol. 74, 371-376.
23. Shek, P.N. and Coons, A.H. (1978) J. Exp. Med. 147, 1213-1227.
24. Azar, M.M., Ranges, G.E., Yunis, E.J. and Clarke, C. (1978) J. Immunol. 121, 1251-1256.
25. Cantor, H., McVay-Boudreau, L., Hugenberger, J., Naidorf, K. Shen, F.W. and Gershon, R.K. (1978) J. Exp. Med. 147, 1116-1125.

DISCUSSION

SISKIND: I would like to mention that in a couple of somewhat different tolerance models we found similar age-dependent changes with probably rather different mechanisms. If you look at DNP-DGL induced tolerance, where, for a variety of reasons, we are really looking at a B cell tolerance, we find a real loss or fall off in either tolerance induction with age. With an ultracentrifuged BGG type tolerance, in which you look at the helper type effect, we see a progressive fall off in tolerizing ability of the helper cell compartment. So it appears that resistance to tolerance reduction is a property of several different mechanisms of tolerance induction.

CINADER: Of course it was fascinating to hear about the B suppressor cell and I wonder whether that could play a role in what you have described in your own B cell tolerance and age-dependent changes.

EFFECTS OF PARAINFLUENZA VIRUS INFECTION ON IMMUNOLOGIC AGING

Marguerite M.B. Kay[+]

[+]Laboratory of Molecular and Clinical Immunology, Geriatric Research, Education and Clinical Center (GRECC), V.A. Wadsworth Medical Center and the Department of Medicine, University of California, Los Angeles, California 90073, USA

INTRODUCTION

The alteration in immune function accompanying aging is associated with increased incidence of infection, autoimmune and immune complex diseases, and neoplasia[1,2]. A crucial issue in aging research is to distinguish changes intrinsic to the aging process from those that are imposed by the environment. For this reason, we studied the temporal relationship between immune function, aging, viral infection and long-term sequelae of viral infection in mice of eight medium and long-lived strains and hybrids.

The virus which we studied was a parainfluenza type 1 virus (Sendai). Parainfluenza viruses commonly cause recurrent infections in humans. The initial infections which occur in childhood are the most severe[3]. Parainfluenza infections occurring in adults are generally subclinical or produce mild symptoms of a "cold"[3]. Adults have relatively high titers of circulating antibodies to all types of parainfluenza virus, which presumably decreases the severity of infections--thus accounting for the usually mild symptoms[3].

Parainfluenza virus (Sendai) infection was brought into the Gerontology Research Center Animal Farm in January, 1976, by a shipment of infected 5-6 week old mice from Bethesda, Md. None of the aging mice had detectable serum antibody titers to the virus prior to the infection, but subsequently had titers of 1:20 to 1:80 by complement fixation tests performed by Microbiological Associates, Bethesda, Md. At the height of the infection (2-3 weeks post infection) the old mice appeared ill, but adult and middle-aged mice appeared normal. However, autopises revealed pulmonary lesions typical of Sendai infection in mice and influenza infection in humans. The following strains, hybrids, and random bred mice were used in this study: $BC3F_1$, $B6D2F_1$, CBA/T6T6, CV1, C3H, C57Bl, C57Bl/6, and DBA/2.

Mortality was highest among untreated weanling and old mice and young adult mice that had been rendered T cell deficient by thymectomy, irradiation, and bone marrow reconstitution. Thus, for for example, mortality in mice of the latter group was > 80% following parainfluenza infection, versus < 5% before infection.

A total of 63 indices were determined on each mouse following infection (i.e., 7 weight, 31 cellular, 18 activity, and 7 autoimmune indices).

Experimentally determined weight indices included body (g), lymph node (mg), spleen (mg), and thymus weight (mg); calculated weight indices derived from experimental determinations included percent organ weight of body weight for lymph nodes, spleen, and thymus.

Cellular indices included the following experimental determinations: cells per tissue, percent dead cells at $4^{o}C$ during routine processing for tissue culture, percent T cells, percent B cells, and percent dead cells after a 30 min. incubation at $37^{o}C$ in culture media with 5% bovine serum albumin for dispersed bone marrow, lymph node, spleen and thymic cells. The following indices were calculated from experimental determinations: cells per mg wet weight for lymph nodes, spleen and thymus; the number of B cells and T cells for bone marrow, lymph nodes, spleen, and thymus.

Activity assays included the ^{3}H-thymidine incorporation in counts per minute (cpm) of unstimulated background cultures (BKG), a phytohemagglutinin (PHA) dose-cpm response curve (0.03, 0.05, 0.10, 0.25, 0.5, 1.0, 2.0, and 3.0 ug PHA) of stimulated cultures from which the dose eliciting the peak response was determined, the response (cpm) of lipopolysaccharide (LPS) stimulated cultures of lymph node and spleen cell, and the number of spleen colony forming units (CFU-S) per 5×10^{4} bone marrow cells. The following indices were calculated from experimental determinations: $\log_{10}cpm_{PHA}-\log_{10}cpm_{BKG}$, $\log_{10}cpm_{LPS}-\log_{10}cpm_{BKG}$, $\log_{10}(cpm_{PHA}-cpm_{BKG})$, $\log_{10}(cpm_{LPS}-cpm_{BKG})$ for dispersed lymph node and spleen cells, and the total CFU in the femoral bone marrow.

Autoimmune indices included: IgM and IgG Coombs' titers, the per- cent dead cells after a 30 min. incubation at $37^{o}C$ in culture media containing 5% guinea pig complement for bone marrow, lymph node, spleen and thymus cells, anti-DNA and RNA antibody titers for CBA/T6T6 mice, and the hematocrit. Direct Coombs' titers were assessed with serially diluted goat antimouse IgG or goat anti-mouse IgM (Meloy). For details of methodology, see reference 4.

RESULTS

The data were analyzed with a computer employing the Spearman correlation coefficient for each index. The data are presented for all mice regardless of genetic background for three reasons. First, we wanted to present data on an "average" or "typical" mouse. Although there were differences between strains and hybrids in the rate or magnitude of the age-related change in a response, each index that correlated best with age for all strains and hybrids tested regardless of genetic background correlated with age for each individual strain or hybrid (see Table 1, footnote a, for the statistical definition of "correlated best" that was used).

Following parainfluenza infection, differences between strains, between hybrids, and between strains and hybrids, were minimal; and the sample size per age group per genetic type was small.

Preinfection Age-related Indices. All nine of the indices which correlated best with age for all mice tested regardless of genetic background prior to infection were thymic or thymic dependent (Table 1). All of these decreased with age.

TABLE 1

INDICES THAT CORRELATE BEST WITH AGE FOR ALL MICE TESTED
BOTH BEFORE AND AFTER PARAINFLUENZA INFECTION[a]

INDEX	CORRELATION COEFFICIENT		P VALUE[b]	
	Time Relative to Infection			
	Pre	Post	Pre	Post
WEIGHT:				
percent thymus wt of body wt	-0.90	-0.78	0.0001	0.0001
thymus wt	-0.86	-0.79	0.0001	0.0001
CELL:				
number of T cells, thymus	-0.86	--	0.0001	--
thymus cellularity	-0.83	-0.83	0.0001	0.0001
cells per mg wet wt, thymus	-0.59	-0.75	0.0001	0.0001
ACTIVITY[c]:				
$\log_{10}$(PHA-BKG), lymph node	-0.63	--	0.0001	--
$\log_{10}$PHA-$\log_{10}$BKG, lymph node	-0.61	-0.39	0.0001	0.05
$\log_{10}$PHA, lymph node	-0.58	--	0.0001	--
$\log_{10}$(PHA-BKG), spleen	-0.52	--	0.0001	--

[a] The data for individual mice tested independent of genetic background were

120

correlated with chronological age. An index is included in this table if the Spearman rank correlation coefficient prior to infection was equal or greater than 0.50 positively or negatively regardless of P value. A correlation coefficient of 1.0 indicates complete agreement in order of ranks and a correlation coefficient of -1.0 indicates complete agreement in the opposite order of ranks.
bThe P value or significance probability of a correlation coefficient is the probability that a value of the correlation coefficient as large or larger in absolute value than the one calculated would have arisen by chance, were the two random variables (age versus the index in this case) truly uncorrelated.
cBKG, cpm Background; LPS, cpm Lipopolysaccharide; PHA, cpm Phytohemagglutinin

Indices Altered by Infection. Fifty-five of the 63 indices examined were abnormal as late as 8 months after the disappearance of clinical symptoms of parainfluenza infection (Table 2).

TABLE 2

EFFECT OF SENDAI INFECTION ON ORGAN, CELLULAR, ACTIVITY, AND AUTOIMMUNE INDICES OF MICE OF 8 STRAINS AND HYBRIDS[a,b]

Index	Relative Change	P value ($\leq$)
Weight		
Body	Decrease	0.0002
Thymus	Decrease	0.0001
Lymph node	Increase	0.0001
Spleen	Not significant	
Thymus wt (g)/body wt (g)	Decrease	0.0001
Lymph node wt (g)/body wt (g)	Increase	0.0001
Spleen wt (g)/body wt (g)	Increase	0.0003
Cellular[c]		
Thymus cellularity ($\times 10^6$)	Decrease	0.0001
Lymph node cellularity ($\times 10^6$)	Not significant	
Spleen cellularity ($\times 10^6$)	Decrease	0.0006
Bone Marrow Cellularity ($\times 10^6$)	Increase	0.0001
Dead Cells, thymus (%) at 4°	Increase	0.0001
Dead cells, lymph nodes (%) at 4°	Increase	0.0001
Dead cells, spleen (%) at 4°	Increase	0.0001
Dead cells, bone marrow (%) at 4°	Increase	0.0001
Dead cells, thymus (%) at 37°	Not significant	
Dead cell, lymph nodes (%) at 37°	Increase	0.0001
Dead cells, spleen (%) at 37°	Increase	0.0001
Dead cells, bone marrow (%) at 37°	Increase	0.0001
B cells, thymus (%)	Not significant	
B cells, lymph node (%)	Decrease	0.0001
B cells, spleen (%)	Decrease	0.0001
B cells, bone marrow (%)	Decrease	0.03
B cells, thymus ($\times 10^6$)	Not significant	
B cells, lymph node ($\times 10^6$)	Decrease	0.0001

TABLE 2 (Continued)
EFFECT OF SENDAI INFECTION ON ORGAN, CELLULAR, ACTIVITY,
AND AUTOIMMUNE INDICES OF MICE OF 8 STRAINS AND HYBRIDS[a,b]

Index	Relative Change	P value ($\leq$)
Cellular[c] (continued)		
B cells, spleen ($\times 10^6$)	Decrease	0.001
B cells, bone marrow ($\times 10^6$)	Not significant	
Cells per mg wet wt, thymus	Decrease	0.0002
Activity[d,e]		
$\text{Log}_{10}\text{cpm}_{PHA} - \text{log}_{10}\text{cpm}_{BKG}$, lymph node	Decrease	0.0005
$\text{Log}_{10}\text{cpm}_{PHA} - \text{log}_{10}\text{cpm}_{BKG}$, spleen	Decrease	0.0001
$\text{log}_{10}\text{cpm}_{LPS} - \text{log}_{10}\text{cpm}_{BKG}$, lymph node	Decrease	0.04
$\text{log}_{10}\text{cpm}_{LPS} - \text{log}_{10}\text{cpm}_{BKG}$, spleen	Not significant	
$\text{log}_{10}\text{PHA}$, lymph node	Decrease	0.01
$\text{log}_{10}\text{PHA}$, spleen	Decrease	0.01
$\text{log}_{10}\text{BKG}$, lymph node	Decrease	0.02
$\text{log}_{10}\text{BKG}$, spleen	Decrease	0.02
$\text{log}_{10}\text{LPS}$, lymph node	Decrease	0.04
$\text{log}_{10}\text{LPS}$, spleen	Decrease	0.05
PHA dose, lymph node	Decrease	0.05
PHA dose, spleen	Decrease	0.05
Autoimmune[f]		
Coombs' titer	Increase	0.01
Coombs' titer	Increase	0.0001
Dead cells, thymus (%) with hematocrit	Not significant	
Hematocrit	Decrease	0.06

[a]For statistical analysis, the general linear model was used to determine
the effect of time (mo) following Sendai infection on each index. The
procedure uses the principal of least squares to fit a fixed-effects model to
data and performs linear regression analysis of variance, analysis of
covariance, and partial correlation analysis.

[b]Young (1.5-2 months), adult (3-7 months), middle-aged (10-12 months),
and old (18-21, 24-26, or 28-31 months) mice of each of 8 strains were tested
prior to the onset of Sendai infection. Six to twelve mice were tested per
age group when available. Following Sendai infection, 3-6 mice were tested in
each age group, when available, at 1, 2, 3, 5, 6 and 8 months postinfection.
Mice which were infected when they were less than 3 months of age are not
included in this table or in Figs. 1 and 2. All assays were performed on each
individual mouse.

[c]The data for ther percent and number of T cells in the thymus, lymph
nodes, spleen, and bone marrow are not presented because the high frequency of
cell death of untreated T cells at 37° rendered the cytotoxicity assay
invalid.

[d]cpm_{BKG} and BKG, counts per minute of unstimulated background culture; cpm_{LPS} and BKG, counts per minute of LPS-stimulated culture; cpm_{PHA}, counts per minute of PHA-stimulated culture.

[e]The data for the CFU-S per 5 x 10^6 bone marrow cells and the tola CFU-S per femur are not presented because the irradiated recipient test mice died before Day 9, the day of splenic CFU determination.

[f]The data for the percent dead lymph node, spleen, and bone marrow cells after incubation at 37^0 in medium with 5% guinea pig complement are not presented in this table because they are presented in Fig. 1.

Reproduced with permission from Kay, M.M.B. (1978), Proc. Soc. Expt. Biol. Med. 158:326.

Weight Indices. The 2 weight indices that correlated best with age for all mice, prior to infection, were thymus weight and percent thymus weight of body weight. They decreased significantly 6 months after the initial infection, as shown in Table 1 and 3. Mice born into the infected colony which were 6 months of age when assayed, were more severely affected than those that were 7 months old when assayed (Table 3).

TABLE 3

PERCENT THYMUS WEIGHT OF BODY WEIGHT AT 3 AND 6 MONTHS FOLLOWING PARAINFLUENZA INFECTION[a]

TIME AFTER INFECTION (mo)	PERCENT THYMUS WT. OF BODY WT.					
	Age (mo)					
	3	6	7	10-12	18-20	24-28
3	0.39 (0.07)	NT	0.16 (0.04)	0.12 (0.01)	NT	0.06 (0.01)
6	NT	0.03 (0.02)	0.07 (0.01)	0.06 (0.01)	0.01 (0.03)	0 (0)

[a]Values expressed as the mean for all mice tested; numbers in parenthesis are ± standard error the the mean. NT, not tested.

Regarding the effect of parainfluenza infection on other weight indices, the body weight decreased, while lymph node weight, percent lymph node weight of body weight, and percent spleen weight of body weight increased significantly ($P \leq 0.0002$). These changes are consistent with chronic infection.

Cellular Indices. Two of the three cellular indices that correlated best with age prior to parainfluenza infection were thymus cellularity and cells per mg we weight thymus. These, too, decreased significantly following infection (Table 1, 4 and 5). Regarding the latter index, old mice were more

severely affected than adult and middle-aged mice. The third index, number of
T cells in the thymus, could not be used because 40-60% of the cells in all
lymphoid tissues died when incubated with complement without the anti-T cell
reagent (Figure 1). This was not the case prior to infection.

TABLE 4

THYMUS CELLULARITY BEFORE AND 6 MONTHS FOLLOWING PARAINFLUENZA INFECTION[a]

TIME RELATIVE TO INFECTION	THYMUS CELLULARITY ($\times 10^6$)							
	Age (mo)							
	2	3-4	6	7.5	10-12	18-20	24-26	28-31
Pre	183 (18)	102 (8)	NT	NT	54 (7)	20 (2)	12 (2)	4 (1)
Post		20 (20)	60 (16)		40 (9)	13 (12)	0 (0)	0 (0)

[a]Value expressed as the mean for all mice tested; numbers in parenthesis are
$\pm$ standard error of the mean. NT, not tested.

TABLE 5

CELLS PER MG WET WEIGHT THYMUS BEFORE AND FOLLOWING PARAINFLUENZA INFECTION[a]

TIME RELATIVE TO INFECTION	CELLS PER mg WET WT. THYMUS ($\times 10^6$)						
	Age (mo)						
	2	3-4	6-8	10-12	18-20	24-26	27-31
Pre	2.80 (0.01)	2.03 (0.11)	NT	1.66 (0.22)	0.98 (0.09)	1.13 (0.17)	0.3 (0.13)
Post	NT	NT	1.37 (0.53)	1.95 (0.32)	0 (0)	0 (0)	0 (0)

[a]Value expressed as the mean for all mice tested; numbers in parenthesis are
$\pm$ standard error of the mean. NT, not tested.

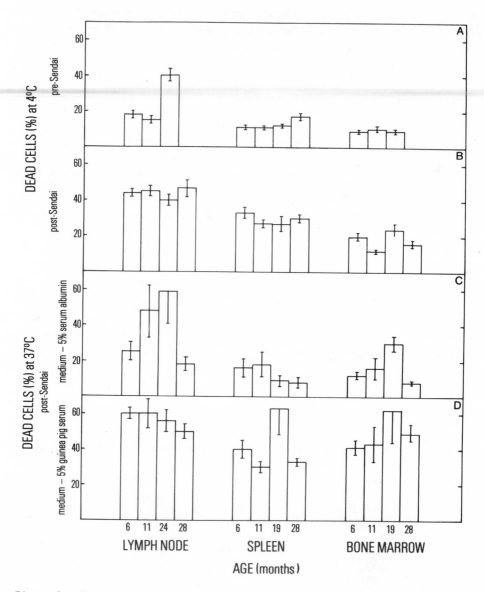

Figure 1. Frequency of cell death pre- (A) and 6 months post-Sendai (B-D) infection at 4 and 37°C. At 4°C, the cells were incubated in medium for 30 min. At 37°C, cells were incubated in medium with either 5% bovine serum albumin (C) or 5% guinea pig serum as a source of complement (D). Cell viability was determined by the trypan blue dye exclusion technique. Bars indicate standard error of the mean. (Reproduced with permission from Kay, M.M.B. (1978), Proc. Soc. Expt. Biol. Med. 158:326.)

Most of the other cellular indices were also affected by parainfluenza infection. For example, the frequency of B cells in lymph nodes, spleen, and bone marrow decreased significantly (P ≤ 0.03); bone marrow cellularily increased; and spleen cellularity decreased (P ≤ 0.001).

Activity Indices. All 4 of the activity indices which correlated best with age prior to Sendai infection decreased following infection (Tables 1 and 2 and Figure 2).

All of the other activity indices except one, the ratio of LPS stimulated to unstimulated spleen cells, decreased following infection (Table 2). Colony forming units could not be assessed even as late as 6 months post infection, because most of the adult recipient mice either died or were moribund before day 9, the day of splenic CFU determination.

Autoimmunity and Immune Complexes. Although Coombs' titer did not correlate best with age for all mice tested prior to infection, by 6 months post infection all old mice were Coombs' positive (Table 6), whereas only 22% of the adult mice were Coombs' positive. The IgM Coombs' titer of 18-20 months old mice and mice 23 months of age was 112 ± 20 and 73 ± 10, respectively. In contrast, the Coombs' titer of adult mice (10-12 months old) was 13 ± 9. Again, mice born into the infected colony or infected within a month of birth were as severely affected as the old mice. Their Coombs' titers were 80 ± 20 and 66 ± 13, respectively.

TABLE 6

EFFECT OF PARAINFLUENZA INFECTION ON IgG and IgM COOMBS' TITER[a]

AGE WHEN TESTED (mo)	AGE WHEN INFECTED (mo)	COOMBS' TITER AND FREQUENCY	
		IgM	IgG
6	in utero	80 ± 20 (56)	3 ± 3 (17)
7-8	1-2	66 ± 13 (82)	5 ± 2 (39)
10-12	7-9	13 ± 9 (22)	1 ± 1 (11)
18-20	12-14	112 ± 20 (100)	12 ± 4 (80)
28	23	73 ± 10 (100)	13 ± 4 (54)

[a]Value expressed as the mean of the dilution⁻¹ ± standard error the the mean; sample size, 6-18 mice per group. Numbers in parenthesis indicate the

frequency of Coombs' positivity. Antisera was titrated in a two-fold manner starting with a 1:10 dilution. Data presented are from 6 mo after infection.

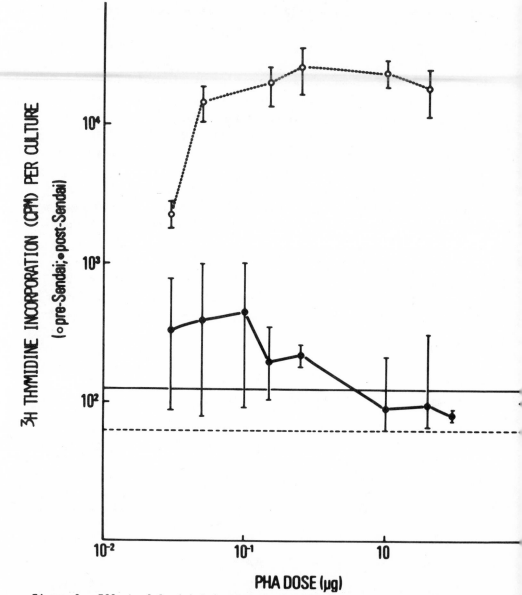

Figure 2. Effect of Sendai infection on the PHA dose-cpm response relationship of young BC3F$_1$ mouse lymph node cells. The horizontal dotted and solid lines represent background prior to and 6 mo after infection. Comparable results were obtained with other strains and hybrids of mice. (Reproduced with permission from Kay, M.M.B. (1978), Proc. Soc. Expt. Biol. Med. 158:326.)

No correlation could be detected between Coombs' titer and the hematocrit for all mice regardless of age. However, the hematocrits of Coombs' positive old mice (33.1 $\pm$ 4.0%) were significantly less than those of Coombs' positive young mice (40.0 $\pm$ 2.7%) and Coombs' negative old mice assayed 1 month after the initial infection (38.4 $\pm$ 2.1%).

The possibility that Coombs' positive erythrocytes could result from parainfluenza virus particles attaching to circulating cells was investigated with scanning electron microscopy (EM) and transmission EM. Viral particles were not detected with either technique on the surface of erythrocytes from any experimental mice, even though they were easily visible on the surface of erythrocytes which had been incubated with parainfluenza type 1 virus (Figures 3A and B). Viral like particles were visible with transmission EM in erythrocytes of the spleen and peripheral blood of old mice, but not of normal adult and middle-aged mice.

The strain CBA/T6T6 was selected for investigation of the effect of parainfluenza virus on antibody titer to DNA and RNA, antibodies to glomerular basement membranes, and antigen-antibody complexes in the kidneys of mice of different ages. CBA/T6T6 mice were selected because they are considered to be resistant to autoimmune disease, as manifested by the fact that (a) they do not develop Coombs' positive erythrocytes and antibodies to DNA and deoxyribonucleoprotein (DNP) even as late as 30 months of age, and (b) neonatal thymectomy does not result in Coombs' positivity even though about a third of the thymectomized mice develop antibodies to DNA and DNP[6]. The study revealed no increase in antibody titer to either DNA or RNA following parainfluenza virus infection.

Immunofluorescent studies of the kidneys performed 9-12 months post infection showed both linear deposits of immunoglobulins along the glomerular basement membrane and "lumpy" or granular deposits outside the basement membrane and in the mesangium of mice which were infected when they were one month old, and granular deposits of immunoglobulins in the glomeruli of old mice (Fig. 4A and B). In contrast, none of the middle-aged mice examined had detectable immunoglobulin deposits in their glomeruli.

DISCUSSION

Sixty-three indices were measured on each individual mouse of 8 medium and long-lived strains and hybrids ranging in age from 3 to 29 months following natural infection with parainfluenza type 1 virus. Fifty-five of these indices were abnormal as late as 8 months postinfection, when compared to values

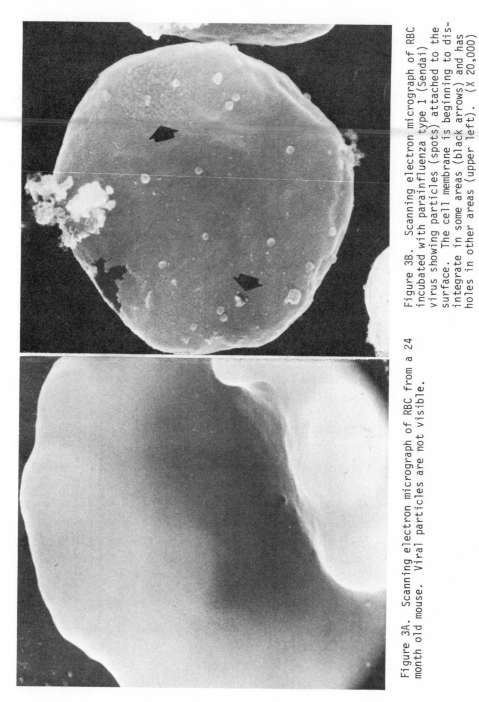

Figure 3A. Scanning electron micrograph of RBC from a 24 month old mouse. Viral particles are not visible.

Figure 3B. Scanning electron micrograph of RBC incubated with parainfluenza type 1 (Sendai) virus showing particles (spots) attached to the surface. The cell membrane is beginning to disintegrate in some areas (black arrows) and has holes in other areas (upper left). (X 20,000)

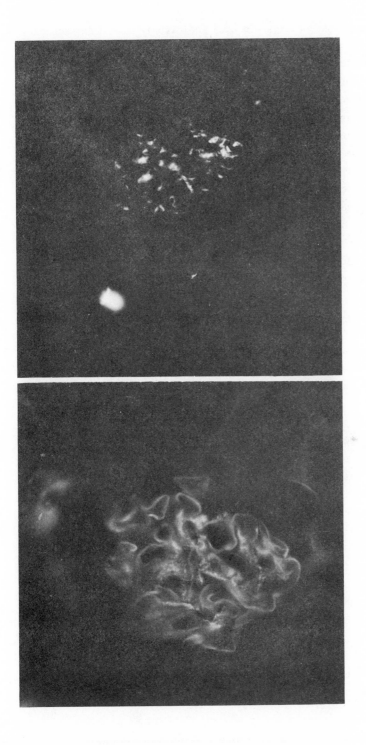

Figure 4A. Kidney section from a 10 month old CBA/T6T6 mouse infected with parainfluenza type 1 virus (Sendai) within a month after birth. Sections were incubated with fluorescein labeled antimouse immunoglobulins (anti IgG, G, and M) as described in the text. Both linear deposits of immunoglobulins along the basement membrane and "lumpy" or granular deposits are visible (X 1484).

Figure 4B. Immunofluorescent staining of a kidney section from a 26 month old CBA/T6T6 mouse showing granular deposits of immunoglobulins in the glomerulus (X 927).

obtained prior to infection. Changes in some indices may have been secondary to changes obtained in others. For example, the decrease in spleen, lymph node, and thymus cellularity may be secondary to increased cell death in vivo similar to that observed in vitro. The apparent decrease in the proportion of B cells could also be an artifact of increased cell death.

The changes in the indices which require culture in vitro for measurement was particularly striking (e.g., PHA response). These changes may well have resulted from decreased viability of cells from infected mice in culture (Table 1 and Fig 1).

It is possible that complement dependent cytotoxicity in the presence of autoantibodies to lymphoid cells contributed to the high frequency of cell death following infection. Data indicating that the frequency of cell death at 4° is associated with IgM Coombs' titer ($P \leq 0.01$) and that cell death at $37^o C$ increases in the presence of complement (Fig 1) lend support to this interpretation. However, a cytopathic effect of the virus remains a possibility.

This study also provides data suggesting that chronic viral infection can accelerate immunologic aging. All indices that correlated best with age prior to infection decreased significantly following infection for all age groups (Tables 1 and 2). For example, cells per mg wet weight thymus (Table 5) declined more rapidly following infection so that it was zero by 18 months of age, at least 12 months earlier than it would be in uninfected animals. Thymus cellularity and percent thymus weight of body weight also exhibited an accelerated decline (Table 3 and 4). Accelerated immunologic aging can be explained on the basis of findings showing that precursor stem cell traffic into the thymus may cease prior to adolescence[7]. Thus, if one assumes that chronic viral infection depletes the T cell population, which can not be replenished by bone marrow stem cells, one would expect an accelerated decline in T cell function. An alterative explanation is that virus infection depresses or terminates synthesis of T cell differentiation factors that are required for transformation of precursor T cells into mature T cells.

In addition, the results suggest that viral infection in utero may suppress or retard the development of the T cell component of the immune system. For example, thymus weight and cellularity of 6 month old mice which had been infected in utero were significantly less than those of uninfected mice. Such an interpretation may be of importance to studies of cell-mediated immunity of animals such as NZB mice, which are chronically infected with viruses and show an early decline in immune indices[8,9].

Although chronic viral infection appears to accelerate immunologic aging, thymus weight and cellular indices still correlated best with age.

Prior to infection, these indices exhibited a statistically significant negative correlation for all mice, independent of genetic background, and they continued to do so following the infection (Table 1 and 3). The proliferative response of lymph node T cells, as determined by the ratio index, still correlated negatively with age following infection. However, the arithmetic index of lymph node and splenic T cell activity and the ^{3}H thymidine uptake of PHA stimulated lymph node cells no longer did so. These results support the view that thymic aging is characteristic of the mouse species[4] since thymus weight and cell indices, and lymph node T cell activity correlated negatively with age even after prolonged exposure to an environmental pathogen.

Previous studies have shown that in long-lived humans and mice immunodeficiency and autoimmunity are often associated with each other, the frequency of individuals with serum autoantibodies increases with age, and the presence of autoantibodies in males is correlated with death from cardiovascular disease[10-12]. Unfortunately, it has been difficult to determine whether a causal relationship exists between the two events because these phenomenological studies were performed at a time when both immunodeficiency and autoimmunity were present. Other studies have shown that certain T cell activities of the immune system decline early in relatively short-lived strains of mice such as NZB and A strain mice which spontaneously develop AID. The decline precedes AID, and the onset of AID can be either accelerated by neonatal thymectomy or retarded by injection of syngeneic thymocytes[13-15]. Although much knowledge has been gained by studies on these short-lived animal models, it is still uncertain whether they are appropriate models for immunodeficiency and AID as they occur in aging long-lived animals and humans. The causes and mechanisms of the decline in normal immune functions and of autoimmune diseases may be different, particularly in view of the evidence that NZB mice carry, throughout life, Gross leukemia virus which participates in the development of AID[16,17].

The results presented here demonstrate that a decline in the T cell component of the immune system precedes AID. This supports the view that immunodeficiency precedes and predisposes an individual to AID. Another important conclusion which can be drawn from these studies is that infection by a common respiratory virus can initiate AID in immunologically old individuals, and in immunologically immature young individuals, but not in immunologically mature adult individuals and immunologically adequate middle-aged individuals[18].

The Coombs' positivity observed in this study was not due to antibodies to viral particles attached to erthyrocytes, since both scanning and transmission EM failed to demonstrate the presence of such particles on cell surfaces. The antibodies may have been directed toward viral proteins in cell membranes or toward membrane antigens exposed by viral enzymes such as neuraminidase[19], since the EM data suggests that the virus persists in cells of old mice.

Regardless of which mechanism is responsible for the Coombs' positive auto-immune hemolytic anemia in naturally aged mice, these experiments indicate that the production of RBC by elderly and immunodeficient individuals may be adequate provided they are not stressed severely, for example, by an infection. Such stress would reveal the deficit in their reserve of progenitor cells as manifested by their inability to maintain homeostasis by increasing RBC production to compensate for increased destruction.

Since the immune response plays a large role in terminating parainfluenza virus infection, natural infection of aging mice with parainfluenza virus might provide us with a physiological assessment in vivo of the immunological parameters which we measured previously in vitro. If the decline in thymic weight, cell, and activity indices observed with age prior to infection is relevant to the survival of the animal, then one would expect old mice to suffer more severe sequelae following viral infection than adult or middle-aged mice. This was observed to be the case as demonstrated by the following:

(a) Morality following infection was highest among old mice.

(b) By 6 months post-infection, all old mice were Coombs' positive, whereas only 22% of the adult mice were.

(c) The IgM Coombs' titer was significantly higher in old mice than in adult mice.

(d) Hematocrits of Coombs' positive old mice were significantly lower than those of Coombs' positive young mice and Coombs' negative old mice assayed 1 month after the initial infection.

(e) Old mice of a strain that is not prone to autoimmune disease had antigen-antibody complexes deposited in their kidneys which was not the case prior to infection.

Once again, young mice which were infected in utero and thus were immunologically immature[4] also developed severe sequelae following viral infection as determined by Coombs' positivity and anti-glomerular basement membrane antibodies and antigen-antibody complex deposits in their kidneys.

This study suggests that the age related decline in immune function is due primarily to a decrease in the T cell component. The finding that indices that correlated best with age prior to Sendai infection do so even after 6 months of chronic viral infection (i.e., 20-25% of the mean life span), and that old mice of all strains and hybrids contracted autoimmune disease following viral infection, lend further support to the view that genetic factors regulating immunologic aging are not easily influenced by environmental factors[20].

ACKNOWLEDGEMENTS

This is publication number 14 from the Laboratory of Molecular and Clinical Immunology and publication number 15 from GRECC, Wadsworth Medical Center, Los Angeles. Work conducted in my laboratory is supported by DOE Contract EY-76-S-03-0034 and NIH Grant HL 22671. This research was performed, in part, at the National Institute of Aging, Baltimore and Bethesda, Md.

REFERENCES

1. Good, R.A. and Yunis, E.J. (1974) Fed. Proc. 33, 2040.
2. Gross, L. (1965) Cancer 18, 201-204.
3. Davis, B.D., Dulbecco, R., Eisen, H.N., Ginsberg, H.S. and Wood, B., ed. (1969) Microbiology. Hoebner Medical Division, Harper and Row, New York.
4. Kay, M.M.B., Mendoza, J., Denton, T., Union, N. and Lajiness, M., Mech. Age. Dev., in press.
5. Kay, M.M.B (1978) Proc. Soc. Expt. Biol. Med. 158, 326.
6. Teague, P.O, Yunis, Y., Rodney, E., Fish, A., Stutman, O. and Good, R. (1970) Lab. Invest. 22, 121.
7. Kay, M.M.B. (1978) Fed. Proc., 37, 1241.
8. Stutman, O. (1972) J. Immunol. 109, 602.
9. Teague, P., Yunis, E., Rodney, G., Fish, A., Stutman, O. and Good, R. (1970) Lab. Invest. 22, 121.
10. Rowley, M.J., Buchman, H. and MacKay, I.R. (1968) Lancet 2, 24.
11. Fudenberg, H.H., Good, R.A., Goodman, H.C., Hitzig, W., Kundel, H.G., Roitt, I.M., Rosen, F.S., Rowe, D.S., Seligman, M. and Soothill, J.R. (1971) Bull. Wld. Hlth. Org. 45, 125.
12. MacKay, I.R., Whittingham, S.F. and Mathews, J.D. (1977) in Immunology and Aging, Makinodan, T. and Yunis, E., ed., Plenum Medical Book Co., New York, pp. 35-49.
13. Yunis, E.J., Hilgard, H., Sjodin, K., Martinez, C. and Good, R.A. (1964) Nature (London) 201, 784.
14. Stutman, O. (1972) J. Immunol. 109, 1204.
15. Gershwin, M.E. and Steinberg, A. (1975) Clin. Immunol. Immunopath. 4, 38.
16. Mellors, R.C. and Huang, C.Y. (1966) J. Exp. Med. 124, 1031.
17. Mellors, R.C., Shirai, T., Aoke, T., Heubner, R.J. and Krawczynski, K. (1971) J. Exp. Med. 133, 113.
18. Kay, M.M.B. (1976) J. Amer. Geriatric Soc. 26, 253.

19. Kay, M.M.B. (1978) in Basic and Clinical Immunology, Fudenberg, H.H., Stites, D.P., Galdwell, J.L. and Wells, J.W. ed., Lange Medical Publications, Los Altos, California, pp. 322-333.
20. Chino, F., Makinodan, T., Lever, W.E., and Peterson, W.J. (1971) J. Gerontol. 26, 497.

DISCUSSION

BASH: It seems to me that a likely explanation for your decrease in responsiveness after virus infection say, the PHA response in the spleen, could be due to induction of a suppressor cell. Have you considered this possibility and have you done co-culture experiments to exclude that?

KAY: We considered that possibility but it is a difficult thing to include or exclude when you have the percentage or frequency of cell death that we had and that is why pinpointing the mechanism in this case was really difficult. If only 20% of your cells survived in culture you cannot say very much.

BASH: I was considering it might be worthwhile looking at suppressor T cell as an index to include. You might find a change with age, an increase rather a depression in T-cell parameter.

KAY: We did not specifically look at suppressor cell function.

GENERAL DISCUSSION: SESSION II

AGING AND IMMUNE REGULATION

CUNNINGHAM: I have always been very interested in Walford's idea that immune dysfunction and autoimmune disease contributes to aging. I wonder if anyone wants to comment on that.

GOOD: I don't think there is any question that autoimmune phenomena of certain types are associated with aging temporally but to really get at Walford's basic concept that some autoimmune process was essential to the aging process itself has been very, very difficult for him as well as for everyone else. I would prefer to think of autoimmunity as being among the diseases or manifestations intimately associated with aging, rather than being pathogenetically important. I think that there is still the possibility of an autoimmune mechanism directed towards a central nervous system function or substance that could be actually very important in the development of what we call the manifestations of aging. I prefer to think of the immunological changes associated with aging as being intrinsic to the immunological system. I am sure that the interaction between the multiple network such as the central nervous system network, the hormonal network and the immunological network, are crucial.

TALAL: I would agree very strongly with what Bob just said. I want to go back to the idea of receptors, both idiotypic receptors and so called non-immunologic receptors, for example neurotransmitters and polypeptide hormones. It seems to me that we are living in a time of immunologic revolution with a question of autoimmunity having moved from horror autotoxicus and forbidden clones to the phenomenon of self-recognition at the central focal point of immune response with the immune system now being seen as not so much outward-looking but rather inward-directed, perhaps in an obsessive way. I feel that normal individuals have autoantigen-binding cells because they subserve a physiological role. Self-recognition even of what are, in the pathologic sense, harmful autoantigen-antibody systems, in a physiologic sense may be part of the normal homeostatic mechanism. Years ago I had the pleasure of working with Pierre Grabar who thought about autoantibodies as transporteurs, as carriers of cellular debris. I am not suggesting necessarily that that idea is correct, but I think that Grabar and others made us aware even before most of us could accept the idea that autoantibodies might be physiologic. Dr. Good is absolutely correct in focussing our attention on the neuro-endocrine system and on the central nervous system. Much of the relationship between autoimmunity and aging can be seen as aspects of a biological clock in which the immune system is really being controlled by higher centres. The next decade will see investigation in that area.

CUNNINGHAM: In a sense there has been a philosophical shift. To state it in an extreme way: anti-self reactions are far from being unwanted. They are mandatory now for development of immune repertoire perhaps in B cells as well as in T-cells.

MAKINODAN: With regard to the aging process, one should keep in mind that, if one looks evolutionarily, the only common denominator that seems to fit regardless of species is a striking correlation between the brain and aging. I think, if you have to gamble and look at a particular organ that may have the biological clock of aging, then in some place in the brain sits the aging clock. The immune system is an arm of this particular clock.

138

GOOD: One of the things that has really surprised us as we have become able to quantify thymic hormones, or thymic humoral factors, or at least substances that are circulating that are derived from the thymus, is how very early in even these long-lived strains of mice one begins to see evidence of declining circulating hormonal concentration. This is certainly true in man as well as in the mice, but in the very long-lived strains like C3H and CBA, one begins to see significant declines in measurable thymic hormone activities by 26 weeks or even earlier. There are ways of manipulating this; for example: just giving the element zinc in a higher concentration can maintain the circulating thymic hormone levels much longer. It looks to me that the changes begin, in the immunologic system, with declining thymic function and then a progressive disorganization of the entire T lymphocyte system first and much later alterations in the B system. This is another reason, for thinking in terms of whatever it is that controls programmed involution of the thymus is a central event, and that's why I look to the endocrinological apparatus and its control in the central nervous system.

CUNNINGHAM: Does it mean that you would put the clock in the thymus rather than in the brain, or that the thymus is a secondary clock?

GOOD: Probably both.

SESSION 111

Potential Approaches to Aging

Chairman: M. Weksler
Cornell University, New York

Singhal, Sinclair, Stiller, eds. Aging and Immunity

NUTRITION, IMMUNOLOGIC AGING, AND DISEASE

ROBERT A. GOOD, GABRIEL FERNANDES AND ANNE WEST
SLOAN-KETTERING INSTITUTE FOR CANCER RESEARCH, 1275 York Avenue, New York,
New York, USA   10021

INTRODUCTION

It is within the genetic capacity of human beings to live for a hundred

years. However, the diseases of aging--including arteriosclerosis, coronary

vascular disease, renal disease, cancer, autoimmunities such as arthritis,

vasculitis, amyloidosis, and infections--shorten most individual's lives

below this potential span. Several of these diseases have already been clearly

linked with involution of immunologic functions, especially of the thymus-

dependent system [1-9]. While a broad genetic framework underlies the processes

by which all biological systems develop and decline, the rate of change in the

immunological apparatus--again the thymus in particular--varies a great deal

among both humans and the strains of mice chiefly used for studies of

these processes.

As the rate of thymic involution, which normally begins shortly after

puberty, is directly correlated both with immunologic aging and in turn with

biological aging in general, it seems clear that factors influencing the func-

tional capacity of the thymus are important determinants of life expectancy.

Recent studies have demonstrated that the diet may be a powerful determinant

of the vigor or frailty of thymic and other lymphoid tissues and functions, at

any period in an animal's life. Further, the composition of the diet from

early life can act as a major determinant both of the tempo of immunologic

aging and of whether and when major diseases develop.

While different theoretical approaches may be taken towards understanding

the association between aging and immunologic malfunction[10-12] an interpretation based on thymic involution would argue that the T-dependent lymphoid system is genetically programmed to decline in effectiveness, possibly through altered endocrine and central nervous system controls. Such an interpretation is strongly supported by the consistent findings of defective cellular immunity functions in aged humans and animals[13-21] as well as the development of the age-related diseases listed above. It has also been demonstrated that while approximately 90% of the decline in immunologic functions with aging appears to be the result of cellular change [22] rather than other factors,[23] it is T-cell populations which primarily reflect immunologic changes, rather than B cells or macrophages[24].

However, we now know that even genetically programmed immunologic decline or insufficiency, in certain inbred strains of mice and in humans with certain inherited disorders, can be counteracted by nutritional elements. Both experimental and clinical studies in our own and other laboratories have begun to outline the relationships between nutrition and the anatomical and functional properties of the thymus-derived immunologic system, with the consequences of these relationships for development of the diseases of aging. As we gain increasingly specific knowledge of the mechanisms by which dietary components exert their influences on immunologic activity, we may eventually devise preventive or clinical approaches which could harness these influences to therapeutic ends. Indeed, key nutrients have already provided solutions to otherwise intractable medical problems. One instance we shall consider here is the trace metal zinc, which apparently operates directly through this element's influence on the functional capacity of the thymus and thus on T-cell immunity.

MALNUTRITION

The role of proper nutrition in long and healthy life has been recognized for centuries by the age-old association of famine with pestilence. Today, malnourished populations throughout the world continue to reflect the vital relationship between nutritional deficiencies, impaired immunity and disease[25-31]. However, since these clinical situations frequently involve multiple disease processes along with multiple dietary deficiencies, they have often been impossible to interpret. For example, while both the B- and T-cell systems were both evidently depressed in severely undernourished Palestinian refugees[32-34] and depressed T-cell function often characterized patients with kwashiorkor or marasmum studied around the world[25-31], a startling enhancement of certain T-cell functions was reported in a group of moderately protein-malnourished Australian aboriginal children[35]. We and others have responded to this complexity by turning to experimental systems, in order to analyse the effects of specific dietary components, precisely controlled, on immunologic function and the diseases of aging. Table 1 lists the strains of mice, along with their characteristic disease processes, in which we have studied these relationships most extensively. Our data strongly support the view that the thymus may be directly influenced by nutritional states, with major consequences for immunologic competence and development of the diseases of aging.

TABLE 1

PATHOLOGICAL PROCESSES ASSOCIATED WITH DISEASES OF AGING IN SEVERAL STRAINS OF MICE

Experimental Model	Disease process associated with aging
NZB	Autoimmunity Thymic involution Renal disease Cardiovascular disease Splenomegaly
NZB/NZW	Autoimmunity Thymic involution Renal disease Cardiovascular disease
C3H	Adenocarcinoma

TABLE 1, CONTINUED

Experimental Model	Disease process associated with aging
kdkd	Nephronophthisis Coomb's positivity
MRL/1	Autoimmunity Renal disease Cardiovascular lesions Amyloidosis Splenomegaly

EXPERIMENTAL DIETARY RESTRICTION

The developmental stage of an animal is a crucial aspect of the relationship between nutritional variables and the immunologic apparatus. A full diet early in life may produce vigorous immunologic function while the animal is young. However, the immunologic mechanisms appear to enter their decline sooner as a result of this early activity, possibly facilitating the genesis of several diseases[36,37]. Such animals consequently die younger than those who receive a restricted diet from the time of weaning. The animals restricted in total food intake early in life maintain an immunocompetence which, though comparatively moderate, persists longer in life.

Since autoimmune processes are closely associated with aging[5,6,38], we chose in our early studies to test the influence of diet on the characteristic autoimmune hemolytic anemia of NZB mice. When the fat component of the diet was lowered while the protein component was raised, these animals' diseases occurred significantly later, were milder, and animals lived correspondingly longer[39] (see Table 2). A lower fat diet was associated with lower titers of autoantibodies, but increased cellular cytotoxicity after tumor immunization[40]. Later studies, in which NZB mice were chronically protein deprived (CPD), showed that their thymic involution was delayed, splenomegaly inhibited and cellular immunities were more vigorous than in normally fed controls. In these animals the capacity to mount antibody responses also remained intact[41,42]. In other

experiments we saw again that while humoral immunity was decreased in
nutritionally restricted mice and rats, cellular immunity was significantly
enhanced [43-45] suggesting that these animals' thymus-dependent immunological
functions were differentially affected by nutritional factors.

TABLE 2

LIFE SPAN OF NZB MICE FED HIGH FAT/LOW PROTEIN OR LOW FAT/HIGH PROTEIN DIETS

	Age(Days)		
Diet	Males (p = < .001)	Females (p = < .05)	p
Protein 17% Fat 11%	295 $\pm$ 20.5	305 $\pm$ 21.0	ns
Protein 23% Fat 4.5%	456 $\pm$ 15.0	367 $\pm$ 18.3	<.001

(Mean $\pm$ SE for all mice, which either died or were sacrificed at 16 months.)

Developing this approach, we have shown that decreasing total food intake,
including carbohydrates, fats, and protein, may more than double the life span
of (NZB x NZW)F_1 mice, a strain which under normal feeding conditions develops
rampant autoimmune renal disease and dies between 8 and 14 months of age. The
hyalinizing kidney disease, in this model, is based on deposits of antigen-
antibody complexes in the glomeruli, which produce inflammation and tissue
injury. However, when male mice were fed 10 calories/day instead of 20, their
life spans were more than doubled whether the diet consisted of normal protein
(22%) with low calories, or low protein (6%) with low calories, or normal
protein/low fat (5%) and low calories[43,46]. Autoantibody formation was
significantly decreased in calorie-restricted animals compared to mice fed a
normal diet. Figure 1 illustrates the strikingly different appearance of

146

glomeruli from mice fed 10 or 20 calories per day. We were even able to prolong the life span of B/W mice, and inhibit development of their renal disease, when we imposed dietary restriction after the autoimmune disease process had already begun[47].

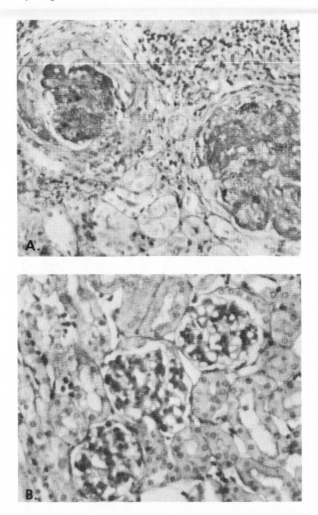

Fig. 1. (A and B) Histologic sections. (A) Typical glomerulus from a B/W mouse fed 20 cal per day. The glomerular tufts show proliferation and sclerosis. Note wire loop lesions similar to those seen in human lupus. (Hematoxylin and eosin; X200.) (B) Typical glomerulus from mouse fed 10 cal per day. Note the well-preserved glomerular architecture and the absence of sclerosis, wire loop lesions, or evidence of proliferation. Minimal increase of mesangial cells is the only abnormality present. (Hematoxylin and eosin; X250.)

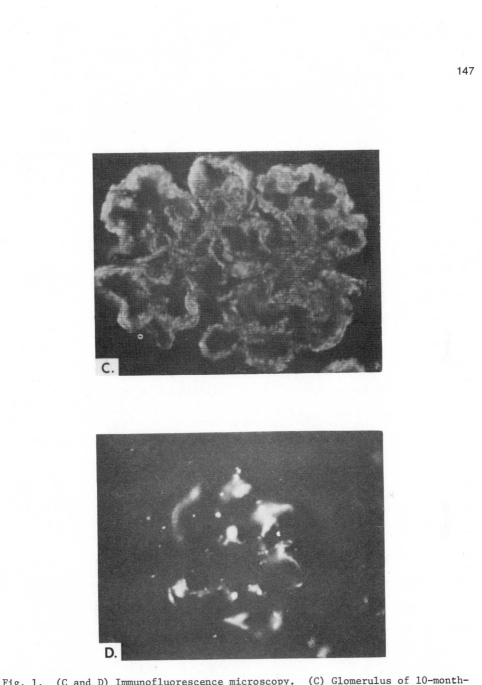

Fig. 1. (C and D) Immunofluorescence microscopy. (C) Glomerulus of 10-month-old 20-cal per day B/W mouse stained with fluorescent antiserum specific for IgG. Note irregular granular deposits of IgG lining cell capillaries of the glomerulus. Every glomerulus of the kidneys of these older B/W hybrids showed these characteristics. (X500.) (D) Glomerulus of 10-month-old B/W mouse fed 10 cal per day. Note that glomerular capillaries are completely free of deposits of IgG. The only IgG demonstrable was present in the mesangium of the glomerular tuft. (X650.) Source: Fernandes, G., Friend, P., Yunis, E.J., and Good, R.A. (1978) Proc. Natl. Acad. Sci. USA 75:1500–1504.

148

The disorganization of immunologic function begins at an early age in mice
of this hybrid strain. It is expressed as several characteristic changes:
progressive decrease in T-cell numbers and in vigor of T-cell responses,
including cell-mediated cytotoxicity after immunization in _vivo_ or in _vitro_;
excessive proliferation of B cells and plasma cells, but decreased antibody
response to T-dependent antigens after stimulation with antigen in _vivo_ and
in _vitro_; appearance of spontaneously activated suppressor T cells, and
progressive loss of inducible suppressor T cells. With aging, the autoimmunity
is expressed, and progressive renal and vascular disease ensues. All of these
changes are forestalled by restricting calorie intake from the time of
weaning [46,48,49]. Similar observations have subsequently been reported by
others, who showed that these vital consequences of early moderate nutritional
deprivation were not consequent to decreased expression of the xenotropic
viruses of Levy and associates [50,51].

Further studies, confirming and extending the work of other investigators[51-55] have shown that dietary restriction profoundly influences the
development of spontaneous mammary adenocarcinoma in mice[56]. When we placed
female C3H mice on calorie-restricted diets and measured their responses to
mitogens, capacity to develop plaque-forming cells after immunization with
SRBC, and activity of splenic suppressor cells, animals maintained vigorous
T-cell function in each of these assays. Most dramatic, however, was our
ability to prevent completely the development of tumors in these animals, which
on normal diets develop malignant disease in more than 70% of cases by
16 months of age, simply by restricting their food intake. The proportion
of fat in the diet has emerged as the crucial nutritional variable in these
experiments[57]. Even when total calories were substantially reduced, if the
percentage of fat in the diet remained high, the incidence of tumors was as
great as in animals on the higher calorie diet (see Figure 2).

149

FIGURE 2

EFFECTS OF HIGH AND LOW PROPORTIONS OF DIETARY FAT ON THE

DEVELOPMENT OF MAMMARY CANCER IN C3H/VIRGIN FEMALE MICE

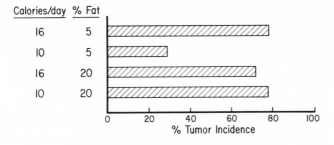

Studies of the short-lived kdkd mutant mouse[55] have also corroborated the direct relationship between diet and immunologic function, although the role of the thymus in this particular model has not yet been fully clarified. These mice regularly die between 7 and 9 months of age of a progressive renal disease associated histologically with chronic interstitial nephritis and nephronophthisis. Restricting protein intake had no effect either on immunologic parameters or length of life in these animals. Restriction of total calories, however, resulted in striking inhibition of the development of renal disease and regularly doubled their life span: in some instances, these mice lived over twice as long as well-fed mice. Microscopic examination of the kidneys from mice in both groups showed, in the normally fed animals, extensive formation of hyaline casts, glomerular sclerosis, severe tubular dilation and damage, as well as interstitial infiltration with round cells and an increased amount of connective tissue. By contrast, the kidneys of mice on the restricted diet were normal or nearly normal in appearance.

When the diet was changed in mid-course, the results were even more dramatic. Mice maintained on the restricted diet until 240 days of age all survived, while nearly all of those fed a higher calorie intake had died by the same age. When half of the former group were then placed on a higher calorie intake, all of them went on to die of renal disease by 300 days of age. Animals maintained throughout on the low calorie intake, however, all lived beyond 300 days and the majority more than 500 days (see Table 3).

TABLE 3

EFFECTS OF RESTRICTING DIETARY INTAKE ON SURVIVAL OF kdkd MICE *

Cal/day	% Protein	No. survivors		
		240 days	300 days	500 days
Ad lib.	17	4/15	0/15	0
16	22	1/20	0	0
16	6	2/20	0	0
8	22	20/20	0/9 (16 cal)	0
			9/9 (8 cal)	5/9

* Restriction began at 60 days

Work with the extremely short-lived MRL/1 mouse has also shown a powerful impact by calorie restriction on the thymus, immunologic stability, and development of disease[59]. On normal diets, both male and female mice develop severe autoimmunity and massive lymphoproliferative disease, dying by 5–6 months of age. Total calorie restriction dramatically inhibits disease development in these animals. Thymic involution is delayed, and spleen cell responsiveness to the mitogens phytohemagglutinin (PHA), concanavalin A (Con A) and lipopolysaccharide (LPS), which declines drastically in well-fed controls. is maintained in restricted mice (see Table 4).

TABLE 4

HIGHER RESPONSE TO MITOGENS BY SPLEEN CELLS FROM MRL/1 MICE FED 10 CAL/DAY

Mice (female)	Diet	Cells	Media	PHA 2.5 µg	Con A 2.5 µg	LPS 10 µg
MRL/1 (5 mo)	20 Cal/day	Spleen	995	4300	3000	3600
		L.N.	250	13725	30220	1500
MRL/1 (5 mo)	10 Cal/day	Spleen	812	35600	39030	28000
		L.N.	270	81300	83000	4600
MRL/1 (3 mo)	Lab chow ad lib	Spleen	890	20450	18000	34150
		L.N.	370	55530	28300	1100

Table 4 shows the sharp drop in responsiveness to mitogens of spleen cells from well-fed mice, by the age of 5 months, in contrast to the sustained or heightened responsiveness of cells from mice on restricted calories.

Other studies have illustrated the effects of nutritional deprivation on immunologic functions which are either deficient or pathologically activated in the diseases of aging. When we placed several strains of laboratory animals on chronic restriction either of total calories or of the protein component in the diet, we saw profound inhibitory effects both on the development of plaque-forming cells and on antibody production[44,60,61]. However, the seeming paradox of increased T-cell mediated functions in deprived mice and rats consistently reappeared[43-45]. Development of delayed hypersensitivity, timing of allograft rejection, proliferative response to the mitogens concanavalin A or phytohemagglutinin, and formation of migration inhibitory factor[44,60-62] were all enhanced in underfed animals.

152

Moreover, the ability of restricted animals to resist different kinds
of infection depended on whether the immunologic response necessary to combat
the challenging pathogen was mediated by humoral or cellular mechanisms[44].
While protein deprivation increased susceptibility to infection with
streptococci, an encapsulated pathogen defended against largely by antibody,
the same diet enhanced resistance to infection with pseudorabies virus
(see Figure 3) presumably through an increased cell-mediated immunity.[44]

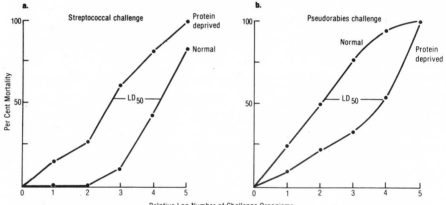

Fig. 3. Differential effects of protein restriction on resistance to infection
by streptococci and pseudorabies virus. Source: Good, R.A., Fernandes, G. and
West, A. (1979) MSKCC Clinical Bulletin 9:3-13.

Studies of tumor immunity confirmed the differential effects of nutritional
deprivation on the B-cell and T-cell systems. When mice and rats on restricted
diets were immunized with syngeneic, allogeneic, or xenogeneic tumors,
hemagglutinating, cytotoxic and blocking antibody production was reduced
compared with responses of normally fed animals, but T killer cell activity was
normal or even heightened[43,45,63].

Guinea pigs and monkeys, on comparable dietary regimens, were also studied
with similar results. While antibody production was inhibited by chronic,

moderate protein restriction, the capacity to mount a delayed hypersensitivity reaction remained intact[62,64]. When the protein component was further reduced to lethal or near-lethal levels in guinea pigs, this T-cell mediated function finally did break down. However, the basis for this functional impairment could be identified as some component of the inflammatory response other than T lymphocytes themselves. Indeed, T-cells from malnourished guinea pigs required smaller doses of antigens in order to develop sensitivity in the migration inhibition factor (MIF) assay than T-cells from normally fed animals require.

DIETARY ZINC DEFICIENCY

These apparent differences between the effects of dietary restriction on humoral and cellular immunologic functions have led us to examine the immunologic effects of restricting a single specific nutrient, the trace metal zinc. Recent experimental and clinical investigations in our laboratories have linked zinc deficiency with altered thymus-dependent immunity and with cancer and other immunodeficiency diseases. For several years, nutritional zinc deficiency has been linked with skin lesions and growth retardation in humans and a number of animals [66,67]. In 1971, published studies began to call the attention of immunologists to an autosomal recessive mutation (A-46) among Holstein-Friesian cattle[67-69] which produces calves unable to absorb the trace metal zinc through the intestinal tract. These animals are stunted, lethargic, and subject to skin lesions resembling acrodermatitis enteropathica; examination shows severe underdevelopment both of the thymus itself and of the thymus-derived immunologic system, including the thymus-dependent areas of the lymph nodes, the Peyer's patches, and the spleen. The calves' T-cell function is profoundly impaired, and they usually die of infection consequent to defective cell-mediated immunity. Treatment with large dietary supplements of zinc,

154

however, cures these animals' disease[70], restoring the thymus and Peyer's patches and the animals' cell-mediated immunity[69,71]. Figure 4 shows an affected calf, the typical hypoplastic thymus, and the normal sized thymus of a reconstituted calf.

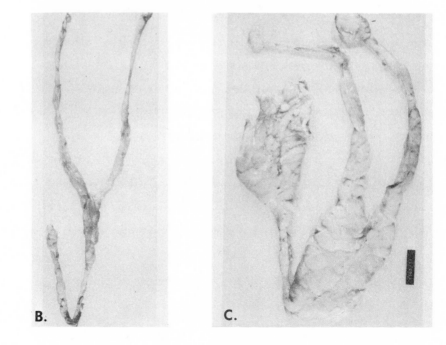

Fig. 4. (A) Calf with hereditary thymus hypoplasia (lethal trait A-46) showing typical late lesions. (B) Hypoplastic thymus (9.5 gm) from affected calf. (C) Normal sized thymus (372 gm) from a reconstituted calf. Source: Brummerstedt, TE., Basse, A., Flagstad, T. and Andresen, E. (1977) Am. J. Pathol. 87:725-728.

The human counterpart of this disease is acrodermatitis enteropathica, defined as a clinical entity by Danbolt and Closs in 1942 [72]. Patients with this frequently lethal malady, also inherited as an autosomal recessive trait, often show thymic involution. Their negligible cellular immunity offers no effective resistance to infecting pathogens, and they develop, among other symptoms, scourge-like skin lesions which are often heavily infected, especially with fungi. Large supplements of dietary zinc completely correct this condition, which is probably also caused by malabsorption of zinc from the gut.

Experimental work with zinc has now begun to document the precise relationship between this element and thymic function. Dietary restriction of zinc produces lymphoid system abnormalities, including severe involution of the thymus and thymus-dependent regions of the lymph nodes, with some involution of the thymus-dependent areas of the spleen as well; zinc-deprived animals also develop acrodermatitis enteropathica[73-76].

Functional thymic and T-cell defects accompanying zinc restriction include deficient production of the thymic hormone Facteur Thymique Serique (FTS) [74,75,77-79] which may be restored by grafting syngeneic thymic epithelium[80]. In addition, the ability of zinc-deprived animals both to develop cytotoxic T killer cells in response to EL-4 lymphoma cells, and to express natural killer cell function, are grossly deficient. Humoral immunity is severely impaired as well in zinc-deficient animals, although B-cell functions are spared to some degree[73,74]. Zinc-positive pair-fed animals respond readily to standard immunological tests measuring thymus-dependent humoral immunity, among them _in vivo_ challenge with sheep red blood cells[75]. In zinc-deficient animals, however, this capacity is progressively undermined. Primary antibody response is also reduced, and the secondary response, requiring helper T lymphocytes, is virtually eliminated. Natural killer cell (NK) function declines with age at a greater rate in zinc-deficient mice than in pair-fed controls. The rather startling finding that lymphocytes from restricted animals show normal or even slightly enhanced antibody-dependent cell-mediated cytotoxicity (ADCC)[75] gives further evidence of heterogeneity among the cellular elements of the lymphoid system with respect to the influence of dietary components, in this case zinc. It is also now clear that these profound immunologic changes especially in T-cell function are not entirely attributable to pituitary adrenal axis hyperactivity consequent to stress, since adrenalectomy does not inhibit the loss of thymic humoral function or the cellular immune functions discussed above[80].

The clinical relevance of these experimental studies is becoming increasingly apparent. At least 70 enzymes in both humans and animals, including DNA polymerase, RNA polymerase, and thymidine kinase[81] which are all necessary for synthesis of DNA and RNA, require zinc in order to function properly. Since both cellular and humoral immunologic responses depend on proliferation of immunocompetent lymphocytes and protein synthesis by these cellular elements, deficiency of zinc must substantially reduce immunologic vigor. It has been reported, however, that many self-selected diets in the United States contain less than the minimum daily requirement of trace metals[82]. Protein and protein-calorie malnutrition syndromes in immunodeficient children who may also have kwashiorkor or marasmus are frequently accompanied by low plasma concentrations of zinc[83-85]. Severely reduced levels of zinc have also been noted in patients with other immunologically based diseases, including 20-30% of patients with epidermoid cancer of the head and neck[86] and common variable immunodeficiency disease[87-90]. The patients in the latter group who have deficient T-cell immunity, along with the characteristic antibody-deficiency syndrome, respond well to dietary zinc supplements, with correction of clinical symptoms as well as T-cell abnormalities[86-90].

Several studies have shown that zinc can function as a mitogen for lymphocytes in both humans and animal models[89,91-94]. Normal human peripheral blood lymphocytes (PBL) proliferate in vitro in the presence of zinc at higher than physiological concentrations, at a response rate comparable to that produced by stimulation with antigens. PBL from certain patients with cancer or hypogammaglobulinemia, whose mitogen responses were depressed, have shown comparably deficient responsiveness to zinc [89,95,96].

Highly significant differences in responsiveness to zinc may be seen, however, when PBL from young and aged individuals are compared[97]. In our studies, zinc suppressed the responsiveness of cells from aged individuals, while young individuals' responses were significantly enhanced. A possible explanation for this difference may lie in the fact that the cell membrane changes with aging[98]. These changes are likely to include alterations in surface receptors[99,100]. Although the exact mechanism of action of zinc is not known, the available data suggest that the cell membrane is likely to be one site of action of zinc ions[101-103]. Consequently, alterations in the cells themselves with aging[9,18] could underlie decreased responsiveness to stimulation by zinc as well as by other elements.

CONCLUSION

These studies extend our understanding of the relationships between nutrition, thymic-dependent immunologic function, and the disease processes associated with aging. Autoimmunity, including arthritis; amyloidoisis and vasculitis; cardiovascular disease and renal disease; cancer, several forms of immunodeficiency, and susceptibility to infection: all have been associated with pathological changes in cell-mediated immunologic activity, often accompanied by involution of the thymus. Nutritional components, including total calories, percentage protein, and dietary zinc have all been shown to have a profound effect on the development and maintenance of the thymus-derived immunity system in both humans and experimental models. Thus it is clear that changes in diet which affect thymus-dependent immunocompetence may be crucial to the tempo at which diseases of aging develop. As a consequence, specific dietary factors may come to be increasingly well understood as determinants of life span.

The processes which link these nutritional causes and immunologic effects are clearly vital subjects for further study. That diet may profoundly alter the maintenance of immunity over time affecting the organization of complex networks of cells and cell products and the specific functions that they serve, surely implies that nutritional components act on neuroendocrinologic modulators of the hormonal network. This system in turn modulates the mechanisms, whether genetically programmed or specifically perturbed, that control involution of the immunologic apparatus. We already know, for instance, that decreased levels of thymic hormones with age[104] may be partially responsible for the failure of thymus-derived lymphocytes from aged persons to differentiate into immunocompetent lymphocytes [18,105]. We also know that dietary zinc may differentially affect functional subpopulations of T lymphocytes: witness the accelerated loss of NK activity in zinc-deprived mice, in contrast with enhanced ADCC in the same animals[75]. Taken together, the relationship between dietary zinc and thymic hormone levels, the specificity of this element's effects on certain T-lymphocyte functions, the necessity of zinc for proper function of the enzymes required for synthesis of DNA and RNA, and the depressed DNA content of the thymus in zinc deficiency[106], all represent an imposing paradigm of how a single nutrient may support or undermine immunocompetence through the thymus-derived branch of the immunity system, throughout an animal's lifetime.

Moreover, our experimental work in restriction of total food intake showed that calories may even differentially affect distinct types of suppressor cell activity[46]. A population of specific suppressor cells are spontaneously active in B/W mice which have developed autoimmune disease. A population of inducible, nonspecific suppressor cells present in young animals, however, is lost with age. We found that reduction of total food intake seemed to facilitate maintenance of the precursor cells from which the inducible, non-specific suppressors were derived, and at the same time to inhibit the appearance of spontaneously activated specific suppressors. Calorie-restricted B/W mice also developed less severe autoimmune disease and preserved a balance of immunologic function similar to what may be observed in longer-lived strains, including ability to make antibody to SRBC and to generate T killer cells after immunization with EL-4 allogeneic tumor cells. These latter modifications, along with our studies of mammary cancer in mice, support the view that development of malignancy, as well as autoimmunity, immunodeficiency disease and other diseases of aging, may be significantly influenced by diet. Future investigations must continue to address these issues, both by classical reduction analyses and by learning in the most rudimentary terms how the major biological systems interact.

We may begin to look forward to a time when dietary manipulation which extends immunologic vigor, particularly through preserving the functional capacity of the thymus and thymus-dependent functions over a longer period, may be incorporated into treatment or even prevention of the diseases of aging.

160

REFERENCES

1. Hammar, J.A. (1926) Z. Mikrosk.-Anat. Forsch. 6, 1.
2. Good, R.A. and Gabrielson, A.E., ed. (1964) The Thymus in Immunobiology. Hoeber-Harper, New York.
3. MacKay, I.R. (1972) Gerontologia 18, 285-304.
4. Yunis, E.J., Fernandes, G. and Stutman, O. (1971) Am. J. Clin. Pathol. 56, 280-282.
5. Yunis, E.J., Stutman, O. and Good, R.A. (1971) Ann. N.Y. Acad. Sci. 183, 205-220.
6. Good, R.A. and Yunis, E.J. (1974) Fed. Proc. Fed. Am. Soc. Exp. Biol. 33, 2040-2050.
7. Roberts-Thompson, I., Whittingham, S., Youngchaiyud, U. and MacKay, I.R. (1974) Lancet 2, 368-370.
8. Fernandes, G., Yunis, E.J. and Good, R.A. (1976) Clin. Immunol. Immunopathol. 6, 318-333.
9. Yunis, E.J., Fernandes, G. and Good, R.A. (1978) in The Immunopathology of Lymphoreticular Neoplasms, Twomey, J.J. and Good, R.A.. ed., Plenum Publishing Corp., New York, pp. 53-80.
10. Hayflick, L. (1965) Exp. Cell Res. 37, 614-636.
11. Burnet, F.M. (1970) Lancet 2, 358-360.
12. Walford, R.L. (1969) The Immunologic Theory of Aging. Munksgaard, Copenhagen.
13. Waldorf, D.S., Willkens, R.F. and Decker, J.L. (1968) J. Am. Med. Assoc. 203, 111.
14. Hallgren, H.M., Buckley, C.E., III, Gilbertsen, V.A. and Yunis, E.J. (1973) J. Immunol. 111, 1101-1107.
15. Friedman, D., Keiser, V. and Globerson, A. (1974) Nature (Lond.) 251, 545.
16. Weksler, M.E. and Hutteroth, T.H. (1974) J. Clin. Invest. 53, 437.
17. Stobo, J.D. and Tomasi, T.B. (1975) J. Chron. Dis. 28, 437.
18. Inkeles, B., Innes, J.B., Juntz, M.M., Kadish, A.S. and Weksler, M.E. (1977) J. Exp. Med. 145, 1176-1187.
19. Makinodan, T. (1977) in Handbook of the Biology of Aging, C.E. Finch and L. Hayflick, ed., Van Nostrand, Rheinhold, New York, p. 379.
20. Kay, M.M.B. (1978) Fed. Proc. 37, 1241.
21. Goidl, E.A., Innes, J.B. and Weksler, M.E. (1976) J. Exp. Med. 144, 1037-1048.
22. Perkins, E.H. and Makinodan, T. (1971) in Proceedings of the 1st Rocky Mountain Symposium on Aging, Colorado State University, Fort Collins, Colorado, pp. 80-103.
23. Makinodan, T. and Adler, W.H. (1975) Fed. Proc. Fed. Am. Soc. Exp. Biol. 34, 153-158.
24. Heidrick, M.L. and Makinodan, T. (1973) in Proceedings of the 1st Rocky Mountain Symposium on Aging, Colorado State University, Fort Collins, Colorado, pp. 80-103.
25. Faulk, W.P. (1975) Trop. Dis. Bull. 72, 89-103.
26. Scrimshaw, N.S., Taylor, C.E. and Gordon, J.E. (1959) Am. J. Med. Sci. 237, 367-403.
27. Stiehm, E.R. and Fudenberg, H.H. (1966) Pediatrics 37, 715-727.
28. Schlesinger, L. and Stekel, A. (1974) Am. J. Clin. Nutr. 27, 615-620.
29. Olson, R.E. ed. (1975) Protein-Calorie Malnutrition, Academic Press, New York.
30. Chandra, R.K. and Newberne, P.M., ed. (1977) Nutrition, Immunity and Infection. Mechanisms of Interactions. Plenum Publishing Corp., New York.
31. Suskind, R.R., ed. (1977) Malnutrition and the Immune Response, Raven Press, New York.

32. Aref, G.H., Badr El-Din, M.K., Hassan, A.I. and Araby, I.I.(1970) J. Trop. Med. Hyg. 73, 186-191.
33. Abassy, A.S., Badr El-Din, M.K., Hassan, A.I., Aref, G.H., Hammad, S.A., El-Araby, I.I. and Badr El-Din, A.A. (1974) J. Trop. Med. Hyg. 77,13-17.
34. Abassy, A.S., Badr El-Din, M.K., Hassan, A.I., Aref, G.H., Hammad, S.A., El-Araby, I.I. and Badr El-Din, A.A. (1974) J. Tro. Med. Hyg. 77, 18-21.
35. Jose, D.G., Welch, J.S. and Doherty, R.L. (1970) Aust. Paediatr. J. 5, 209-218.
36. Walford, R.L.(1974) Fed. Proc. 33, 2020-2027.
37. Walford, R.L., Liu, R.K., Gerbase-Delima, M., Mathies, M. and Smith, G.S. (1974) Mech. Ageing Dev. 2, 447-454.
38. Fernandes, G., Good, R.A. and Yunis, E.J. (1976) in Immunology and Aging, Makinodan, T. and Yunis, E, ed.,pp. 111-133.
39. Fernandes, G., Yunis, E.J., Smith, J. and Good, R.A. (1972) Proc. Soc. Exp. Biol. Med. 139, 1189-1196.
40. Fernandes, G., Yunis, E.J., Jose, D.G. and Good, R.A. (1973) Int. Arch. Allergy 44, 770-782.
41. Fernandes, G., Yunis, E.J. and Good, R.A. (1976) J. Immunol. 116, 782-790.
42. Good, R.A., Fernandes, G., Yunis, E.J., Cooper, W.C., Jose, D.G., Kramer, T.R. and Hansen, M.A. (1976) Am. J. Pathol. 84, 599-614.
43. Jose, D.G. and Good, R.A. (1971) Nature 231, 323-325.
44. Cooper, W.C., Good, R.A. and Mariani, T. (1974) Am. J. Clin. Nutr. 27, 647-664.
45. Jose, D.G., Stutman, O. and Good, R.A. (1973) Nature 241, 57-58.
46. Fernandes, G., Friend, P., Yunis, E.J. and Good, R.A. (1978) Proc. Natl. Acad. Sci. USA (75)3, 1500-1504.
47. Friend, P.S., Fernandes, G., Good, R.A., Michael, A.F. and Yunis, E.J. (1978) Lab. Invest. 38, 629-632.
48. Fernandes, G., Friend, P.S., Good, R.A. and Yunis, E.J. (1976) Fed. Proc. 35, 437 (Abstr).
49. Fernandes, G., Yunis, E.J. and Good, R.A. (1976) Proc. Natl. Acad. Sci. USA 73, 1279-1283.
50. Dubois, E.L. and Strain, L. (1973) Biochem. Med. 7, 336-342.
51. Gardner, M.B., Ihle, J.N., Pillarisetty, R.J., Talal, N., Dubois, E.L., and Levy, J.A. (1977) Nature 268, 341-344.
52. Rous, P. (1914) J. Exp. Med. 20, 433-451.
53. Tannenbaum, A. (1940) Am. J. Cancer 38, 335-350.
54. Visscher, M.B., Ball, Z.B., Barnes, R.H. and Silbertsen, I. (1942) Surgery 11, 48-55.
55. Carroll, K.K. (1975) Cancer Res. 35, 3374-3383.
56. Fernandes, G., Yunis, E.J. and Good, R.A. (1976) Nature 263, 504.
57. Fernandes, G. (1978) Ph.D. Thesis in Applied Biology, Institute for Research in Reproduction, University of Bombay, Bombay, India.
58. Fernandes, G., Yunis, E.J., Miranda, M., Smith, J. and Good, R.A. (1978) Proc. Natl. Acad. Sci. USA 75, 2888-2892.
59. Fernandes, G. and Good, R.A. (1979) Fed. Proc. 38, 1370 (Abstr.).
60. Cooper, W.C., Mariani, T.M. and Good, R.A. (1975) in Immunodeficiency in Man and Animals; Proceedings, Bergsma, D., ed., Sinauer Associates, Inc., Sunderland, Mass., pp. 223-228.
61. Good, R.A., Fernandes, G., Yunis, E.J., Cooper, W.C., Jose, D.G., Kramer, T. and Hansen, M.A. (1977) in Food and Immunology, Hambraeus, L., Hanson, L.A. and McFarlane, H. ed., Almqvist and Wiksell International, Stockholm, pp. 11-22.
62. Kramer, T.R. and Good, R.A. (1978) Clin. Immunol. Immunopathol. 11, 212-228.
63. Jose, D.G. and Good, R.A. (1972) Lancet 1, 314 (Letter to the Editor).

162

64. Good, R.A., unpublished data.
65. Prasad, A.S. (1976) in Trace Elements in Human Health and Disease, Prasad, A.S., ed., Academic Press, New York, pp. 1-20.
66. Luecke, R.A. (1966) in Zinc Metabolism, Prasad, A.S., ed., Thomas, Springfield, Illinois, pp. 202-214.
67. Brummerstedt, E., Flagstad, T., Basse, A. and Andresen, E. (1971) Acta. Pathol. Microbiol. Scand. (A), 79, 686-687.
68. Andresen, E., Basse, A., Brummerstedt, E. and Flagstad, T. (1974) Nord. Vet. Med. 26, 275-578.
69. Brummerstedt, E., Andresen, E., Basse, A. and Flagstad, T. (1974) Nord. Vet. Med. 26, 279-293.
70. Legg, S.L. and Sear, L. (1960) Nature 186, 1061.
71. Weisman, K. and Flagstad, T. (1976) Acta Derm. Venereol. (Stockh) 56, 151-154.
72. Danbolt, N. and Closs, K. (1942) Acta Derm. Venereol. (Stockh) 23, 127-169.
73. Fraker, P.J., Haas, S.M. and Luecke, R.W. (1977) J. Nutr. 107, 1889-1895.
74. Tanaka, T.. Fernandes. G., Tsoa, C., Pih, K. and Good, R.A. (1978) Fed. Proc. 37, 931.
75. Fernandes, G., Nair, M., Onoe, K., Tanaka, T., Floyd, R. and Good, R.A. (1979) Proc. Natl. Acad. Sci. USA 76, 457-461.
76. Swenerton, H. and Hurley, L.S. (1968) J. Nutr. 95, 8-18.
77. Bach, J.F., Dardenne, M., Pleau, J.M. and Bach, M. (1975) Ann. N.Y. Acad. Sci. 249, 186-210.
78. Iwata, T., Incefy, G.S., Tanaka, T., Fernandes, G., Menendez-Botet, C.J., Pih, K. and Good, R.A. (1978) Fed. Proc. 37, 1827.
79. Iwata, T., Incefy, G.S., Tanaka, T., Fernandes, G., Menendez-Botet, C.J., Pih, K. and Good, R.A. (1979) Cell. Immunol. 46,
80. Bach, J.F., Bach, M.A., Charreire, J., Dardenne, M., Fournier, C., Papiernik, M. and Pleau, J.M. (1975) in The Biological Activity of Thymic Hormones, van Bekkum, D.W., ed., Kooyker Scientific Publications, Rotterdam, p. 145.
81. Kirchgessner, M., Roth, H.P. and Weigand, E. (1976) in Trace Elements in Human Health and Disease. Vol. 1. Zinc and Copper, Prasad, A., ed., Academic Press, New York, pp. 189-225.
82. Wolf, W.R., Holden, J. and Green, F.E. (1977) Fed. Proc. 36, 1175.
83. Khalid, M., Kabiel, A., El-Khateeb, S., Aref, K., El-Lozy, M., Johin, S. and Nasr, F. (1974) Am. J. Clin. Nutr. 27, 260-262.
84. Golden, M.H.N., Golden, B.E., Harland, P.S.E.G. and Jackson, A.A. (1978) Lancet 1, 1226-1227.
85. Kramer, T. and Good, R.A., unpublished data.
86. Strong, E., Cunningham-Rundles, S., Erlandson, E., Menendez-Botet, C., Schwartz, M. and Good, R.A. (1979) Fed. Proc. 38, 713.
87. Oleske, J. (1978) Cutis 21, 297-298.
88. Oleske, J.M., Westphal, M.L., Shore, S., Gorden, D., Bogden, J. and Nahmias, A. (1979) Am. J. Dis. Child., in press.
89. Cunningham-Rundles, S., Cunningham-Rundles, C., Dupont, B. and Good, R.A. (1979) Fed. Proc. 38, 936 (Abstr).
90. Cunningham-Rundles, C., Cunningham-Rundles, S., Iwata, T., Incefy, G., Twomey, J. and Good, R.A. (1979) Fed. Proc. 38, 1222 (Abstr).
91. Ruhl, J., Kirchner, H. and Bochert, G. (1971) Proc. Soc. Exp. Biol. Med. 137, 1089-1092.
92. Chesters, J.K. (1972) Biochem. J. 130, 133-139.
93. Williams, R.O. and Loeb, L.A. (1973) J. Cell. Biol. 58, 594-601.
94. Berger, N.A. and Skinner, I.A.M. (1974) Cell. Biol. 61, 45-55.
95. Ruhl, H., Scholle, H. and Kirchner, H. (1971) Acta. Hematol. 46, 326-337.
96. Garofalo, J.A., Cunningham-Rundles, S., Braun, D.W. and Good, R.A. (1979) Cancer Research (submitted).

97. Rao, K.M.K., Schwartz, S.A. and Good, R.A. (1979) Cell. Immunol. 42, 270-278.
98. Grinna, L.S. (1977) Gerontology 23. 452.
99. Meredith, P., Gerbase-DeLima, M. and Walford, R.L. (1975) Exp. Gerontol. 10, 247.
100. Price, G.B. and Makinodan, T. (1972) J. Immunol. 108, 403.
101. Chvapil, M. (1973) Life Sci. 13, 1041.
102. Phillips, J.L. (1976) Biochem. Biophys. Res. Commun. 72, 634.
103. Brewer, G.J., Schoomaker, E.B., Leichman, D.A., Kruckeberg, W.C., Brewer, L.F. and Meyers, N. (1977) in Zinc Metabolism: Current Aspects in Health and Disease, Brewer, G.J. and Prasad, A.S., ed. Allan R. Liss, New York, p. 241.
104. Bach, J.F., Dardenne, M. and Salomon, J.C. (1973) Clin. Exp. Immunol. 14, 247.
105. Basch, R.S. and Goldstein, G. (1975) Cell. Immunol. 20, 218.
106. Ku, P.K., Ullrey, D.E. and Miller, E.R. (1970) in Trace Element Metabolism in Animals, Mills, C.F., ed., Livingstone, Edinburgh and London, p. 158.

ACKNOWLEDGEMENTS

Original work described in this paper was supported by grants CA-17404, CA-08748, AI-11843, and NS-11457 from the National Institutes of Health; the National Foundation March of Dimes; the Special Projects Committee of Memorial Sloan-Kettering Cancer Center; the Zelda R. Weintraub Foundation; the Richard Molin Memorial Foundation; and the Fund for the Advanced Study of Cancer.

DISCUSSION

YAMAMURA: What do you think about the effect of the fiber in a low fat diet?

GOOD: Well, we certainly recognize this as a serious problem and issue in nutrition. We haven't studied directly the fiber situation. We do intend to do that. In our first experiments in the two diets the low fat intake prolonged the life of the NZB mice. Those diets were higher in fiber. But that variable by itself has to be analyzed and so far as I know it hasn't been analyzed. The influence of already established disease has to be further studied. I'm not at all convinced that things are as irreversible as we have always thought them to be, but we know the difficulty of reversing established vascular lesions of the atherosclerotic type. I don't know of any new way of doing that. The most interesting work that I have found is that the combined restriction of calories and fat had been associated in monkeys with reversal of the coronary lesions.

SINCLAIR: What is the result of reducing fat and calorie intake in mice that can withstand obesity and inactivity? There are mice that live to a ripe old age under normal conditions.

GOOD: Well, the best data have been those of Walford in both mice and rats of about 20-25% prolongation of life in the long-lived strains so that it is not nearly as dramatic. But there is some evidence that maybe their rectangle isn't entirely square.

Published 1979 by Elsevier North Holland, Inc.
Singhal, Sinclair, Stiller, eds. Aging and Immunity

THE ROLE OF THE THYMUS IN THE SENESCENCE OF THE IMMUNE RESPONSE

MARC E. WEKSLER, JUDITH B. INNES AND GIDEON GOLDSTEIN
Department of Medicine, Cornell University Medical College, New York, New York,
10021.

The involution of the thymus gland after puberty had been recognized (1)
before the immunological function of the thymus was recognized in the early
1960's by Miller (2) and Good (3). It seemed reasonable to relate the age-
associated defects in immune function to the loss of thymic mass and decline in
the serum concentration of thymic hormone with age (4, 5). We shall review
several age-associated changes in immune function that can be related to a loss
of thymic function. More important, certain age-associated defects in immune
function can be reversed by a young thymus gland, young thymocytes or
thymopoietin. This observation provided strong support for the relationship
between waning thymic function and the immune deficiency that accompanies aging.

Cell-mediated immunity declines with age. Thus, graft versus host reactivity (6), the generation of cytotoxic T-lymphocytes (7) and the proliferation
of T-lymphocytes (8) are all impaired in lymphoid preparation from old mice.
T-cells from old carrier-primed mice are less capable than T-cells from young
carrier-primed mice of cooperating with young syngeneic B-cells from hapten-
primed young mice (9). It is not clear whether this observation reflects a
failure of T-cell "carrier-priming" in old mice, a failure of cooperative interaction between old T-cells and B-cells, or both.

We have studied the anti-dinitrophenyl (DNP) plaque forming cell (PFC) response of mice induced by the T-dependent antigen, DNP-bovine gamma globulin
(BGG) and the T-independent antigen DNP-Ficoll. The methods used to measure
direct, indirect PFC and the heterogeneity of the PFC response with respect to
affinity have been previously described (10). BALB/c mice of various ages were
immunized by the intraperitoneal (IP) injection of 500 micrograms of DNP-BGG in
complete Freund's adjuvant or by the IP injection of 50 micrograms of DNP-
Ficoll.

Effects of Age and Thymectomy on Anti-DNP PFC Response of BALB/c Mice.

Mice of different ages were immunized with DNP-BGG and splenic anti-DNP PFC
determined 2 weeks later (Table 1). Older mice showed a preferential loss of
indirect and high affinity PFC. The fall of the heterogeneity index reflects
the loss of high affinity PFC. Thymectomy accelerated the loss of indirect and
high affinity PFC. Thus, intact 12 month old mice showed a 22% decline in

indirect and 15% decline in direct PFC compared with the PFC response of 4
month old mice, whereas 12 month old mice, thymectomized at the age of 2 months,
had a 60% loss of indirect PFC and 48% loss of direct PFC.   In addition, intact
12 month old mice had a normally heterogeneous PFC response, whereas thymectomized 12 month old mice had a highly significant (p<0.01) loss of high affinity
PFC.   The PFC response of four month old mice which had been thymectomized at
2 months of age was comparable to intact age-matched animals.   This indicates
that thymic deprivation for more than 2 months is necessary before the loss of
indirect or high affinity PFC can be demonstrated.
Effect of the Young Thymus Gland or Young Thymocytes on the Immune Response of
Old Spleen Cells.

TABLE 1

Effect of Age and Thymectomy on the Anti-DNP PFC Response of BALB/c Mice[*]

	Age of intact animals		
	4	12	24
		mo	
Direct PFC	4,130	3,494	1,018
Indirect PFC	4,935	3,872	810
Heterogeneity index	2.55	2.49	1.25

	Age of thymectomized animals	
	4	12
Direct PFC	4,325	2,443
Indirect PFC	5,185	2,109
Heterogeneity index	2.54	1.72

*A group of mice were thymectomized at 2 mo of age. Age-matched nonthymecto-
mized and thymectomized mice were immunized with DNP-BGG in CFA at 4, 12, and
24 mo of age. 2 wk later, the number of anti-DNP PFC/spleen and their
distribution with respect to affinity were determined. The data presented are
the mean heterogeneity index and PFC/spleen.

As the immune deficiency observed during aging could be accelerated by thymectomy, the capacity of a young thymus gland to reverse the loss of indirect
and high affinity PFC of spleen cells from old mice was tested (Table 2).
Intact or thymectomized, irradiated, syngeneic 2 month old mice were reconstituted with spleen cells from 2 or 24 month old mice. Recipients were immunized
7 weeks after cell transfer. Intact recipients of old spleen cells produced
more indirect and high affinity PFC than did thymectomized recipients. Old
spleen cells in the presence of a young thymus gland generated a normally
heterogeneous PFC response. The increase in indirect PFC, although highly
significant statistically, did not equal the indirect PFC response of young
spleen cells.

Restoration of the indirect and high affinity PFC response of old spleen
cells was also achieved when young thymocytes were transferred with old spleen
cells to young, irradiated, thymectomized, syngeneic mice (Table 2). This
effect could be demonstrated as soon as 2 weeks after transfer, at a time when
no effect of a young thymus gland (which required 6 or 7 weeks) could be
demonstrated.

TABLE 2

Effect of the Thymus Gland on Anti-DNP PFC Response of Spleen Cells from
Old and Young Mice[*]

Donors	Thymus Gland	Indirect Anti-DNP PFC/spleen	Heterogeneity index
mo			
2	Present	$5,153 \pm 523$	2.56 ± 0.63
	Removed	$3,955 \pm 760$	2.53 ± 0.33
24	Present	$1,798 \pm 275$	2.43 ± 0.48
	Removed	941 ± 170	1.39 ± 0.50
24	Removed	603 ± 120	1.55 ± 0.48
	Removed Thymocytes Added	$1,050 \pm 210$	2.17 ± 0.41

[*] Spleen cells from 2- or 24-mo-old mice were transferred into 2-mo-old
irradiated intact, or thymectomized syngeneic animals. All recipients were
immunized with DNP-BGG in CFA 7 wk after transfer and the splenic anti-DNP
PFC response measured 2 wk later. The data presented are the mean $\pm$ the SEM.

Effect of Thymopoietin Administration to Old Mice on the PFC Response.

The capacity of a young thymus gland to augment the PFC response of spleen cells from old mice did not distinguish between the activity of the gland itself and an effect of thymic hormone on the transferred cells. The effect of treating 24 month old mice with thymopoietin was tested. The thymopoietin preparation used in these studies was the biologically active pentapeptide Arg-Lys-Asp-Val-Tyr. This is the sequence from 32 to 36 of the 49 amino acid protein (11). The pentapeptide was prepared by organic synthesis. Thymopoietin was given to 24 month old mice by IP route in doses of 1 microgram for 5 days before immunization and for the 10 working days in the 2 weeks after immunization. The PFC response of young, old, and thymopoietin-treated old mice was compared (Table 3). Injection of thymopoietin produced a highly significant increase in the indirect PFC response and a complete reconstitution of the normal heterogeneity of the PFC responses with respect to affinity.

Response of Young and Old Mice to DNP-Ficoll.

The preferential loss of high affinity and indirect PFC of old mice immunized with the T-dependent antigen (DNP-BGG) might result from a defect in the T and/or B-lymphocyte populations. The capacity of aged mice to generate an anti-DNP PFC response to the T-independent antigen DNP-Ficoll was tested (Table 4). Although the number of anti-DNP PFC was less in 24 month old mice, this was not statistically significant. Furthermore, there was no difference in the distribution of PFC with regard to affinity in old as compared to young mice. Thus, in aged mice, the thymic independent anti-DNA PFC response was less compromised than the thymic-dependent anti-DNP PFC response.

TABLE 3

Effect of Thymopoietin Administration on the Anti-DNP PFC Response of Old Mice[*]

Age of Mice	Thymopoietin-treated	Indirect anti-DNP PFC/spleen	Heterogeneity index
mo			
2	No	$5,916 \pm 213$	2.78 ± 0.20
24	No	385 ± 79	1.09 ± 0.05
24	Yes	977 ± 102	2.48 ± 0.33

[*] 24-mo-old mice were given 1 μg of thymopoietin by the intraperitoneal route for 5 days before and 10 days after immunization. The thymopoietin-treated 24-mo-old mice and untreated 2- and 24-mo old mice were all immunized with DNP-BGG in CFA. The number of splenic anti-DNP PFC was determined 2 wk after immunization. The data presented are the mean $\pm$ the SEM.

TABLE 4

Response of Old and Young Mice to the T-Independent Antigen DNP-Ficoll[*]

Age of mouse	Direct anti-DNP PFC/spleen
mo	
2 (9)	9,422 (3,000 - 15,000)
24 (6)	7,086 (6,000 - 13,000)

[*]2- and 24-mo-old mice were given 50 µg of DNP-Ficoll by the intraperitoneal route. 2 wk later, the splenic anti-DNP PFC response was assayed. The number of animals in each group is given in parentheses. The data presented are the mean and range of response.

Discussion.

The production of indirect and high affinity anti-DNP PFC, following immunization with DNP-BGG is preferentially lost during aging. These immune deficiencies occur more rapidly in thymectomized mice. The age-associated defects are stable on transfer to syngeneic, thymectomized mice. The impaired PFC response of spleen cells from old mice can be reversed by the presence of a young thymus gland, young thymocytes or thymopoietin (12). In contrast, the anti-DNP PFC response, following immunization with DNP-Ficoll is little impaired in old mice. Thus, the T-dependent and DNP PFC response is severely impaired in old mice, while the T-independent anti-DNP PFC response was little impaired. Previous studies have reported that T-independent responses are either not impaired in old mice (13) or less impaired than T-dependent responses (14). In some studies both T-dependent and T-independent responses were impaired (15). In this context, it is important to review the usual definition of a "T-independent" response. Most investigators use this term when a B-cell response is not impaired in the absence of a thymus gland, thymocytes and/or peripheral T-cells. This operational definition of T-independence does not address an influence of the thymus gland on the maturation of the B-lymphocyte. Siskind and his colleagues (16) have demonstrated that the thymus is critical in the development of B-lymphocyte function. The capacity of fetal B-cells to generate a heterogeneous response was shown to depend on the presence of a mature thymus gland or adult thymocytes. Recently (17) we have found that the capacity of the thymus cell population to induce this differentiation step declines with age. Thymocytes from 7 month old

C57B1/6 mice are significantly less capable of effecting the differentiation of B-cell precursors, as compared with equal numbers of thymocytes from 1 or 2 month old mice. In this way the thymus gland may influence "T-independent" B-cell function. Consequently the involution of the thymus with age might affect B-cell functions which do not require contemporaneous T-cell cooperation.

Certain age-associated immune defects can be ameliorated or reversed by grafts of young thymus glands or by the administration of thymic factors. Transplantation of thymus glands has been reported to reverse the age-associated formation of auto-antibodies (18) and to prolong the life of autoimmune prone NZB/W mice (19). Furthermore, old spleen cells which have lost in vitro graft-versus-host reactivity are reactivated by incubation with a thymic humoral factor (6). The restoration of immune function by these techniques have, in some circumstances, been incomplete. This may indicate that age-associated phenomena unrelated to the involution of the thymus, e.g. contraction of the immunological repertoire with age may limit immune competence. It is also possible that the age-associated immune deficiencies might be more easily prevented than reversed. Experiments which aim to determine whether lifelong maintenance of serum thymic hormone levels found during early life by repeated and lifelong administration of thymic hormone will prevent the senescence of the immune response are now underway.

Acknowledgements

Supported in part by grants AG 00541 and AG 00239 from the National Institutes of Health.

Marc E. Weksler, recipient of Research Career Development Award CA 32102 from the National Institutes of Health.

REFERENCES

1. Boyd, E. (1932) Amer. J. Dis. Children, 43, 1162-1214.

2. Miller, J.F.A.P. (1961) Lancet, 2, 748-749.

3. Good, R.A., Dalmasso, A.P., Martinez, C., Archer, D.K., Pierce, J.C. and Papermaster, B.W. (1962) J. Exp. Med., 116, 773-796.

4. Bach, J.F., Dardenne, M., Pleau, J.M. and Bach, M.A. (1975) Ann. N.Y. Acad. Sci., 249, 186-210.

5. Lewis, V.M., Twomey, J.J., Bealmear, P., Goldstein, G., and Good, R.A. (1978) Journal of Clinical Endocrinology and Metabolism, 47, 145-150.

6. Friedman, D., Keiser, V. and Globerson, A. (1974) Nature, 251, 545-546.

7. Alder, W.H., Jones, K.H. and Nariuchi, H. (1977) in Recent Advances in Clinical Immunology, Thompson, R.A. ed., p. 77.

8. Hori, Y., Perkins, E.H., and Halsall, M.K. (1973) Proc. Soc. Exp. Biol. Med., 144, 48.

9. Krogsrud, R.L. and Perkins, E.H. (1977) J. Immunol., 118, 1607-1611.

10. Goidl, E.A., Innes, J.B. and Weksler, M.E. (1976) J. Exp. Med., 144, 1037-1048.

11. Schlessinger, D.H. and Goldstein, G. (1975) Cell., 5, 361.

12. Weksler, M.E., Innes, J.B. and Goldstein, G. (1978) J. Exp. Med., 148, 996-1006.

13. Smith, A.M. (1976) J. Immunol., 116, 469.

14. Gerbase-DeLima, M., Wilkinson, J., Smith, G.S. and Walford, R.L. (1974) J. Geront., 29, 261.

15. Abraham, C.Y., Tal, Y. and Gershon, H. (1977) Eur. J. Immunol., 7, 301.

16. Sherr, D., Swewczuk, M.R. and Siskind, G.W. (1978) J. Exp. Med., 147, 196.

17. Swewczuk, M.R., DeKryuff, R.H., Weksler, M.E. and Siskind, G.W. (1979) Unpublished Observations.

18. Teague, P.O., and Friou, G.J. (1969) Immunol., 17, 665.

19. Kysela, S. and Steinberg, A.D. (1973) Clin. Immunol. Immunopath., 2, 133.

DISCUSSION

SINGHAL: Mark, do you think you have a deficiency of thymopoeitin in these animals and that you are converting some pre T-cells into cells that can express T-cell function which would push the affinity up?

WEKSLER: We have really been totally unsuccessful in affecting very much of a change by incubating cells either from old humans or old mice with thymic factors in vitro. The real question I feel is: can we take lymphocytes and expose them to thymic factor and then return them to the animal? If you take the cells and put them into a test tube we are hard pressed to find any effect. I would suggest that there are several stages of differentiation in the functional capacity.

PAUL: It would be very interesting to know whether thymopoeitin might act not so much to encourage, let's say, primitive cells in the aged animals to become mature - but rather perhaps by eliminating a suppressor which should be considered. For example, if you co-transfer thymopoeitin treated and non-thymopoeitin treated old cells with old and young cells, or if you transfer thymopoeitin treated cells into the aged animal directly without any other manipulation, do any of those activities reconstitute a response?

WEKSLER: I think it is a critical question. It is extremely difficult to approach. I think our findings are in complete agreement with Kim Singhal's. There is no doubt the response observed with the co-transfer is very much less than expected. However, the suppressor activity in our hands is only modestly removed by anti-theta treatment.

PAUL: Does the thymic hormone treatment of the cells being transferred in vivo relieve a substantial fraction of the disability? If that disability is due to suppression as Kim has suggested, then you have to come to terms with how that could be. For example, maybe the thymopoeitin treated T-cells are less susceptible to suppressive action of the cells. It may be paradoxical that the problem with old animals is that there are too many young cells.

Published 1979 by Elsevier North Holland, Inc.
Singhal, Sinclair, Stiller, eds. Aging and Immunity

INTERVENTION OF IMPAIRED IMMUNE FUNCTIONS AS AN APPROACH TO UNDERSTAND
IMMUNOLOGIC AGING

TAKASHI MAKINODAN[+]
[+]Geriatric Research, Education and Clinical Center (GRECC), V.A. Wadsworth
Medical Center, Los Angeles, CA 90073, and the Department of Medicine,
U.C.L.A., Los Angeles, CA 90024, USA

INTRODUCTION

There are two major issues confronting us on the problem of Aging and
Immunity, one at the cellular level and the other at the organismic level. At
the cellular level, the issue concerns the nature of decline in normal immunologic vigor with age, commonly referred to as immunologic aging. Studies to
date, as emphasized earlier by Singhal, Kay and Weksler at this symposium,
clearly show that the cause is multifactorial, involving the regulatory components of the immune system preferentially. This should not be surprising,
for the immunologic network is highly complex, as emphasized by Wigzell and
Cantor at this symposium. At the organismic level, the issue concerns the
causal nature of the inverse relationship between immunologic aging and
increase in the susceptibility to infectious, autoimmune, immune complex and
cancerous diseases; i.e., whether immunologic aging predisposes individuals to
diseases, or alternatively, whether the diseases cause immunologic aging.

Since the former issue has already been discusssed at great length in
reviews and at workshops and symposia[1-4], I wish to addresss myself to the
latter issue. This latter issue is centered about the hypothesis that since
immunologic aging predisposes an individual to various disesaes, and, therefore, that perturbation of immunologic aging should alter the pattern of diseases in terms of their onset, rate, severity and multiplicity. The immune
system can be perturbed either by further reducing, by preventing, or by
restoring the immunologic activities. Since the latter two approaches have
the added advantage of lending themselves more effectively to the understanding of the mechanism of immunologic aging, only they will be considered.

INTERVENTION BY PREVENTIVE METHODS

Four different methods have been attempted to date. They are: (a) internal
body temperature control[5], (b) tissue ablation[6,7], (c) genetic manipulation[8-11]

and (d) dietary control[12-15]. Only the latter two will be discussed, as they appear the most promising.

Genetic manipulation

Genetic manipulation has been performed in long-lived and short-lived strains of mice. With long-lived mice, it was reasoned that aging is influenced genetically by only a limited number of regulatory genes[16], that the immune system plays a major role in aging[17], and that the major histocompatibility complex (MHC) system represents a "super-regulatory gene complex system" of the immune system[18], i.e., the H-2 region of chromosome 17 in the mouse and the HLA region of chromosome 6 in the human. Inbred strains of mice differing only at the H-2 region, commonly referred to as congenic mice, were therefore assessed for their age-related immune functions, age-specific diseases and life spans[8-9]. The results revealed that variation in these parameters between these congenic mice within a given inbred strain was as great as that observed between different inbred strains of mice. If the MHC system in the mouse did not exert a significant influence upon aging, age-related immunologic abnormalities and life span, one would have expected a greater uniformity in life span, immunologically associated disease pattern, and immunologic activities between congenic sets of mice within an inbred strain than between inbred strains. It can be argued, therefore, that the MHC system plays a major role in age-associated immunologic abnormalities and life span in mice.

With short-lived mice, the focus has been on susceptibility to autoimmune and immune complex manifestations[10]. These studies revealed that susceptibility to autoimmune and immune complex diseases involves more than one gene. An example is reflected in the life span of different inbred strains of mice and their hybrids; e.g., the mean life span of autoimmune-susceptible NZB, NZW, (NZB x NZW)F$_1$, (NZB x CBA)F$_1$ and nonautoimmune-susceptible CBA mice were 12, 21, 12, 29, and 28 months, respectively.

Obviously, genetic manipulation is not a practical method in humans. However, it can be used to dissociate the relative roles genetic and environmental factors play on aging, and from such studies practical methods could arise. To this end, Greenberg and Yunis have undertaken studies on the influence of HLA on immune responsiveness in aging humans[11], which will be discussed by Greenberg at this symposium.

Dietary manipulation

About 45 years ago, McCay, et al.[19] first discovered that the life span of rats can be extended significantly by restricting their caloric intake during growth. Recently a more exhaustive study was carried out, also in rats, by

Ross and Bras[20-21], which confirmed and extended the classical work. Thus, they found that early caloric restriction decelerates the aging rate, as judged by age-related biochemical and pathological changes. Walford, et al.[12] then showed that the immune system of long-lived mice, subjected to the life-extending, calorically restricted but nutritionally supplemented diet, matures more slowly and begins to age later in life. Fernandes et al.[13-14] showed that a diet high in fat and relatively low in protein, which favors reproduction in experimental rodents, significantly increased cell-mediated autoimmune manifestations and shortened the life expectancy of short-lived, autoimmune-susceptible mice. In contrast, a diet low in fat and relatively high in protein, which is less favorable for reproduction, decreased autoimmune manifestations and prolonged the life expectancy of these mice. Fernandes et al. further showed that the life span of these short-lived autoimmune-susceptible mice can be dramatically extended by restricting their caloric intake[15].

These, as well as other results have been discussed earlier by Good at this symposium and therefore need not be elaborated on any further.

INTERVENTION BY RESTORATIVE METHODS

Three different methods have been attempted to date, and they all appear promising.

Tissue ablation

The tissue ablation approach, mentioned earlier, has been used as a preventive method, but recently, it has also been used effectively by Bilder and Denckla[22] in their attempt to restore normal immune functions. Rats were used in their study to test the hypothesis by Denckla[23] that hypothyroidism in old individuals could be caused by a substance(s) secreted by the pituitary that competes with thyroid hormones for the same receptors of target cells, including those of the immune system, and that secretion of the substance begins shortly after sexual maturity. They reasoned that if the hypothesis were correct, hypophysectomy of aging individuals, supplemented with the standard hormone replacement therapy should have a beneficial effect. Accordingly, they hypophysectomized old and young rats and subjected them to hormone therapy. The results revealed that hypophysectomy had a pronounced immunorestorative effect on old, but not young rats.

This method is not practical in humans. However, hypophysectomized old rats could be used to resolve the problem of the relationship between the immune system's "aging clock" and its extrinsic "pacemaker." Moreover, if the pituitary substance can be purified, a specific antiserum reagent could be prepared and used clinically. Thus, it would appear that this type of tissue ablation study has both basic and clinical importance.

Cell Grafting

Grafting of thymus, spleen. lymph nodes and bone marrow has been attempted individually or in combinations in genetically compatible old recipients with varying success in terms of immunologic restoration and extension of life span.

Fabris et al. demonstratrated most impressively that the life span of short-lived, growth-hormone deficient, hypopituitary dwarf mice can be extended as much as 3- to 4-fold by injecting large doses of lymph node cells[24]. A comparable life-prolonging effect was obtained by injecting growth hormone and thyroxin into these dwarf mice with intact thymus, but not into dwarf mice whose thymi had been removed beforehand. These results indicate that the pituitary "turns on" the immune system through the thymus, and the T cells "turn on" the endocrine system through the pituitary. Injection of young spleen or thymus cells into old, autoimmune-susceptible, short-lived mice has had less spectacular results. It did delay, but not prevent permanently, the appearance of certain types of autoantibodies[25], and it had a minimal life-prolonging effect[26]. Similarly, multiple thymus grafts did extend the life expectancy of the mice, but only by 1 month[27]. Furthermore, the age-associated pathological changes were unaltered by these treatments[28].

The first attempts to graft young thymus or bone marrow cells into old non-autoimmune-susceptible, long-lived mice were also not very encouraging, as the life span was not extended appreciably, nor was the immune response elevated[29-30]. Subsequent studies on the mechanism of decline with age in normal imlune functions suggested to us why these earlier cell grafting attempts were not successful. These studies revealed that the loss of immunologic vigor is due in part to changes in the T cell population[31], in part to the reduced rate at which stem cells can self-generate and generate progeny cells[32], and in part to the inability of involuted thymus to transform precursor cells to T cells efficiently[33]. Therefore, we exposed long-lived old mice to low dose radiation to destroy most of their immune cells and grafted into them both new born thymus and young adult bone marrow stem cells. This treatment restored their immune functions to levels approaching those of adult mice for at least six months after graft treatment in mice with a normal mean life-span of 27 months (an equivalent to 0.22 of a mean mouse life span, or about 15 human years)[34]. Current immunorestorative studies by cell grafting should resolve what extent, if any, grafting will have on the frequency and severity of diseases of the aged and whether cell grafting can alter the life expectancy of short-lived and long-lived mice.

Studies by Perkins et al.[35] on susceptibility to infection have also
generated encouraging data. These showed that old mice can be made to resist
lethal doses of virulent Salmonella typhimurium by injecting them beforehand
with spleen cells from young genetically compatible mice which had been immunized with the vaccine. Their findings also indicated that sensitized spleen
cells can persist in the recipients for a long time after injection, and that
spleen cells can be stored cryogenically for an extended period of time without loss of immunologic activity. This means that the method of Perkins et
al.[35] may have a practical application in random bred species.

Chemical Therapy

Only a few chemical agents have been shown to possess immunorestorative
activity. These include thymic hormones, certain free radical inhibitors
(antioxidants), double-stranded polynucleotide, and mercaptoethanol.

It would seem obvious that thymic hormones would be used to prevent or
restore immunologic aging, since the loss of immunologic vigor has been
clearly shown to be associated with the failure of thymus to continue vigorously synthesizing T cell maturation hormone after sexual maturity[33,36]. Sur-
prisingly, however, there has been no systematic study on their effectiveness
in preventing immunologic aging, and studies on their use as immunorestorative
agents have been meager. Nevertheless, the results have been encouraging.
Thus, Friedman et al.[37] found that thymus humoral factor (THF), prepared by N.
Trainin, can enhance the T cell dependent graft-vs-host activity in vitro of
spleen cells of old but not young mice. This would indicate that THF is not
acting as a nonspecific adjuvant agent. Otherwise, THF would also have enhanced the graft-vs-host activity of young spleen cells. Less encouraging are
the preliminary findings of Bach[38] using T cell-dependent lymphocyte-mediated
cytotoxicity (LMC) as the assay. She found that circulating thymic factor
(TF) treatment in vivo is effective in preventing the accelerated decline in
LMC activity of adult thymectomized mice, but ineffective in normal young and
middle-aged (75-86 weeks old) mice. It would appear that TF may be promoting
the emergence of suppressor cells in these normal mice. Whether or not it
would be effective in old mice, as demonstrated by Friedman et al.[37], remains
to be resolved.

Using another preparation of thymic hormones, thymopoietin, Weksler et
al.[39] were able to restore partially the antibody-forming capacity of old
spleen cells by exposing them to it. In contrast, Martinez et al.[40] failed to
demonstrate the effectiveness of thymopoietin, ubiquitin and synthetic serum

thymic factor, prepared by G. Goldstein, as judged by T cell mitogenic response and resistance to tumor cells. The test mice were thymectomized at neonatal age or at 1 month of age and then subjected to treatment with one of the
hormones. No attempt was made to assess the effectiveness of a mixture of
these hormones, which could have been effective, because T cell maturation
requires many transformation steps. Therefore several different types of thymic differentiation hormones would be necessary for the generation of mature
functional T cells, according to A. Goldstein[41].

A. Goldstein et al.[41] using still another preparation of thymic hormone,
thymosin, have found that repeated injection of the hormone can alleviate many
of the symptoms in mice and humans manifesting immunodeficiency diseases.
That repeated injection of thymosin may also have immunorestorative effect on
elderly humans manifesting reduced T cell-dependent immune functions comes
from a recent preliminary report showing that the number of T cells of old
individuals can be increased by exposing their white blood cells to thymosin
in vitro[42]. However, before assessing the effect of thymosin on elderly individuals, it would seem prudent to carry out animal studies assessing the
effects of repeated injection into aging short-lived and long-lived mice on
their normal immune functions, disease patterns and life spans. For further
discussion on thymic hormones, the reader is referred to the presentation of
Weksler at this symposium.

The use of free radical inhibitors stems from the hypothesis that aging is
caused by somatic mutation[43] and consequently high levels of free radicals
should enhance aging and low levels delay aging[44]. It was further reasoned
that since the immune system plays a major role in aging[45], these agents
should enhance immune functions of aging individuals. This notion was tested
by Harman et al.[46] by incorporating these agents into the diet of aging mice.
Their preliminary results indicate that vitamin E and other free radical inhibitors can enhance the antibody response of adult and middle-aged (88 weeks)
mice. Studies are being extended to assess the effectiveness of these agents
on immune functions, disease pattern and life span of older mice. In a related study, Bliznakov[47] found that coenzyme Q_{10}, a nonspecific stimulant of
mitochondrial electron transport process of respiration, can enhance the level
of antibody response of old mice to a level approaching that of adult mice.
Both of these studies will require further investigations to identify the target cell(s) and the mechanism of action of these agents.

Braun et al.[48] were the first to demonstrate that double-stranded polynucleotides (e.g., polyadenlic-polyuridylic acid complexes) can restore the

T cell-dependent antibody response of middle-aged mice to that of young adult mice. Han and Johnson[49] not only confirmed this observation, but proceeded to demonstrate that the supernatant of cultures of thymocytes treated with double-stranded polynucleotides is equally effective as an immunorestorative agent. This would suggest that the double-stranded polynucleotide restores immunologic vigor of aging mice by acting on T cells. Further studies are required to determine the mechanism of its action on T and other immune cells and on the disease pattern and life span. An insight into the possible mechanism of action at the membrane level comes from the observation of Schmidt and Douglas[50], who found that double- and triple-stranded, but not single-stranded, polynucleotides increase the IgG binding activity of human monocytes in vitro. This would indicate that multi-stranded polynucleotides stimulate either by unmasking or promoting more synthesis of surface IgG binding receptors.

About a decade ago when we became interested in intervention, we decided on the restorative method for we felt that a successful immunorestorative method would lend itself more effectively to the study of both cellular and molecular mechanisms responsible for the decline in normal immunologic activities with age. In our initial effort, immunorestoration of old mice was attempted by replacing their immune cells with those from syngeneic young mice[35]. This was done by injecting into them spleen cells from young donors which had been previously immunized with Salmonella typhimurium vaccine. Following such a treatment, these old mice were able to resist lethal doses of virulent Salmonella typhimurium for an extended period of time. We then found that the combined treatment of old mice with 400 R of X-rays to destroy most of their radiosensitive immune cells, followed by injection of bone marrow cells of young syngeneic donors and implantation of thymic tissues of young syngeneic donors elevated their T cell dependent antibody response and T cell proliferative activity to levels approaching those of young adult mice for an extended period[34]. These results suggest that cell replacement method could be used as a probe to identify the cell(s) responsible for the decline in immunologic vigor with age. However, its effectiveness as a molecular probe appears to be limited.

We therefore decided to focus our effort on a chemically defined agent that is effective at the cellular level. Mercaptoethanol (2-ME) was chosen as an immunorestorative agent in old mice because sulfhydryl compounds have been employed effectively in enhancing various nonimmunologic and immunologic cellular activities in vitro[51-57] and because 2-ME is a simple 2-carbon compound effective at very low concentrations. Our findings revealed that the reduced

in vitro T cell-dependent antibody forming activities of spleen cells from
four out of four genetically-defined old long-lived mice can be restored to
levels approaching those of young adult mice by exposing the cells to 2-ME at
very low concentration (4 ug/ml)[58-59]. The demonstration that the enhancing
effect of 2-ME of old spleen cells is greater than that of young spleen cells,
as judged by 2 different criteria, is most encouraging. That is, in terms of
its magnitude of enhancement of the antibody forming capacity of an optimum
number of spleen cells, the effect of 2-ME on old spleen cells was an order of
magnitude greater than that on young spleen cells (i.e., 500 versus 30% enhancement). In terms of its ability to transform antigen-stimulated, nonantibody-
responding cultures with limiting numbers of spleen cells into antibody-respon-
ding cultures, the effect of 2-ME on old spleen cells was 6.5 times greater
than that on young spleen cells.

That mercaptoethanol is also an effective immunorestorative agent in intact
old mice was demonstrated by restoring the T cell-dependent antibody responding capacity of long-lived old to that of young mice with appropriate doses of
2-ME[60]. These results would suggest that 2-ME and related chemicals may have
practical applications.

The mode of action of 2-ME is not known. This is not surprising in view of
the multitude of possible biochemical effects sulfhydryl compounds can have on
cell structure and functions, ranging from SH/SS exchange reactions at the
membrane level to the antioxidant and metal chelating effects[51-52,56]. Moreover, various types of immunologic processes have been shown to benefit from
the presence of 2-ME, including antibody response[53], mitogentic response of T
and B cells to plant lectins[52,54,61], B cell colony formation[62], mixed lymphocyte reaction[55,63] and cytolytic killer T cell formation[64-65]. All three major
cell types have been implicated as the target of 2-ME[52,55,61-65], as well as
serum factor(s) in the tissue culture medium[61,66]. Finally, it should be
emphasized that in previous immunoenhancing studies of 2-ME, the source of
immune cells has been limited to young adult donors, whose magnitude of response in the presence of 2-ME, as demonstrated here, does not exceed by more
than two-fold (100%). Logistically, this could make it difficult to resolve
the molecular mechanism of the enhancing action of 2-ME. The use of immune
cells of old donors is therefore of obvious advantage, for, as demonstrated
here, 2-ME, at a concentration as low as 4 ug/ml, can enhance the primary antibody response of old spleen cells by as much as 11-fold (1100%).

CONCLUSION

Six model intervention approaches have been attempted to prevent and to restore normal immunologic aging. These studies are very preliminary, but overall, the findings are most encouraging.

Of the six model approaches, genetic manipulation and chemical therapy appear to be most promising in serving as probes to understand the biochemical nature and mechanism(s) of the decline. The former approach should enable one to determine which gene(s) is primarily reponsible for the decline in normal immune functions with age and the diseases associated with it. The latter approach should enable one to determine the cell type(s) that is most severely affected functionally and the nature of changes associated with it at the sub-cellular level.

In terms of practical application, dietary manipulation appears to be the most promising in controlling immunologic aging and the diseases associated with it. Chemical therapy could also serve as an effective preventive method. Perhaps the most effective approach in controlling immunologic aging may be a combination of dietary manipulation, chemical therapy and cell grafting.

ACKNOWLEDGEMENTS

This is publication no. 024 from GRECC, V.A. Wadsworth Medical Center, supported in part by the Medical Research Service of V.A., the Department of Energy (EY76-S-03-0034 P.A. 264), and the Glenn Research Foundation.

REFERENCES
1. Siegel, M.M. and Good, R.A. ed. (1972) Tolerance, Autoimmunity and Aging. Charles C. Thomas, Springfield, Ill.
2. Mackay, I.R. (1972) Gerontologia, 18, 285-304
3. Kay, M.M.B. and Makinodan, T. (1976) Clin. Immunol. Immunopathol., 6 394-413.
4. Makinodan, T. and Yunis, E.J. ed. (1977) Immunology and Aging. Plenum Medical Book Company, New York.
5. Liu, R.K. and Walford, R.L. (1975) J. Gerontol., 30, 129-131.
6. Furth, J. (1946) J. Gerontol., 1, 46-52.
7. Albright, J.W., Makinodan, T. and Deitchman, J.W. (1969) Exp. Gerontol., 4, 267-276.
8. Smith, G.S. and Walford, R.L. (1977) Nature, 270, 727-729.
9. Meredith, P.J. and Walford, R.L. (1978) Immunogenetics, 5, 109-128.
10. Fernandes, G., Good, R.A. and Yunis, E.J., (1977) in Immunology and Aging, Makinodan, T. and Yunis, E.J. ed. Plenum Medical Book Company, New York, pp. 111-133.
11. Greenburg, L.J. and Yunis, E.J. (1978) Fed. Proc., 37, 1258-1262.
12. Walford, R.L., Liu, R.K., Mathies, M., Gerbase-DeLima, M., and Smith, G.S. (1974) Mech. Ageing Dev., 2, 447-454.
13. Fernandes, G., Yunis, E.J., Jose, D.G. and Good, R.A. (1973) Int. Arch. Allergy Appl. Immunol., 44, 770-782.

182

14. Fernandes, G., Yunis, E.J., Smith, J. and Good, R.A. (1972) Proc. Soc. Exp. Biol. Med., 139, 1189-1196.
15. Fernandes, G., Yunis, E.J. and Good, R.A. (1976) Proc. Nat. Acad. Sci., 73, 1279-1283.
16. Cutler, R.G. (1975) Proc. Nat. Acad. Sci., 72, 4664-4668.
17. Walford, R.L. (1974) Fed. Proc., 33, 2020-2027.
18. Benacerraf, B. ed. (1975) Immunogenetics and Immunodeficiency, University Park Press, Baltimore.
19. McCay, C.M., Crowell, M.F. and Maynard, L.A. (1935) J. Nutrition, 10, 63-79.
20. Ross, M.H. (1969) J. Nutrition Suppl. 1, part 2, 97, 565-601.
21. Ross, M.H. and Bras, G. (1971) J. Nat. Cancer Inst., 47, 1095-1113.
22. Bilder, G.E. and Denckla, W.D. (1977) Mech. Ageing Dev., 6, 153-163.
23. Denckla, W.D. (1974) J. Clin. Invest., 53, 572-581.
24. Fabris, N., Pierpaoli, W., and Sorkin, E. (1972) Nature, 240, 557-559.
25. Teague, P.O. and Friou, G.J. (1969) Immunology, 17, 665-675.
26. Yunis, E.J. and Greenberg, L.J. (1974) Fed. Proc., 33, 2017-2019.
27. Kysela, S. and Steinberg, A.D. (1973) Clin. Immunol. Immunopath., 2, 133-136.
28. Yunis, E.J., Fernandes, G. and Stutman, O. (1971) Am. J. Clin. Path., 56, 280-292.
29. Albright, J.F. and Makinodan, T. (1966) J. Cell Comp. Physiol., 67 (Suppl. 1), 185-206.
30. Metcalf, D., Moulds, R. and Pike, B. (1966) Clin. Exp. Immunol., 2, 109-120.
31. Makinodan, T. and Adler, W.H. (1975) Fed. Proc., 34, 153-158.
32. Albright, J.W. and Makinodan, T. (1976) J. Exp. Med., 144, 1204-1213.
33. Hirokawa, K. and Makinodan, T. (1975) J. Immunol., 114, 1659-1664.
34. Hirokawa, K., Albright, J.W., and Makinodan, T. (1976) Clin. Immunol. Immunopathol., 5, 371-376.
35. Perkins, E.H., Makinodan, T. and Seibert, C. (1972) Infect. Immunity, 6, 518-524.
36. Bach, F.J., Dardenne, M. and Solomon, J.C. (1973) Clin. Exp. Immunol., 14, 247-256.
37. Friedman, D., Keiser, V. and Globerson, A. (1974) Nature 251, 545-547.
38. Bach, M-A. (1977) J. Immunol., 119, 641-646.
39. Weksler, M.E., Innes, J.B. and Goldstein, G. (1978) J. Exp. Med., 148, 996-1006.
40. Martinez, D., Field, A.K., Schwam, H., Tytell, A.A. and Hilleman, M.R. (1978) Proc. Soc. Exp. Biol. Med. 159, 195-200.
41. Goldstein, A.L., Thurman, G.B., Low, T.L., Trivers, G.E. and Rossio, J.L. (1979) in Physiology and Cell Biology of Aging, Cherkin, A., Finch, C.E., Kharasch, N., Makinodan, T., Scott, F.L. and Strehler, B.L. ed., Raven Press, N.Y.
42. Rovensky, J., Goldstein, A.L., Holt, P.J.L., Pwkarek, J., and Mistina, T. (1977) Cas. Lek. Ces., 116, 1063-1065.
43. Strehler, B. (1977) Time, Cells and Aging, Academic Press, N.Y.
44. Harman, D. (1969) J. Am. Geriatrics Soc., 17, 721-735.
45. Walford, R.L. (1969) The Immunologic Theory of Aging, Munksgaard, Copenhagen.
46. Harman, D., Heidrick, M.L. and Eddy, D.E. (1977) J. Am. Geriatrics Soc., 25, 400-407.
47. Bliznakov, E.G. (1978) Mech. Ageing Dev., 7, 189-197.
48. Braun, W., Yajima, Y. and Ishizuka, M. (1970) J. Reticuloendothel. Soc., 7, 418-424.
49. Han, I.H. and Johnson, A.G. (1976) J. Immunol., 117, 423-427.

50   Schmidt, M.E. and Douglas, S.D. (1976) Proc. Soc. Exp. Biol. Med. 151, 376-379.
51.   Braun, W., Lichtenstein, W.M. and Parker, C. ed. (1974) Cyclic AMP, Cell Growth and the Immune Response, Springer-Verlag, New York.
52.   Broome, J.D. and Jeng, M.W. (1973) J. Exp. Med., 138, 574-592.
53.   Chen, C. and Hirsch, J.G. (1972) J. Exp. Med., 136, 604-617.
54.   Fanger, M.W., Hart, D.A., Wells, J.V. and Nisonoff, A. (1970) J. Immunol., 105, 1043-1045.
55.   Heber-Katz, E. and Click, R.E. (1972) Cell. Immunol., 5, 410-418.
56.   Johnson, N., Jessup, R. and Ramwell, P.W. (1974) Prostaglandins, 5, 125-136.
57.   Lands, W., Lee, R. and Smith, W. (1971) Ann. N.Y. Acad. Sci., 180, 107-122.
58.   Makinodan, T., Deitchman, J.W., Stoltzner, G.H., Kay, M.M. and Hirokawa, K. (1975) Proc. 10th Internat. Cong. Gerontol., 2, 23.
59.   Makinodan, T. and Albright, J.F. Mech. Ageing Dev., in press.
60.   Makinodan, T. and Albright, J.F. Mech. Ageing Dev., in press.
61.   Goodman, M.G. and Weigle, W.O. (1977) J. Exp. Med., 145, 473-489.
62.   Metcalf, D. (1976) J. Immunol., 116, 635-638.
63.   Bevan, M.J., Epstein, R. and Cohn, M. (1974) J. Exp. Med., 139, 1025-1030.
64.   Engers, H.D., MacDonald, H.R., Cerottini, J.-C. and Brunner, K.T. (1975) Eur. J. Immunol., 5, 223-225.
65.   Igarashi, T., Okada, M., Kishimoto, T. and Yamamura, Y. (1977) J. Immunol., 118, 1697-1703.
66.   Opitz, H.G., Opitz, U., Lemke, H., Flad, H.D., Hewlett, G. and Schlumberger, H.D. (1977) J. Immunol., 119, 2089-2094.

184

DISCUSSION

WEKSLER: Have you been able to identify whether it's a T-cell, or a macrophage? Are you able to pretreat a subpopulation before your in vitro culture?

MAKINODAN: Yes, we are doing these kind of studies now and it looks like the main target is the T cell, but we haven't been able to identify the subpopulation.

SINGHAL: What does mercaptoethanol really do? It has been shown to promote cell growth and replace macrophage function.

MAKINODAN: I don't know. As you know it is very volatile at 37° so the half-life of mercaptoethanol is very short and the concentration we are using is very small and the effect seems to be almost instaneous. My bias is that the defect in the target cell is transductional, i.e. along the pathway of the information from the receptor into the nucleus something is screwed up and I think mercaptoethanol is doing something to this defect in the pathway. So for this reason, mercaptoethanol may not be a good probe and so we are looking at something that is a little more stable than this messy compound.

TALAL: Mac (Mackinodan), my comment is related to Kim's statement just before. Several years ago, we showed that there was a defect in the macrophage population in the NZB spleen. This is most easily demonstrated in Mishell Dutton cultures because paradoxically they give very poor in vitro responses. We could restore full competence in vitro by 2-mercaptoethanol or macrophages from the peritoneal cavity or combinations of those two. We interpreted our results to be consistent with the mercaptoethanol affect acting on a macrophage.

MAKINODAN: The reason I say that the primary target seems to be in these long-lived T-cells is that there is no question that there are other target cells of mercaptoethanol. Perhaps at least in these long-lived animals that we are using, the target of mercaptoethanol are the T cells.

GOOD: I'm really interested in this last point as well because we have found that the proportion or the numbers of macrophages that can be washed out of the peritoneum in these autoimmune susceptible strains goes up progressively with age. There are plenty of macrophages available in the animal, but they are just not in the places where we like to study them and putting in the 2-mercaptoethanol may really just take the place of those cells.

Published 1979 by Elsevier North Holland, Inc.
Singhal, Sinclair, Stiller, eds. Aging and Immunity

MORPHOLOGY OF THE AGING BRAIN AND DEMENTIA - HUMAN AND ANIMAL

HENRYK M. WISNIEWSKI
New York State Institute for Basic Research in Mental Retardation, 1050 Forest
Hill Road, Staten Island, NY 10314, USA

The aged brain is characterized by atrophy and loss of neuronal elements.
The functional deficit, however, is sometimes greater than weight and neuronal
loss would imply, indicating that much of the remaining tissue is abnormal.
The list of pathologic findings is long and it includes:

A. Fibrosis of the leptomeninges

B. Changes in the neuronal perikarya

    1. Neurofibrillary degeneration

    2. Granulovacuolar degeneration

    3. Lipofuscin accumulation

    4. Lewy bodies

    5. Hirano bodies

C. Changes in the neuropil

    1. Neuritic (senile) plaques

    2. Axonal spheroids

    3. Amyloid deposits

    4. Wallerian degeneration

    5. Shrinkage of dendrite arbor

    6. Loss of dendritic spines

    7. Decrease of extracellular space

D. Glial Changes

    1. Corpora amylacea

    2. Myelin remodeling

E. Arteriosclerosis and vascular lesions

F. Viruses

Until recently it was not clear which of these changes was the major correlate with deteriorating brain function (disorders of memory with disorienta-
tion in time and space, fixation and recall amnesia, confabulation, false
recognitions, language impoverishment and difficulties to find the right word).
Clinicians and the public most often ascribe senile dementia to arteriosclerosis. Corselles in 1962[1], and Tomlinson et al.[2], have examined significant numbers of affected specimens and find that on an anatomic basis, arteriosclerosis
with consequent ischemic infarction is a significant factor in only a small
minority of cases. The work of the Newcastle group indicates that vascular
disease with gross cerebral infarcts is responsible for 12 to 17% of cases,
whereas 50% of their patients were demented with plaques and tangles. About
18% had mixed lesions, but in this latter group the impression was that the
neuronal lesions were the operative factor.

The effect of small vessel pathology (thickening of the basement membranes,
perivascular deposits of amyloid, perivascular gliosis, and increased cellularity of the vessel wall) on the well-being of the neuronal elements is not
known. Also unknown is the extent to which extracerebral factors, such as
cardio-vascular malfunction and pulmonary pathology, contribute to the abnormal
findings in the aged brains. In aged animals, neuronal loss and changes of the
type observed in brains of old humans are found without the occurrence of large
vessel atherosclerosis. There is also the fact that the high percentage (32%)
of age-dependent loss of myelinated fibers in the human ventral roots cannot be
attributed to atherosclerosis, because spinal atherosclerosis is minimal, if
present at all[3].

Because out of the above list of pathological findings only neurofibrillary
changes and neuritic (senile) plaques appear to be the major cause of age-
associated dementia, these lesions will be discussed. As for the other lesions
they will be omitted; however, the reader can find this information in the

following sources of references[3-11].

Electron microscopic studies revealed that normal neurons have three types of fibrillar structures: ± 24 nm neurotubules, 10 nm neurofilaments and few 60-70 nm microfilaments. The neurotubule is a structure consisting of about 75-90% tubulin and a variety of other proteins. Tubulin protein is a dimer formed of dissimilar peptides. The faster migrating peptide on SDS-PAGE (polyacrylamide gel electrophoresis in buffer system containing sodium dodecyl sulfate) is termed β— tubulin (53,000 daltons), the slower α-tubulin (56,000 daltons)[12]. Neurofilaments are considered as a type of intermediate filament. Recent reports[13] suggests that neurofilaments differ from other intermediate filaments in that they are formed of a "triplet" of polypeptides of molecular weights of 68,000-70,000; 115,000-160,000 and 200,000-220,000 daltons, respectively. The microfilaments probably represent the actin and myosin proteins.

In people suffering from senile dementia of the Alzheimer type (SDAT) and to a much lesser degree in normal aged people, tangles of neurofibrils, formed of paired helical filaments (PHF) are found in nerve cells and their processes[14]. These pathological fibers are each made up of a pair of filaments (about 10 nm each) with periodic twists every 80 nm. The tangles of PHF do not appear to disrupt the cytoplasmic organelles other than to displace them from the space the tangles occupy. They are much more commonly seen in nonmyelinated processes than in myelinated. It is not clear whether accumulation of PHF leads to neuronal death. Although neurofibrillary change is one of the most common histologic features of Alzheimer's disease and senile dementia, and is found in lesser numbers in the normal aged brain, it may also be present in other pathological conditions such as mongolism[15], postencephalitic Parkinsonism, and the amyotrophic lateral sclerosis-Parkinsonism dementia complex (ALS-P-D)[16]. The latter disease is essentially indigenous to the Chamorro population of Guam in the Mariana Islands. The topographic distribution of neurofibrillary

tangles in these disorders is of great interest because it appears that certain
areas of the nervous system are invariably spared. For example, the Purkinje
cells, the primary sensory nuclei such as the mesencephalic nucleus of the
trigeminal nerve, the Gasserian, and the spinal dorsal ganglia are never involved. The areas which are affected in one or another disease are the hippocampus, especially the pyramidal cells in Sommers' sector and the glomerular
formation of the hippocampal gyrus, the fronto-temporal cerebral cortex,
various hypothalmic nuclei, the substantia nigra and locus caeruleus, and the
reticular formation of the brainstem[17]. The occurrence of Alzheimer's fibrillary cells in various diseases seem to indicate that the PHF can be induced
by various pathological agents. Furthermore, the fact that certain neurons
produce PHF in large quantities, and others do not in spite of the fact that
they show other degenerative changes (e.g., the anterior horn cells in the
spinal cord in ALS-P-D complex), indicates that not all nerve cells respond in
the same way to the etiological factor. Therefore, one must recognize the
possibility that the same agent in one area of the brain will induce PHF
whereas elsewhere it might cause neurons to die without going through the stage
of neurofibrillary degeneration.

The paired helical filaments have been described only in human nerve cells.
On rare occasions (in one aged Rhesus monkey and in Wobbler mice) small aggregates of helically wound paired 10 nm filaments with a twist about every
50 nm have been reported[18]. However these differ from the abnormal fibrillar
elements found in human diseases where, as indicated above, the twists occur
every 80 nm.

The PHF are structurally stable with regard to postmortem time, formalin
and osmic acid fixatives, and a variety of physical disruptive procedures such
as are used for cell isolation.

There are several compounds which cause accumulation of fibrillar profiles
in nerve cells. The best known are the spindle inhibitors (colchicine, pod-

phylltoxin and vinblastine) and aluminum salts[19]. Electron microscopic studies

of neurons from animals treated with these compounds reveal, however, that the

experimentally induced neurofibrillary tangles are made of 10 nm filaments and

not of the PHF. Both PHF and 10 nm filaments stain readily with silver salts,

however, only PHF shows the Congo red birefringence. The silver impregnation

technique is, therefore, used by the light microscopist to identify the af-

fected neurons. Irrespective of the ultrastructural features the condition

characterized by an excess of fibrillary profiles in neurons is termed "neuro-

fibrillary degeneration" or "neurofibrillary changes." On the basis of peptide

mapping and serological affinities the protein purified from paired helical

filaments (PHF) appears to be similar to β-tubulin[20]. The chemical composition

of the experimentally induced neurofilaments is not known. However, tangles

of filaments induced by anti-mitotic agents in cultured cells have recently

been isolated[21]. They are formed of a peptide which may be distinguished from

tubulin both by its behavior on SDS-PAGE and by its antigenic properties. In

these cells the colchicine induced tangles are apparently formed of inter-

mediate filaments whose constituent peptides have molecular weights of 54,000

and 55,000 daltons.

Let us now turn to the other leading lesion in the aging brain – the

neuritic or senile plaque.

It has been known since the report of Divry[22] that amyloid is present in

neuritic plaques and this has been confirmed electron microscopically[23].

Furthermore in aged individuals this substance is known to be present in the

walls of cerebral vessels both with and without associated plaques. Morpho-

logical studies of neuritic (senile) plaques have revealed that beside amyloid

they consist of degenerative neuronal processes and reactive cells. The

primary mechanism that leads to the formation of neuritic plaques and the

significance of cerebral amyloid deposition remain unclear. Some investigators

think that the amyloid itself is a direct toxic cause of neuritic degeneration and senile plaque formation[24], while others point out that amyloid does not act as a neurotoxic substance[25]. The latter group suggests that whatever causes amyloid formation may also cause terminal degeneration. It should be recalled at this point that there are at least 2 types of amyloid. Amyloid B is said to be a complex of light chains of immunoglobulins. Amyloid A is a "nonimmunoglobulin" protein called also amyloid of unknown origin. There is some evidence that the amyloid associated with aging is amyloid B, an immuno-globulin[26]. Recently Glenner and Page[27], discussing the mechanisms of amyloid formation theorized that antigen–antibody complexes may be catabolized by phagocytes, and the immunoglobulin fragments degraded in lysosomes in a manner leading to extracellular amyloid production. Our recent studies showed a close association between vessels and plaques; therefore, the following sequence of events leading to formation of the plaque can be postulated: antigen–antibody complexes are formed in the brain or leak out from the blood and stream into the perivascular space; various morphological pictures develop according to the amount of the extravascular complexes and their neurotoxicity; leakage of small amounts lead to focal deposits of amyloid in the pericytes and the base-ment membrane; a large quantity can give a picture of congophilic angiopathy; toxic antigen–antibody complexes may be responsible for degeneration of neu-rites and formation of neuritic plaques[28].

As mentioned above in normal aged people and in SDAT we find both neuro-fibrillary tangles made of PHF and neuritic plaques. Morphological and chem-ical studies of these lesions showed that they do not look alike. However, they share one property in common, the Congo red birefringence. The fact that neurofibrillary tangles and plaque amyloid shows green polarization color after Congo red staining was known for years and is used by the neuropathologist for diagnosis of SDAT. The same technique is being used to identify deposits of systemic or focal amyloid. Physico-chemical studies of the amyloid fibres revealed that they are made of protein consisting of polypeptide chains arranged in β-pleated sheet conformation[29]. In addition, it has been shown that the synthetic polypeptide, poly-1-lysine, and some synthetic protein fibres when converted into their β-form have tinctorial and optical properties after Congo red staining identical to those of amyloid fibrils. Glenner[29] in his review on β-pleated sheet fibrils stated that "at the present limited stage of our knowledge it is not possible to state unequivocally that all β-pleated sheet fibrils are Congo red birefringent or that all Congo red birefringent tissue protein components are composed of β-pleated sheet fibrils." However his group and other studies suggested that the optical properties of Congo red stained fibrillar proteins are dependent directly or at least in part on the β-pleated sheet conformation of the fibrillar component. If the above is true then both PHF and the plaque amyloid are β-pleated sheet fibrils. Insolubility of β-pleated fibrils under physiologic conditions and their resistance to proteolytic digestion is a well-known fact. Because cells do not have efficient enzymatic machinery to remove β-proteins the PHF and amyloid can be considered a proteolytic enzymes deficiency storage product.

Biochemical analysis of the β-pleated fibrils revealed that they are made of heterologous group of proteins. Ultrastructural studies of the β-pleated sheet fibrils have shown that, when the optimal conditions of fibril formation are varied, Congo red birefringent, β-pleated sheet fibrils can be produced with different ultrastructural appearance[27]. Results of these experiments indicate that the differences in fibrillar morphology, do not necessarily signify per se differences in chemical composition. Conversely, fibrils of similar chemical composition may differ ultrastructurally if the local environmental conditions during their formation are changed. Therefore, it is theoretically possible that the amyloid fibrils of the neuritic plaques and the PHF are made of similar protein. However, they may also derive from different protein precursors by different mechanism displaying similar physical nature - the β-pleated sheet structure. Our and other data indicate that in SDAT the latter situation is true.

How the β-proteins in SDAT are formed is not clear, however if further studies will show that the plaque amyloid is of immunoglobulin origin, a common infectious etiology of PHF and neuritic plaques can be postulated[30]. According to this concept as a result of persistent viral infection, viral protein could form complexes with unpolymerized tubulin, and the tubulin, instead of polymerizing and making normal neurotubules forms PHF. Antibody against the same virus will form immuno complexes which will lead to neurite degeneration and amyloid deposits as described above.

ACKNOWLEDGMENT

The author wishes to thank Marjorie Agoglia for secretarial help. The work itself was done largely in collaboration with Dr. R. D. Terry.

REFERENCES

1. Corsellis, J.A.N. (1962) Mental Illness and the Aging Brain. Oxford University Press, London.

2. Tomlinson, B.E., Blessed, G. and Roth, M. (1970) J. Neurol. Sci. 11, 205-242.

3. Buetow, D.E. (1971) in Cellular and Molecular Renewal in the Mammalian Body, Cameron, I.L. and Thrasher, J.D. ed., Academic Press, New York pp. 87-106.

4. Wisniewski, H.M., Ghetti, B. and Terry, R.D. (1973) J. Neuropath. Exp. Neurol. 32, 566-584.

5. Wisniewski, H.M. and Terry, R.D. (1973) in Progress in Brain Research Ford, D.H. ed., Elsevier, Amsterdam, pp. 167-186.

6. Wisniewski, H.M., Johnson, A.B., Raine, C.S., Kay, W.J. and Terry, R.D. (1970) Lab. Invest. 23, 287-296.

7. Schwartz, P. (1970) Amyloidosis: Cause and Manifestations of Senile Deterioration. Thomas, Springfield, Illinois.

8. Lampert, P., Blumberg, J.M. and Pentschew, A. (1964) J. Neuropath. Exp. Neurol. 23, 60-77.

9. Machado-Salas, J., Scheibel, M.E. and Scheibel, A.B. (1977) Exp. Neurol. 54, 504-512.

10. Scheibel, M.E., Lindsay, R.D., Tomajasu, J. and Scheibel, A.B. (1975) Exp. Neurol. 47, 392-403.

11. Glees, P. and Hasan, M. (1976) Lipofuscin in Neuronal Aging and Disease, G. Thieme Publishers, Stuttgart, Germany.

12. Wisniewski, H.M. and Soifer, D. (1979) Mechanisms of Ageing and Develop. 9, 119-142.

13. Schlaepter, W.W. (1978) J. Cell Biol. 76, 50-56.

14. Wisniewski, H.M., Narang, H.K. and Terry, R.D. (1976) J. Neurol. Sci. 27, 173-181.

15. Wisniewski, K., Howe, J., Williams, D.G. and Wisniewski, H.M. (1978) Biol. Psychiatry 13, 619-627.

16. Hirano, A. (1970) in Alzheimer's Disease and Related Conditions, Wolstenholme, G.E.W. and O'Connor, M. ed., Churchill, London, pp. 185-207.

17. Ball, M.J. (1978) Acta Neuropath. 42, 73-80.

18. Wisniewski, H.M. and Terry, R.D. (1976) in Neurobiology of Aging, Terry, R.D. and Gershon, S. ed., Raven Press, New York, pp. 265-280.

19. Wisniewski, H.M., Terry, R.D. and Hirano, A. (1970) J. Neuropath. Exp. Neurol. 29, 163-176.

20. Grundke-Iqbal, I., Johnson, A.B., Wisniewski, H.M., Terry, R.D. and Iqbal, K. (1979) Lancet I, 578-580.

21. Starger, J. and Goldman, R. (1977) Proc. Natl. Acad. Sci. (USA) 74, 2422-2426.

22. Divry, P. and Florkin, M. (1927) C.R. Soc. Biol. (Paris) 97, 1808.

23. Terry, R.D. and Wisniewski, H.M. (1970) in Alzheimer's Disease and Related Conditions, Wolstenholme, G.E.W. and O'Connor, M. ed., Churchill London, pp. 145-168.

24. Schwartz, P. (1968) in Proceedings of the Symposium on Amyloidosis, Mandema, E., Ruinen, L., Scholten, J.H. and Cohen, A.S. ed., Excerpta Medica, Amsterdam, p. 31.

25. Wisniewski, H.M. and Terry, R.D. (1973) in Progress in Neuropathology, Zimmermann, H.M. ed., Grune and Stratton, New York, Vol. 2, pp. 1-26.

26. Ishii, T. and Haga, S. (1976) Acta Neuropath. (Berl.) 36, 243-249.

27. Glenner, G.G. and Page, D.L. (1976) in International Review of Experimental Pathology, Richter, G.W. and Epstein, M.A. ed., Academic Press, New York, Vol. 15, pp. 1-92.

28. Wisniewski, H.M., Bruce, M.E. and Fraser, H. (1975) Science 190, 1108-1110.

29. Glenner, G.G., Eanes, E.G., Bladen, H.A., Linke, R.P. and Termine, J.D.

(1974) J. Histochem. Cytochem. 22, 1141–1158.

30. Wisniewski, H.M. (1978) in Alzheimer's Diseases: Senile Dementia and Re-
    lated Disorders, Katzman, R., Terry, R.D. and Bick, K.L., Raven Press,
    New York (Aging Vol. 7) pp. 555–557.

DISCUSSION

MORRELL: First, I would like to congratulate Dr. Wisniewski on a very
thorough and succinct review of an extremely complex area. Those of us who
work in this area can admire the thoroughness and succinctness in his
presentation. I have three questions: In connection with the Parkinson
dementia, have there been any observations on neural fibrillary pathology
and/or neuritic plaque formation? Could you comment a little further on the
reactive cells in the margin of the plaque, particularly are these of
monocytoid or pericytic origin? Finally, in connection with the viral
pathology, is there any indication that this is related to altered T-cell
immunity in the aged?

WISNIEWSKI: With respect to the Parkinson dementia complex - it is a very
fascinating pathological disease. It occurs on the Island of Guam and around
40% of the population is dying because of the disease. They present themselves with a profound dementia and many neurons in the classical area show
the presence of parahelical filaments. However, it is a complex disease,
amyotrophic lateral sclerosis, meaning that the neurons in a spinal cord are
disappearing without going through a stage of neurofibrillar degeneration.
Thus, whatever agent is affecting the central nervous system can in one
area induce a parahelical filament and in another will not induce the parahelical filament. Now let us go back to our beta-pleated configuration because
it is very interesting. The same proteins in various areas of the brain may
or may not go into beta conformation and the beta conformation is of two
types: (1) the fibrillar and (2) the globular. The globular can be degraded
quite easily but fibrillar cannot. Whatever the agent causing the proteins
to go into the beta-pleated conformation causes a globular form in the spinal
cord, and a fibrillar form in the brain. With fibrillar changes, neurons are
vanishing without going through the stage of neurofibrillar degeneration.
Now we will have to find conditions which lead to beta-pleated protein
pathology because obviously many more agents than virus will lead to a beta-
pleated protein in the test tube. I was fascinated hearing of zinc deficiency
in areas where the neurofibrils are formed, particularly in amyloid. So
trace metals may have a lot to do with the way these proteins are being
assembled and disassembled. Now, with respect to the cells involved, it is a
microglia type of cell - a very odd cell. If you look at a part of the
cytoplasm it almost looks like a plasma cell, it is so rich in rough endoplasmic reticulum. These are the cells from which amyloid streams out of the
cytoplasm. They are in a perivascular area and I think they are microglia
cells.

GOOD: I know that the light chains themselves have an alphahelical
structure. I don't know about the SAA protein, you know, the serum amyloid
protein. Can you study just the beta-pleated sheet structure, which you can
easily do by circular dichroic analysis in tissues other than the brain, and
show its correlation with aging?

WISNIEWSKI: Yes, in skin where the keratin is increasing and in the lens,
where sure enough, they are all beta. All the cataracts are showing beta
configurations.

GOOD: Has SAA protein got beta-pleated sheet structure?

WISNIEWSKI: No, it is a heterogeneous group of proteins.

BALL: I've just a comment and a quick question. We have quantified neurofibrillary tangle formation in 5 old Down's syndrome patients from age 29 to 63 and they all have markedly elevated numbers of tangles in the hippocampus in the same range as the Alzheimer's patients - up to 40 times as many as in age-matched controls. So I re-emphasize your comment that it is a very good model to ask why Down's syndrome people have this premature aging predisposition. My question is with regard to the virus notion, do you think the gross topography of the disease which has predilection for the temporal lobes, especially mesiotemporal, tells us anything about a slow or latent virus hiding in the trigeminal ganglia?

WISNIEWSKI: Yes, but you must also consider hypoxia, because, you see, every stress will push the neuron to form the abnormal parahelical filaments and, as you know, the hippocampus is very susceptible to hypoxic stress which leads to this type of pathology. Around metastic tumor or scars, not in all cases, but in many, there are increased number of parahelical filaments. So the local change in the environment has a lot to do with polymerization of fibrillar proteins into abnormal products.

Published 1979 by Elsevier North Holland, Inc.
Singhal, Sinclair, Stiller, eds. Aging and Immunity

BIOLOGICAL AGING OF CULTURED HUMAN FIBROBLASTS:
RELEVANCE TO IMMUNOLOGICAL AGING

SAMUEL GOLDSTEIN AND CALVIN B. HARLEY
Departments of Medicine & Biochemistry, McMaster University, Hamilton,
Ontario, Canada L8S 4J9.

In this report we review some recent work on the human fibroblast model of
biological aging.   These studies were selected because we believe they are
germane to the immune system. We will describe four areas. First, we
summarize the experiments which provide evidence for the validity of the model.
Second, we discuss studies on the nature of the biological clock.   Third, we
touch on the response of aging cells to insulin-like growth factors. Finally,
we present data on how fibroblasts respond to prostaglandin E_1 (PGE_1) and
epinephrine during growth and senescence.

METHODS

Human fibroblast cultures were established following skin biopsy of the
anterior forearm of several donors including normal individuals, juvenile- and
maturity-onset diabetics, and subjects with the premature aging syndromes of
Werner and Hutchinson-Gilford, using established techniques.[1-3]   Studies to
evaluate the biological clock were carried out as described.[4]   Insulin-like
growth factors were purified from human plasma[5] and assayed as described.[6-8]
Studies on the response to PGE_1 and epinephrine using cyclic AMP were also
described earlier.[9]

I. Limited replicative lifespan of human fibroblasts: A model for biological
   aging
   The finite replicative capacity of human fibroblasts was first documented
by Hayflick and Moorehead nearly 20 years ago.[10]   Despite various manipulations with cells and growth media, these cells began to proliferate more
slowly after repeated subculture, and inevitably lost their ability to divide.
Hayflick later showed that the replicative limit was related to the age of the
donor.[11]   Thus, cultures derived from 9 adults showed an average replicative
lifespan of 20 mean population doublings (MPD) while cultures from 13 fetal
donors had an average of 50 MPD before phase-out.

In 1969 we showed that an inverse correlation exists between the replicative lifespan of fibroblasts and the age of the donor[12] and this has been confirmed by others (e.g. refs.13-15). We also demonstrated and have since confirmed that diabetes mellitus has an adverse although more subtle effect on the fibroblast replicative capacity.[12,16,17]

What seems clear is the enormous variance that exists in growth potential of fibroblast cultures derived from populations at large. It is now evident that this "scatter" in replicative potential primarily reflects the unique genotype of each donor. Thus, the establishment of cultures from specific donors with premature aging syndromes of Werner and progeria leads to a sharp decrease in the replicative potential.[3] On the other hand, fibroblast strains derived from normal subjects with no evidence of diabetes in the family history and repeatedly normal glucose tolerance tests give a "better than average" replicative performance. We believe that these two examples are exceptions that prove the rule. Accordingly, cultures from subjects with premature aging syndromes skew downwards from the inverse correlation seen in the general ("average") population because they are physiologically effete while cultures from normal donors skew upward because they are physiologically elite.[7,16]

Additional validation of the cultured fibroblast model emanates from comparative biological studies. In brief, it appears that a direct correlation exists between the maximum lifespan attainable by a species in vivo and the lifespan of fibroblasts in vitro.[18,19] In summary, therefore, a significant relationship exists between an individual's aging rate in vivo and his fibroblast "aging" rate in vitro. This system now serves as a powerful model to probe the origins of biological aging and age-dependent diseases.

II. Nature of biological clock

An important issue has recently been resolved regarding the limited fibroblast lifespan, namely, the answer to two related questions: does the replicative lifespan depend on events related to cell division such that all cells have a critical limit up to a maximum number of generations? Or, does "metabolic time" independent of cell division lead to exhaustion of replicative potential? Two early definitive studies have been published. In the first case[20] reducing the serum content of growth media from the normal 10% to 0.5% brought about virtually total arrest of DNA synthesis and mitosis while cellular viability was preserved. After holding some cultures in this stationary phase for up to 6 months (equal to about 1 lifespan of continuously replicating cells) followed by restoring the serum concentration to the usual 10%, cultures were able to resume normal proliferation and go on to achieve the

same number of maximum MPD as cultures that were uninterrupted by serum deprivation. In the other study[21] cells were maintained in normal growth medium
(containing 15% fetal calf serum in this case) but in the confluent density-
inhibited state for up to 3 months with complete replacement of medium weekly.
After this time cells were freed from the stationary phase, subjected to
continuous subculture, and went on to achieve virtually the same maximum number
of MPD before phase-out as uninterrupted cells. In both cases[20,21], the
additional calendar time accruing was highly significant. This clearly indicates that cells record or "count" each round of division rather than other
kinds of metabolic events.

More recent experiments in our laboratory have confirmed and extended the
concept of a replicative counter.[4] In brief, this work involves inoculating
a small drop containing 40,000 cells into the center of a petri dish. On
incubation, cells first adhere, then proliferate in a circular expansion such
that the radial growth is linear with time. Autoradiographic studies with
^{3}H-thymidine incorporation as an index of DNA synthesis showed that virtually
all of the DNA replication occurs within a small rim of cells at the circum-
ferential edge. After some 3 or 4 weeks, cells at the circumference decreased
their growth rate and ultimately ceased dividing due to senescence.

We then asked whether the centrally located cells (which were density-
inhibited and hence did not divide) had a greater replicative capacity remaining than peripheral cells? An additional question was: did cells at intermediate radial positions show a continuous distribution of replicative
capacities? To answer these questions, we harvested several areas of the
circular outgrowth at different radial positions (Fig.1) and subcultured each
of these cell isolates until senescence. The additional number of MPD to
senescence was then determined for each isolate and the results plotted in
Figure 2. Regression analysis indicated that the proliferative capacity
remaining decreased linearly with distance from the centre of the outgrowth
at a rate of 1.33±0.14 MPD/mm. The theoretical generation distribution for
such a circular outgrowth of cells was also determined[4] and revealed a linear
distribution spanning 31 generations (Fig.3). Knowing the initial MPD level
of fibroblasts used to initiate the outgrowth (MPD 18) and the maximum MPD
attainable prior to senescence of replicate cells subcultured in parallel
(MPD 55) we could predict the number of additional MPD accruing before
senescence. This was 37 MPD for the most central cells (r' < 5 mm from the
center) and 6 MPD for the most peripheral cells (at r' = 25 mm). The
predicted value (Fig.2) for the replicative capacity remaining in cells at a

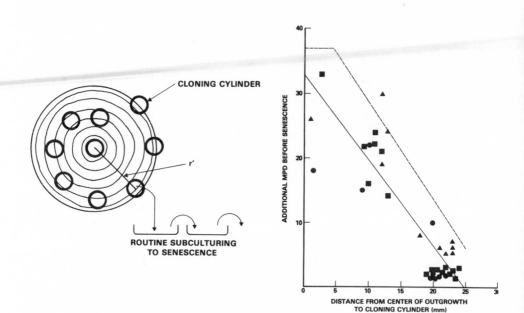

Fig.1. Schema of a circular outgrowth showing how multiple areas can be harvested at different radial positions. Circular cloning cylinders were applied with silicone grease followed by liberation of cells with trypsin, recovery with a pasteur pipet and transfer to separate petri dishes. Individual isolates were then continuously subcultured until senescence at 1:8 splits giving 3 MPD for each such maneuver. The total number of additional MPD accruing between harvest and senescence was thus determined for cells as a function of radial position (Fig.2).

Fig.2 Additional MPD accruing before senescence versus radial position of cells selected at various points within the outgrowth. Additional MPD before senescence were determined for cells from 3 individual circular outgrowths (●,▲,■). The least squares line, r = -0.87 (——) and the theoretical line (---) are shown. Reproduced from ref.4 with permission.

given radius showed a decline of 1.55 MPD/mm which is remarkably close to the experimental value of 1.33 MPD/mm above. That experimental points lie 6 MPD below the theoretical line likely reflects a minor loss of proliferative capacity due to a slight residue of cell division in the density-inhibited central region.

These data clearly indicate that cells "count" the number of replicative events to a uniform maximum limit. Also important is the observation that cells in the circular outgrowth exist along a heterogeneous but ordered scale of MPD (Fig.3). Thus, a relatively young "stem cell pool" resides at the center of the circular outgrowth and is available for proliferative bursts.

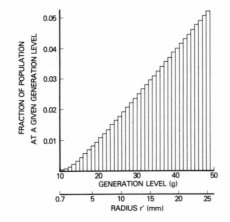

Fig.3. Distribution of cell generations created by a clonal outgrowth. The number of cells occupying each generation level (g) at a radius r' was determined by an iterative procedure.[4] Since all cells undergo 10 divisions before r' > 0.7 mm the abscissa begins at t = 10, r = 0.7. Reproduced from ref.4 with permission.

Nonetheless, these vigorous cells are increasingly depleted with repeated cell division. More abundant are cells at successively higher generation levels but they proceed continuously toward senescence in both their proliferative and functional capacities (see below). A similar mechanism likely exists in three dimensions in vivo with the capacity to produce asynchronous cell division and generate a large population of functional cells. This would, in the case of solid tissues, surround the smaller stem cell pool, or if released into the circulation, become widely disseminated. We emphasize that this model obviates the need to postulate that stem cells are immortal.

There is a coda on the nature of the biological clock. We have found that late-passage fibroblasts lose a fraction of their highly reiterated DNA sequences.[22,23] More specifically, in two tandem repeat arrays of DNA seen following Eco-RI endonuclease digestion there is a 25% loss of 350 and 700 base pair sequences. These data are exciting because they provide the first direct evidence for the marginotomy theory of cellular aging.[24] Accordingly, with each round of cell replication a consecutive loss occurs of sequences at the DNA termini. This mechanism could act as a molecular counter and not only regulate cellular senescence but also play a critical role in differentiation. Taken together, our results are also overwhelmingly in favor of a model of cellular aging based on intrinsic genetic processes that lead to "terminal differentiation"[25] rather than an error process based on stochastic events.

III. Decreased response to insulin-like growth factors (IGF) in aging cells

Explosive advances have recently occurred in the field of IGF. Many of these factors share sequence homology with insulin and also have overlapping receptor reactivities.[26,27] It appears that during evolution we have generated a diverse array of related IGF (including the somatomedins) each likely having a specific target tissue but with considerable interaction and overlap. Thus, among the several factors already described it seems clear that some have predominant effects on adipose tissue, others on chondryocytes, while others favor the fibroblast. It is also likely that insulin or related factors are important with respect to certain immune cells.[28,29]

Certain IGF are potent stimulators of human fibroblast metabolism and thus provide a probe to examine hormone responsiveness in aging cells.[7,8] We have found, using stimulation of DNA synthesis by specific IGF, that dose-response curves "shift to the right" at late passage levels in vitro. Thus a greater concentration of IGF is required to effect stimulation of DNA synthesis to a reference level. A similar shift to the right is seen as a function of donor age in normals (Table). Further, in fibroblasts taken from a subject with the premature aging syndrome, progeria, there is also a blunted response (Table). This strain, derived from a 9 year old boy, resembled considerably older normal donors.

These studies on IGF are most pertinent to the severe growth stunting seen in progeric subjects, the pronounced insulin resistance seen clinically in progeria, and the resistance to insulin and similar hormones seen as a function of normal aging.[30] Thus, the steady increase in diabetes seen in older people is not related primarily to a deficit of circulating insulin but rather to

TABLE

EFFECT OF DONOR AGE AND PROGERIA ON $[IGF]$ REQUIRED TO STIMULATE
DNA SYNTHESIS TO 50% AND 95% OF MAXIMUM RESPONSE*

DONOR AGE (YEARS)	$[IGF]_{50}$	$[IGF]_{95}$
Normal (n):		
9-13 (2)	0.36±0.05	1.13±0.42
19-30 (4)	0.27±0.07	1.38±0.13
55-88 (4)	0.54±0.05	2.90±0.30
Progeria:		
9 (1)	0.88±0.08	3.10±0.10
Ratio		
progeria / normal ≠	2.4±0.1	2.7±0.4

*Measured by ^{3}H-thymidine incorporation into trichloracetic acid-precipitable
material; n = number of subjects in each age group; data are the mean ± S.D.
on 3-14 experiments carried out on each cell strain. ≠ 9-13 years.
Reproduced from ref.7 with permission.

decreased responsiveness to insulin.[31] Analogies may also be drawn to aging
of immune cells and their response to specific immune hormones such as
exogenous thymopoietin. Thus, while one can increase the stimulation of
immune cells using exogenous thymopoietin,[32] the extent of response seen in
younger cells cannot be achieved. Therefore, one salient point bears
repetition. Cellular responsiveness to most hormones and growth factors is
decreased with age and while exogenous factors can promote and partially
restore cell responsiveness, they cannot abrogate or reverse what must be an
intrinsic genetic process.

IV. Response of cyclic AMP levels in fibroblasts to PGE$_1$ and epinephrine:
    Effects of cell density and senescence.

Cyclic AMP (cAMP) has been implicated in various aspects of cell growth
and in hormonal responsiveness.[33] We have, therefore, sought to determine
whether hormonal sensitivity changes during the growth cycle from logarithmic
growth to confluence, and while a culture traverses its lifespan from early-
passage (young) to late-passage (old) cells. With young confluent cells PGE$_1$
induced a large (500-fold) increase above basal levels in intracellular cAMP
(Fig.4). In contradistinction, maximum levels stimulated by epinephrine were
substantially less (note decrease in scale). Peak levels of cAMP following

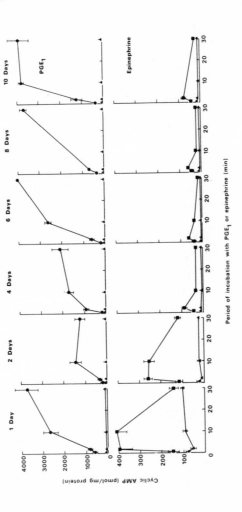

Fig.4. Effects of PGE$_1$ and epinephrine (adrenalin) on cAMP levels in young fibroblasts at different times after subculture. A normal strain of confluent young fibroblasts was subcultured at a 1:8 split ratio in 60 mm dishes and grown for 1 day (a,g), 2 days (b,h), 4 days (c,i), 6 days (d,j), 8 days (e,k) and 10 days (f,l) (see growth curves in Fig.6). The effects of 1 μM-PGE$_1$ (●) and of 10 μM-adrenaline (■) on cAMP levels were determined in incubations lasting 0.5, 2, 10 and 30 min. Control incubations without these hormonal additions were also performed (▲). Mean cAMP values of dishes are given; the S.E.M. is shown where it extends beyond the symbol. Reproduced from ref.9 with permission.

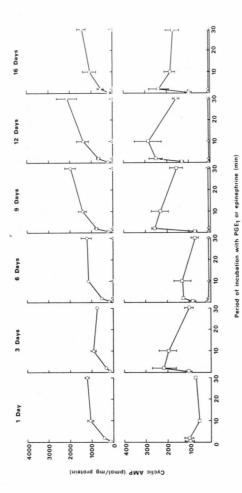

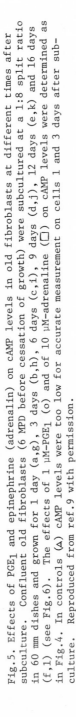

Fig.5. Effects of PGE₁ and epinephrine (adrenalin) on cAMP levels in old fibroblasts at different times after subculture. Confluent old fibroblasts (6 MPD before cessation of growth) were subcultured at a 1:8 split ratio in 60 mm dishes and grown for 1 day (a,g), 3 days (b,h), 6 days (c,i), 9 days (d,j), 12 days (e,k) and 16 days (f,l) (see Fig.6). The effects of 1 μM-PGE₁ (o) and of 10 μM-adrenaline (□) on cAMP levels were determined as in Fig.4. In controls (Δ) cAMP levels were too low for accurate measurement on cells 1 and 3 days after sub-culture. Reproduced from ref.9 with permission.

PGE_1 stimulation occurred between 10 to 30 mins. while epinephrine-induced elevations peaked around 2 mins. Results obtained during the growth of cells from sparse cultures to confluent density-inhibited cells were most interesting. While the response of PGE_1 in day 1 cultures was similar to that observed in confluent cells, epinephrine response was far greater. During exponential growth of young fibroblasts (about 2-4 days following subculture) responses to both PGE_1 and epinephrine were depressed. However, while the response to PGE_1 recovered, for epinephrine it declined further.

In old cells, PGE_1 induced smaller increases of cAMP levels than in young cells (Fig.5). In contrast, epinephrine caused a larger and more persistent increase in cAMP in old compared to young cells, particularly during confluence. In early periods following subculture, old cells responded variably to epinephrine but in general the opposite trend to that of young cells was observed, i.e. the effect of epinephrine increased during growth.

The peak responses to PGE_1 and epinephrine are summarized in Figure 6. The ratio of hormonal responses changed much more during growth of young than of old cells. While initially similar at both ages the ratios diverted sharply as growth of the young cells accelerated. With confluent young cells PGE_1 increased cAMP about 60-fold versus epinephrine, whereas in old cells the ratio was about 8. Comparison of Figs. 6a and 6b indicates that the relative effect of PGE_1 and adrenalin correlated remarkably well with density of cells.

It is evident that cAMP responses to PGE_1 and epinephrine change independently of each other during cellular growth and senescence. This suggests that changes occur in the relative amounts or activities of membrane receptors for each hormone because changes in the adenylate cyclase or in the cAMP phosphodiesterase should alter the cAMP responses to the two hormones in the same direction. These results, therefore, are best reconciled with modulation in the expression of genes responsible for synthesis of hormone receptors during growth and senescence. Similar observations have also been made on human fibroblasts by others using related catecholamines,[34,35] and on the insulin receptor of human fibroblasts as a function of donor age.[36]

Thus, our studies may explain why the immature immune system fails to respond to specific stimuli perhaps because it has not yet expanded to a sufficient critical mass. By the same token, depletion of cell compartments in old age due to cell dropout and/or impaired proliferation could also reduce the immune response.[37,38] In short, the response to various forms of communication between cells and between molecules and cells can depend,

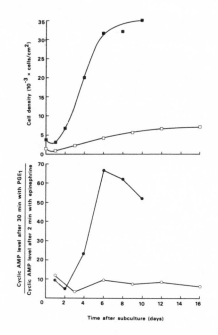

Fig.6. Ratio of peak cyclic AMP levels obtained with PGE₁ and epinephrine (adrenalin) in relation to growth of young and old fibroblasts. (a) Increases in cell density associated with the growth of young (■) and old (□) normal fibroblasts used in the experiments described in Figs. 4 and 5. (b) Ratios of the cAMP levels observed 30 minutes after addition of 1 μM PGE₁ to levels observed 2 minutes after addition of 10 μM epinephrine during the growth of young (●) and old (o) fibroblasts. Reproduced from ref.9 with permission.

as shown here, on cell density and age. This has important implications with respect to cell recruitment and the integrity of circuits in the immune system.

CONCLUSIONS

While the principles elaborated here derive from cultured skin fibroblasts it seems clear that they also apply to the immune system. For example, continuously replicating fibroblasts lose viability significantly before non-dividing but otherwise actively metabolizing cohorts. This suggests that excessively rapid cellular turnover will accelerate clonal senescence and its pathologic sequelae. Perhaps prolongation of the lifespan in vivo by with-holding nutrients[39,40] and delaying senescence of the immune system[41-43] is

mediated by a diminished secretion of insulin and related IGF, thereby
retarding cellular proliferation and terminal differentiation. The paradoxically increased epinephrine stimulation in aged fibroblasts may also have
an in vivo counterpart in the post-denervation sensitivity to catecholamines
that occurs in the tissues of aging animals.[44,45]

Lastly, it is important to emphasize that through the agency of tissue
culture we are able to establish cell strains that are genetic replicas of
any given donor. Thus, we can study personal risk to a specific disease and
even evaluate various modalities of treatment specifically tailored to the
individual genotype. This system of cultured human fibroblasts continues to
provide important insights into the functional decline that accompanies
biological aging and into the cellular and molecular origins of age-dependent
disease.

REFERENCES

1. Goldstein, S. and Littlefield, J.W. (1969) Diabetes, 18, 545-549.
2. Cooper, J.T. and Goldstein, S. (1973) Lancet, 1, 673.
3. Goldstein, S. (1978) in The Genetics of Aging, Schneider, E.L. ed.,
   Plenum Press, New York, pp. 171-224.
4. Harley, C.B. and Goldstein, S. (1978) J.Cell.Physiol. 97, 509-516.
5. Posner, B.I., Guyda, H.J., Corvol, M.T., Rappaport, R., Harley, C. and
   Goldstein, S. (1978) J.Clin.Endocrinol.Metab. 47, 1240-1250.
6. Goldstein, S. and Harley, C.B. (1978) Clin.Res. 26, 416A (abstract).
7. Goldstein, S. and Harley, C.B. (1979) Fed.Proc. 38, 1862-1867.
8. Harley, C.B., Goldstein, S., Posner, B.I. and Guyda, H.J.
   Submitted for publication.
9. Haslam, R.J. and Goldstein, S. (1974) Biochem.J. 144, 253-263.
10.Hayflick, L. and Moorehead, P.S. (1961) Exp.Cell Res. 25, 585-621.
11.Hayflick, L. (1965) Exp.Cell Res. 37, 614-636.
12.Goldstein, S., Littlefield, J.W. and Soeldner, J.S. (1969)
   Proc.Nat.Acad.Sci.USA, 64, 155-160.
13.Martin, G.M., Sprague, C.A. and Epstein, C.J. (1970) Lab.Invest. 23,
   86-92.
14.LeGuilly, Y., Simon, M., Lenoir, P. and Bourel, M. (1973)
   Gerontologia 19, 303-313.
15.Schneider, E. and Mitsui, Y. (1976) Proc.Natl.Acad.Sci.USA 73, 3584-3588.
16.Goldstein, S., Moerman, E.J., Soeldner, J.S., Gleason, R.E. and Barnett, D.M.
   (1978) Science 199, 781-782 and 202, 1217-1218.
17.Goldstein, S., Moerman, E.J., Soeldner, J.S., Gleason, R.E. and Barnett, D.M.
   (1979) J.Clin.Invest. 63, 358-370.
18.Hayflick, L. (1977) in Handbook of the Biology of Aging, Finch, C.E. and
   Hayflick, L. eds., Van Nostrand Reinhold Co., New York, pp.159-186.
19.Goldstein, S. (1979) in Endocrinology, DeGroot, L.J. et al eds.,
   Grune & Stratton, New York (in press).
20.Dell'Orco, R.T., Mertens, J.G. and Kruse, P.F.Jr. (1973) Exptl.Cell
   Res. 77, 356-360.
21. Goldstein, S. and Singal, D.P. (1974) Exp.Cell Res. 88, 359-364.
22.Shmookler Reis, R.J. and Goldstein, S. Submitted for publication.
23.Shmookler Reis, R.J. and Goldstein, S. (1979) Fed.Proc.38, 535 (abstract).

24. Olovnikov, A.M. (1973) J.Theor.Biol.41, 181-190.
25. Martin, G.M. (1977) Amer.J.Pathol. 77, 484-512.
26. Rechler, M.M., Nissley, S.P., Podskalny, J.M., Moses, A.C. and Fryklund, L. (1977) J.Clin.Endocrinol.Metab. 44, 820-831.
27. Sato, G. and Ross, R. eds. (1979) Hormones and Cell Culture, Cold Spring Harbor Conference on Cell Proliferation, Cold Spring Harbor Lab. New York (in press).
28. Olefsky, J. and Reaven, G.M. (1974) J.Clin.Endocrinol.Metab. 38, 554-560.
29. Helderman, J.H. and Strom, T.B. (1977) J.Clin.Invest. 59, 338-344.
30. DeFronzo, R.A. (1979) Fed.Proc. 27, 364A (abstract).
31. Goldstein, S. and Podolsky, S. (1978) Med.Clin.N.Amer. 62, 639-654.
32. Weksler, M. these proceedings.
33. Pastan, I.H., Johnson, G.S. and Anderson, W.B. (1975) Ann.Rev.Biochem. 44, 491-522.
34. Manganiello, V.C. and Breslow, J. (1974) Biochem.Biophys.Acta 362, 509-520.
35. Polgar, P., Taylor, L. and Brown, L. (1978) Mech.Ageing & Develop. 7, 151-160.
36. Rosenbloom, A.L., Goldstein, S. and Yip, C.C. (1977) Science 193, 412-415.
37. Makinodan, T., Good, R.A. and Kay, M.M.B. (1977) in Immunology & Aging, Makinodan, T. and Yunis, E. eds., Plenum Publishing Corp., New York, pp. 9-22.
38. Singhal, S.K. et al, these proceedings.
39. McCay, C.M., Crowell, M.F. and Maynard, L.A. (1935) J.Nutr.10, 63-79.
40. Ross, M.H. (1976) in Nutrition and Aging, Winick, M. ed., Wiley, New York, pp. 43-57.
41. Fernandes, G., Yunis, E.J. and Good, R.A. (1976) Proc.Natl.Acad.Sci.USA, 73, 1279-1283.
42. Weindruch, R.H., Kristie, J.A., Cheney, K.E. and Walford, R.L. (1979) Fed.Proc. 38, 2007-2016.
43. R.A.Good et al, these proceedings.
44. Frolkis, V.V., Bezrukov, V.V., Bogatskaya, N.S., Verkhratsky, N.S., Zamostian, I.V., Shevtchyk, V.G. and Shtchegoleva, I.V. (1970) Gerontologia 16, 129-140.
45. Tannen, R.H. and Domino, E.F. (1977) Gerontology 23, 165-173.

DISCUSSION

TANNER: There may be an in vivo correlate in the change in response to epinephrine.   In older animals where presynaptic stimulation caused a smaller response than in the younger animals direct application of epinephrine to the post-synaptic neuron caused a greater response so this may be an in vivo correlation.   One other related question – how long does it take to measure the final diameter in your in vivo measurement of fibroblast proliferation?

GOLDSTEIN: It is variable.   It depends at what age of the culture you begin.   If you start very early, after initiating the culture, there is a lot more "oomph" in the cells, so you can get radial expansions that are sometimes as large as 3 cm.   Another point that I didn't bring out if that of course this outgrowth represents quite a heterogeneous collection of cells with different life spans at different population levels.   Therefore, those at the centre are still stem type cells and have a lot of time to go ahead and divide.   Those at the periphery have used up just about everything and those in between represent a progression of cellular generation levels.

LEON: Do these fibroblasts express any viral antigens on their surface and do you find any differences in such expression if you take central as opposed to peripheral samples or early and late passage cells?

GOLDSTEIN: That's a good question but I am not aware of any studies on that.

SISKIND: What is the morphology of the late cells in these circles versus the early ones?

GOLDSTEIN: The morphology is very interesting and this has been looked at under both light microscopy and electron microscopy.   The cells tend to be larger, much more bloated; they contain more protein, more RNA, but the DNA content as far as you can measure seems to be the same.   I've just told you that the DNA content goes down but that is in a very small part of the genome. There seem to be some problems in the number of ribosomes that are bound to the endoplasmic reticulum, i.e. there seems to be a reduction.   There seems to be an increase in glycogen.

WISNIEWSKI: Do they have a type of storage disease?

GOLDSTEIN: I had forgotten one very important thing.   They do pile up lysosomes.   It has been said by some that if the lysosome is the disposal sack, then the cells are constipated.

TURKER: I have several questions regarding the biological clock and, if we assume that there is a biological clock in that space of reiterated DNA sequences, do you think it is necessary for cells to replicate in order to eliminate copies of this DNA in vivo to tick off the clock so to speak?   In view of the findings that ribosomal RNA copies are reduced in older animals, do you think it is possible that the clock might be ribosomal RNA?

GOLDSTEIN: Very possible.   Hutchinson was interested in the ribosomal RNA.

MAKINODAN: Did you look at the HLA antigens in this circle of cells?

GOLDSTEIN: No we haven't.   We have been interested in HLA expression too, and we do find an instability of expression of HLA antigens in progeria and in

Werner's syndrome. There is a loss or alteration of recognition of the specific antiserum that was present on the lymphocytes of these people. In normal cells, we have found stability of HLA antigenic expression as you go right through the culture life span.

CINADER: What are the time changes in the progeria cell during cultivation? For instance you get clot retraction changes already in the very early culture cells.

GOLDSTEIN: Yes, everything seems to be telescoped in the progeria situation. First of all, they have a shortened replicative life span. Depending on the case, it seems as if some of them are just about border line normal but most of them are somewhat depressed in their culture life span. Everything else that has ever been reported on aging fibroblasts seems to appear earlier than progeria in the culture and be more severe.

CINADER: How much earlier?

GOLDSTEIN: Almost as soon as you can look, as soon as you can grow cells out of the explant you see the problem.

SISKIND: In view of the morphological changes of the culture cycle could one think of these cells in an alternative hypothesis as sick cells dying as opposed to healthy cells which are using up a clock?

GOLDSTEIN: It is possible. Do you want to elaborate a little more?

SISKIND: Are they in culture in an environment unhealthy for the cells, consequently, are they having accumulative insults, which are being manifested by stimulation of lysosomes?

GOLDSTEIN: That is very possible; they may have a deficiency disease and that is what brings on late passage and termination of the culture.

WEKSLER: This is probably so, because, as you know, addition of hydro-cortisone can double the length of survival in these cells.

GOLDSTEIN: Not quite double, one can get about a third more, but this is the point that I made earlier. You can increase the life span a little bit by adding various factors to this medium. You really can't exaggerate this final event and I believe that this has a lot of in vivo parallels. People are often loathe to accept this in the culture sense but I think there is plenty of evidence in vivo that we are depleting cells all the time in many stem cell compartments.

GOOD: I just wanted to ask what is the situation with respect to reiter-ative DNA in the immortalized cells, the cells that have undergone trans-formation?

GOLDSTEIN: There is a real problem. The immortal cell that you have to look at would be something like a HeLa cell or an SV40 transformed cell and there is so much chromosomal rearrangement and damage that I don't think that it would perhaps have much bearing on this.

THE AGING HUMAN

RONALD D. T. CAPE
Professor and Co-ordinator, Section of Geriatric Medicine, Department of
Medicine, University of Western Ontario, Parkwood Hospital, 81 Grand Avenue,
London, Ontario, Canada, N6C 1M2

There is a stereotype suggesting that the aging human is a deprived, disa-
bled depressed person awaiting his/her end. Robert Butler[1] has underlined
the various myths of aging, unproductivity, disengagement, inflexibility, se-
nility and serenity which are regarded as characteristic of old age. There are
many studies in medical literature on problem areas of this time of life empha-
sising pathology, clinical syndromes and general disability. There are few
which aim to illustrate a broader view.

At the invitation of two Ontario District Health Councils, anxious to establish the needs of the communities which they serve, Dr. P. J. Henschke and I,
with the assistance of four summer students carried out two studies in 1978.
They were designed to provide information on the incidence of significant disability and demonstrate any deficiencies in health care systems which affect
the elderly. The studies were undertaken in the City of London, Ontario and in
the Counties of Grey and Bruce 100 miles to the North. There were no significant differences between the three groups of subjects - London (130), Grey-
Bruce urban (153) and Grey-Bruce rural (102) in the parameters to be described.
These will, therefore, relate to the total group of 385 individuals.

One of our main purposes was to assess the degree of independence of those
continuing to live in their own homes. To determine this, we examined 5 different activities. These were walking, dressing, going up or down stairs, having a shower or bath, and walking around an average city block. The details
are shown in Table 1.

1. Remarkably few of the 385 subjects were unable to perform all 5 of the activities illustrated. 1-2% of the total group were unable to dress without
assistance, about 5% were unable to walk across a small room, 6% were unable to
shower or bath without assistance, 8-9% were unable to go up and down stairs
and 14% were unable to walk around a city block.

2. It is clear that the incidence of failing ability to perform activities of
daily living increases with age. This point is demonstrated in Table 1 in
which a mean for each age-group is shown. Figure 1 illustrates these means

plotted against age from which one can see that the level of developing depend-
ence, due presumably to the incidence of significant disability, increases
slowly from under 5% at age 65 to almost 8% at age 75, at which level it remains stationary until beyond the age of 80.   Thereafter, it increases quite
steeply.   All subjects were randomly selected individuals continuing to live in
their own homes.   The method of selection is explained elsewhere[2].

TABLE 1

SUBJECTS UNABLE TO PERFORM ACTIVITIES OF DAILY LIVING WITHOUT ASSISTANCE

Activity	Sex			Age Category				
	Male	Female	Total	65-69	70-74	75-79	80-85	85+
Number of Subjects	167	218	385	146	97	79	32	31
Dressing	3	3	6 (1.5%)	2	1	0	0	0
Walking Indoors	9	11	20 (5.2%)	4	6	3	2	5
Shower/Bathing	6	18	24 (6.2%)	2	4	4	3	11
Climbing Stairs	11	22	33 (8.5%)	8	5	8	3	9
Walking Outdoors	21	34	55 (14.2%)	9	13	13	6	14
Mean of Subjects Unable to Perform Five Activities	5.9%	8.0%	7.2%	3.4%	5.9%	7.1%	8.7%	27.1%

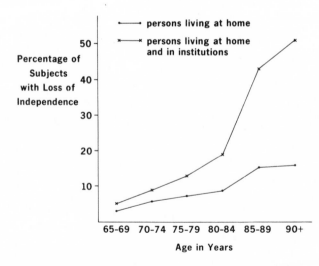

Fig. 1. Loss of Independence with Age

While these results indicate a considerable degree of independence in the elderly people studied, there was also evidence that they required much support from their physician. Only 59 or 15% of the total sample had not visited him/her within the previous year. Of the 326 who had, 139 or 36% had visited the physician on three or more occasions.

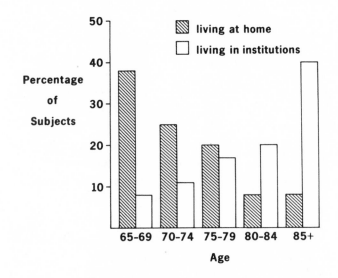

Fig. 2. Comparison Of Age Between Subjects At Home Or In Institutions

To complete the picture of the aging human in the community it is known, from these studies and an earlier one[3], that 6.5% of the elderly in the three areas concerned are in institutions. One striking difference between samples of old people (i.e. over the age of 65) who are living in their own homes and those in institutions, is the age pattern (see Figure 2). The institutional group have a much higher proportion of very old people. Thus, to reach a realistic view of total disability from age 65 onwards we have to add on proportionately for the residents in institutions at each age group. This has been done in Figure 1. In broad terms, disability is present in about 5% of those between 65 and 69 and reaches levels ranging between 25 and 30% at age 85 and beyond. Remembering that it is the oldest cohorts in the population which are now the fastest growing, one can envisage the problems facing the medical services in the next few decades. The aim of physicians is to maintain the independence of the old and they are looking to the scientists, researching into

216

the processes of aging, to produce some answers to help them to achieve their goal.

From the 'human' part of my title, let me turn to the 'aging'. Throughout our lives, from a biological standpoint, we are constantly changing. The genetic impulse which gives us our initial developmental thrust comes from our parents. This results in a rapid process of growth and development which achieves its optimum state as we reach maturity in the early twenties. That is the point at which all of our bodily functions have the greatest potential, the greatest reserve of function and optimum capacity. Thereafter, the decremental effect of time begins to exert its influence on us from maturity onwards. Figure 3 represents the general pattern as it affects both the human body as a whole and each of its organ systems. Some of the latter lose more functional capacity than others. During the first twenty to thirty years beyond the point of optimum maturity, deterioration in biological systems is slow and gradual, but beyond that period, it speeds up. In youth and maturity, there is a range of function between individuals which slowly widens during senescence. As a result, there are individuals at age 90 who constitute a biologically elite group, still within 10% of their optimum function, while others of the same age have lost all but 10% of it.

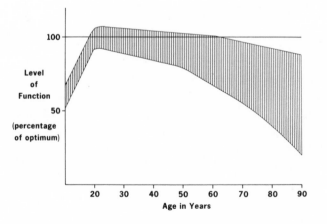

Fig. 3. Effect Of Age On Level Of Function

This can be illustrated by a few examples of physiological changes with age. One of the first functions in which these were examined, was the excretion of urine through the kidneys by Nathan Shock and his colleagues in Baltimore. Demonstrating unequivocally that aging per se can cause significant and consistent changes, Davies and Shock's study[4] of renal function was published in 1950. Seven groups, each of 9 - 12 men, one group from each decade from the 3rd to 9th, were studied. No subject had evidence of previous renal, cerebrovascular, or coronary artery disease, was hypertensive or had any recent alteration in body weight. The authors studied inulin and diodrast clearances which represent filtration through glomeruli and excretion through tubules respectively. Their results indicated that, by the age of 80, the average clearances were approximately 67% of that of 30 year old individuals.

This original study was a cross-sectional one. Since then, the same Gerontological Institute has carried out a longitudinal study on almost 300 men[5], who were examined and re-examined in the same way on no less than three occasions over a period of 10 years, and virtually the same results were obtained. It is likely that the cause of these changes is loss of nephrons.

As an illustration of variations in the degree of loss of function, one can contrast the renal study with the fact that basal metabolic rate is slowly reduced by 20% between the ages of 20 and 80. Maximal breathing capacity, on the other hand, which requires the integrated activity of cardiovascular, nervous, musculoskeletal and respiratory systems is reduced at age 80 by 60%.

There is a widespread belief among physicians that all the ills of the elderly stem from inadequate circulation. It is true that heart disease is the commonest cause of death in most of Europe and North America and that it is directly responsible for almost one-third of mortality in the old. To balance the picture, however, over a quarter of octogenarians will not have diseased hearts when they die. With an old heart, exercise tolerance will be adequate for most purposes, including quite vigorous activity, if it is undertaken slowly. The cardiovascular concomitants of aging can be summed up as[6]:

1. A decrease in the contractility of the heart muscle.
2. An increased stiffness of large arteries which is compensated to some extent by aortic enlargement, and
3. An increased peripheral resistance.

Finally, during the past day and a half we have heard much of the evidence that is currently available on age changes in the immunologic system which again indicates deterioration with time. All systems, thus, have in common a remorseless sequence of diminishing function.

Biological gerontology is the scientific base of geriatric medicine. As knowledge has accummulated, theories about the nature of the aging process have abounded. Some have favoured a hypothesis that there is a programmed pre-planned deteriorating process which affects us all[7], while others have ex-pressed a view that, unlike development, aging is an unplanned stochastic se-ries of disasters[8,9].

One theory, which has not received much attention, but which is certainly of interest was developed by Bullough[10]. He believes that the key to an ani-mal's lifespan lies in its tissues which, no matter how they vary in detailed structure and function, have to be maintained at a mass which is constant rela-tive to the total mass of the body and must preserve a rate of function which is appropriate to the body's needs at any given moment. The former control is achieved through varying the rate of mitosis in tissues consisting of cells which retain this potential. A number of tissues have been studied including epidermis, sebaceous glands, lung, kidney and lymphocytes. In all cases, these cells synthesize a tissue specific antimitotic messenger molecule, a chalone, which controls new cell production. Every tissue which consists of cells cap-able of mitosis is constantly changing, because, as new cells are created, old cells are dying. After a certain period, which varies from tissue to tissue, 14-21 days for epidermal cells, but only 2 days for those of duodenal mucosa, they lose the capacity for division and become aged and post-mitotic. This process is achieved through the chalone antimitotic messenger agent acting to inhibit further mitoses and move the cell into a final senescent phase. Its demise signals the arrival of a new cell into the mitotic circle. The faster the rate of mitosis, the shorter the life-span of the cell, allowing the bal-anced size and function of the tissue to be maintained.

Non-mitotic tissues, the neurons, skeletal and cardiac muscle react to the increasing size and maturity of their host by each individual cell enlarging to the necessary degree. Because the process of mitosis has been completely blocked off, the aging and death of such cells is considerably slowed down. Throughout life, however, there is a loss of both neurons and muscle cells.

Why should there be mitotic and non-mitotic tissues? The former are poten-tially immortal, the latter are not. Bullough suggests that the reason may be to set a limit on the life-span of the animal, because this has an ultimately beneficial effect on the species. If an evolutionary process is to continue there must be a discarding to encourage recreating. If this is the purpose of our non-mitotic tissues it is probable that they have a critical role to play in determining one's life-span. Bullough postulates that the brain is the most probable site for determination of life-span.

Cerebral function involves sensory input and its translation into intellectual, motor and neuro-regulating activity. The brain achieves its optimum potential at maturity after which there will be a slow decline in its capabilities (see Figure 3). An important characteristic of the human brain is its ability to create from many sensory stimuli, complex muscle movements which control, inter alia, posture and bladder function. It is such integrative systems which will tend to fail to the greatest extent as Shock[11] has suggested. He has pointed out that nerve conduction velocity, which involves measurements in a single organ system, shows an average decrement of 15% between the ages of 30 and 80 years while renal function, depending on cardiovascular system and kidneys, falls by twice as much. The brain acts as a regulating centre for a variety of homeostatic mechanisms to maintain temperature, blood pressure and blood acid- base state at normal levels. Deterioration of cerebral function, therefore, leads directly to the three commonest features of illness in old people, mental confusion, urinary incontinence and a tendency to fall and it reduces the efficiency of homeostatic control. To these, one can add a fifth. Multiple pathology, common in the elderly, leads to polypharmacy. Crooks, Shepherd and Stevenson[12] have suggested that, partly because of this, half of all adverse drug reactions occur in elderly patients.

Thus, falling, confusion, incontinence, homeostatic disturbance and iatrogenic illness form the geriatric quintet[13]. They constitute what I call the O-Complex of old age syndromes which are the essence of geriatrics. Based largely on deteriorating cerebral function, they offer some clinical support to the belief that the brain has a crucial role to play in the aging process.

One of the most intriguing observations reported by Bullough was that chalone activity occurred only in the presence of adrenaline. The inhibition of mitosis in epidermis is achieved by a chalone-adrenaline complex, this combined action being strengthened in the presence of a glucocorticoid hormone[14,15]. The life-span of post-mitotic epidermal cells in mice fed on a restricted diet is prolonged[14]. In animals fed in this way the suprarenal glands become greatly enlarged. There is, therefore, a close link between rate of mitosis in epidermal cells, and hence their life-span, and activity of the suprarenal glands. Stimulation of the latter producing increased circulating stress hormones may thus affect the species life-span. Bellamy[16] has shown that giving short-lived strains of mice prednisolone fortified drinking water doubled the life-span of the animals. The influence of stress on the aging process thus becomes of considerable interest.

220

"Science is a first-rate piece of furniture for a man's upper chamber, if he has common sense on the ground floor" said Oliver Wendell Holmes. Let me descend from the loft to a safer ground floor level. Medicine, after all, remains more of an art than a science. Stress is always with us, from the cradle to the grave - some thrive on it, some fight it and some are almost overwhelmed by it. What do I mean by stress? Any type of physical or mental challenge no matter how trivial, which demands thought, decision and action, in addition to more obvious biological disturbances from disease processes or physical accidents. By this definition stress can be initiated by activities as different as climbing Mount Everest or preparing a pot of tea.

For many years I, in common with others practising geriatric medicine, have been perplexed by a simple fact. Two patients with equivalent disabilities may respond to similar rehabilitative efforts quite differently; one will do well, the other badly. Even more surprising is the situation in which an individual with a severe disability will maintain independence to a much greater degree than a person of comparable age and much less handicap. Let me describe two cases to illustrate my point.

Mr. Soames is a 68-year-old man who lives alone. He sustained a devastating right hemisphere cerebral infarction in early 1978. He was transferred to a continuing care institution for further rehabilitation and treatment from an acute hospital. He did well, but continued to have considerable difficulty with spatial orientation and, because of this and a left hemianopsia, he tended to bump into things and was not safe with cooking appliances. An attempt was made to return him home in July 1978. He went on a visit with the occupational therapist and social worker and this proved to be a disaster. He could not manage. After a further two months of continuing rehabilitation he improved to a point at which a second attempt could be made. This was in September of 1978 and he has now been satisfactorily settled back at home for eight months, in spite of considerable physical disability. Somehow, in his case, this acted as a stimulus, and he was able to overcome it. He is representative of many in whom the obvious stress of a physical illness calls forth a more than adequate response.

There is the other side of the coin. Mrs. Bland, aged 79, lived with a male cousin, about ten years her junior in a rural setting on the edge of London, Ontario. She had previously kept a boarding house but had abandoned this and come to live with her cousin a few months earlier because of failing health. Her admission to hospital occurred after repeated falls which severely damaged her confidence. Investigation of the falling episodes revealed no remediable causative factors. Mrs. Bland had a variable degree of hypertension, which was at times severe, and required treatment with antihypertensive medication, but, at other times, subsided to within normal limits. Apart from these problems her only other consistent complaints were of painful knees, with a moderate degree of osteoarthritis, and a 'sick' stomach.

Mrs. Bland was admitted to the continuing care institution. There, she became, and remained for many months, independent, able to dress herself, walk to the washroom, look after her own toilet and feed herself. Pleased with her progress we made several attempts to discharge her. She would go home for the weekend on a Friday afternoon but by Sunday she reached a state of such panic that she could not wait to return to the institution. There was no obvious physical disturbance to account for this. It was only in the security of the continuing care hospital that she felt comfortable and relaxed. Eventually she was transferred to a nursing home and had great difficulty in settling into the new situation.

The difference between these two individuals, is just a matter of personality, it may be said, and, in the sense that this reflects genetic make up this may be true. The other difference lies in each one's self-confidence. This is regarded as a behavioural trait but nonetheless it is likely to be represented at a cellular or neurotransmitter level by an appropriate hormonal or enzymatic substance. After all, it now seems likely that the devastating behavioural changes of dementia may stem, at least partly, from deficiency of acetyl choline transferase[17]. The ability to overcome stress hinges on confidence. The first patient had it, the second did not.

One might postulate that it is, therefore, linked in some way to the stress hormones. Think of the athlete consciously encouraging his adrenaline to flow in preparation for his moment of supreme stress, or the humble physician screwing up his courage to plunge out of his depth to talk to his scientific peers! Unfortunately the central effector of this stimulus to overcome stress is almost certainly peculiar to man, with his highly developed forebrain, and is unlikely to be revealed by animal experiments.

Aging can be defined as the deterioration of a mature organism resulting from, time dependent, essentially irreversible changes, intrinsic to all members of a species, such that with passage of time they become increasingly unable to cope with the stresses of the environment, thus increasing the probability of death.

The clinician recognizes this and the statement returns me to my point of beginning - our studies on old people. Think, for a moment, of the differences in elderly relatives or friends who live in their own homes, and those who are in institutions. The first group struggle on triumphantly, the second have lost zest for living and are content to eke out their lives in a protected almost stifling atmosphere. Somewhere in that maze of emotional turmoil and physical disability the influence of stress and our ability to overcome it plays a critical role.

Nothing is more satisfying than achieving a difficult goal and this will mean overcoming the stresses imposed by the difficulties. Does such an accomplishment follow increased production of stress hormones, and does the difference between the two patients, who have been described, lie in their ability to produce such substances? As a working hypothesis, one might therefore state that stress can be beneficial by stimulating the production of hormones which potentially can reduce the rate of mitosis and increase the life-span of some tissues and, possibly, of the whole animal. Such a concept would not be inconsistent with the immunologic system playing a key role in the aging process. To study the hypothesis a method of measuring stress would be required and the means to define physiologically such behavioural attributes as motivation and self-confidence.

If we are to achieve independence for our old patient we need to be able to influence confidence factors. One of the most exciting developments of the past five years has been that scientist and physician are at last beginning to talk a little of each other's language in the field of aging. Perhaps the former can help the latter to find the means of re-establishing confidence, motivation and independence in patients who have become, for the moment, overwhelmed by what appears to be a minimal stress.

The first Earl of Chatham, a distinguished statesman who played a considerable role in the events of 1759, when Wolfe gained control of the heights of Abraham, and who was a vocal sympathiser with the American rebels in the House of Lords in his own old age, neatly summed up the problem when he declared:

"Confidence is a plant of slow growth in an aged bosom"

223

REFERENCES

1. Butler, R.N. (1975) Why Survive? Being Old In America. Harper and Row, Hagerstown, Maryland, pp. 6-11.
2. Cape, R.D.T., Henschke, P.J. (1979) Perspective of Health in Old Age. J. Am. Geriatr. Soc. [In Press].
3. Cape, R.D.T., Shorrock, C., Tree, R., Pablo, R., Campbell, A.J., Seymour, D.G. (1977) Can. Med. Assoc. J. 117, 1284-1287.
4. Davies, D.F., Shock, N.W. (1950) J. Clin. Invest. 29, 496-506.
5. Rowe, J.W., Andres, R., Tobin J.D., Norris, A.H., Shock, N.W. (1976) J. Geront. 31, 155-163.
6. Kohn, R.R. (1977) in Handbook of the Biology of Aging, Finch, C.E., Hayflick, L. ed., Van Nostrand Reinhold Co., New York, pp. 281-317.
7. Burnett, F.M. (1970) Lancet 11, 358-360.
8. Burch, P.J.R. (1974) in Symposia of Geriatric Medicine, Cape, R.D.T. ed., West Midlands Institue of Geriatric Medicine and Gerontology, Birmingham, England, Vol. 3, pp. 3-14.
9. Bromley, D.B. ibid, pp. 16-23.
10. Bullough, W.S. (1971) Nature 229, 608-610.
11. Shock, N.W. (1977) in Handbook of the Biology of Aging, Finch, C.E., Hayflick, L. ed., Van Nostrand Reinhold Co., New York, pp. 639-665.
12. Crooks, J., Shepherd, A.M.M., Stevenson, I.H. (1975) Health Bull. (Edinb) 33, 222-227.
13. Cape, R.D.T. (1978) Aging: Its Complex Management. Harper and Row, Hagerstown, Maryland, pp. 81-82.
14. Bullough, W.S., Laurence, E.B. (1964) Exp. Cell Res. 33, 176-194.
15. Bullough, W.S. (1967) The Evolution of Differentiation. Academic Press, London, p. 106
16. Bellamy, D. (1968) Exp. Geront. 3, 327-333.
17. Davies, P., Maloney A.J.F. (1976) Lancet II, 1403

SESSION IV

General Discussion
and summation of symposium.

Chairman: **W. Paul**
National Institute of Health
Bethesda

Published 1979 by Elsevier North Holland, Inc.
Singhal, Sinclair, Stiller, eds. Aging and Immunity

AGING AND IMMUNITY: SUMMARY AND PERSPECTIVES

WILLIAM E. PAUL
Laboratory of Immunology, National Institute of Allergy and Infectious Diseases,
National Institutes of Health, Bethesda, MD   20205

The immune system in its role as the major defense mechanism of vertebrate
organisms against pathogenic agents clearly must command attention by individuals interested in the biology of the aging process and in the possibility of
ameliorating some of the debilitating illnesses faced by aged persons.   Over
the last several years, there has been a marked increase in interest in the
immune system of aging humans and animals.   One striking example of this is
the fact that the field could so successfully mount two major meetings on this
general topic during the past week, a National Institute on Aging Workshop on
immunological aspects of aging, held in Bethesda and the international symposium
on Aging and Immunity which we have had the privilege of attending.

Although I have not personally participated in studies of immunity and aging,
attending these two meetings and attempting to relate the problems of the immune
system of the aged to the general problems of immunobiology may allow me to
summarize the current state of immunological research in this area and to make
comments from the perspective of an interested bystander.   As an opening point,
it seems to me absolutely essential to obtain a precise description of the
immune systems of both mature and aging individuals, with particular attention
to the development of quantitative approaches which can be reproduced from
laboratory to laboratory and to the careful delination of the regenerative and
regulatory aspects of the immune system.   I emphasize these two areas because
they seem the most likely sites of specific "lesions" occurring in the course
of aging.

Indeed, we can both summarize the symposium and comment on these principal
issues at the same time as these are the very subjects most intensively dealt
with by the individual speakers.   The fundamental problems of regulation of the
immune systems were very cogently addressed by both Hans Wigzell and Harvey
Cantor in their lectures.   Dr. Cantor reviewed for us the developing concepts
that the immune system is a highly regulated group of interdependent cellular
elements involving certain key regulatory cells which have the capacity to
augment the functions of both helper and suppressor cells through a series of
feedback loops.   The tools which have made possible the appreciation of the
existence of these loops have been antibodies to the differentiation antigens

228

which are markers of individual cell types and the existence of congenic pairs
of mice allowing decisive evaluation of the role of differentiation antigen-
bearing cells. Thus far such unambiguous cellular markers exist in mice only;
studies of changes in the relative proportion and function of individual cell
types in normal aged mice and mice with syndromes consistent with accelerated
aging are beginning to yield interesting results. A good bit of effort is
being expended on mice with autoimmune states, partly with the expectation that
the situation in these mice represents an exaggerated or accelerated form of
the normal aging process. Although this may well be a reasonable interpretation, I am far from confident that the basic immunologic lessons of autoimmunity and aging are similar. I think we must be quite careful to maintain
a balanced research effort and not to place undue reliance on these autoimmune
strains, despite the apparent advantages offered by them. I should also point
out at this time that major progress is being made in the development of
antibodies directed at the differentiation antigens of the human lymphoid
system. This progress is based on the recognition that human lymphoid tumors
offer sources of the individual cell types for antibody preparation and
characterization and that hybridoma technology makes possible the preparation
of truly monospecific antisera directed at human cells. Some of these
hybridoma products will certainly prove to identify differentiation antigens
of the human immune system. Indeed, very promising initial efforts have
already been described by several groups.

Hans Wigzell developed for us the concept that the antigen-binding receptors
of lymphocytes constitute a key target for the regulatory systems described by
Cantor. More precisely, the fact that the antigen-binding receptors on
individual clones of T and B lymphocytes must have distinct structures
allowing them their unique binding specificity, leads to these receptors
displaying unique antigenic determinants or idiotypes against which both
specific antibodies and regulatory lymphocytes can develop. It is now clear
that such regulatory elements do develop and that the interaction of regulatory antibodies and cells with idiotypes on receptors plays a substantial role
in the normal functioning of the immune system. Results presented by Siskind
suggest that abnormalities in such idiotype specific regulation may, in fact,
develop in the course of aging. Further attention to the idiotype-antiidiotype
regulatory system in aging may lead to most interesting insights into the
aberrations of immunity which occur in aged animals and humans.

Before leaving the general topic of regulation, it seems important to
point out that the immune system appears to devote a very substantial fraction

of its cells to such purposes, suggesting that it concerns itself almost as much with regulating an immune response as it does with developing such responses. Norman Talal recently pointed out that the immune system spends an inordinate amount of its energy in "talking to itself". Clearly, such energy must be spent because of the danger that a dysregulated system will lead to immunopathologic consequences.

The next group of presentations, those by Lawton and Siskind, introduced the second of the major themes of the symposium - the generation of immuno-competent cells. As we will discuss later, the question of whether the aging individual possesses stem cells with adequate regenerative capacity is absolutely critical to an appreciation of the potential life expectancy of the immune system. To appreciate the regenerative potential of aged stem cells, we must clearly develop an understanding of the normal development of lymphocytes. Lawton emphasized that B lymphocytes pass through an ordered series of differentiation events which can be appreciated through the identi-fication of unique sets of cellular markers associated with each developmental step. Most interestingly, an example of a human leukemia or lymphoma which appears to be a malignant counterpart of normal cells of virtually every developing phase has also been identified. The latter should provide sources of material for biochemical and antigenic analysis of cells of appropriate types.

Siskind developed for us the concept that developing subsets of cells have distinctive antigenic reactivity. More particularly, he showed that the acquisition of clonal diversity is an age dependent process and that this process is regulated not only by the development of the B lymphocytes themselves but also through the development of the T lymphocyte system.

From this point in the symposium, we turned our attention to a more specific discussion of the aging immune system itself. This was introduced by Greenberg's consideration of the determination of immunologic reactivity by genes of the major histocompatibility complex. In particular, certain very provocative points concerning the possibility that HLA gene products may directly or indirectly influence aging and longevity were developed in this presentation. Singhal and Talal then introduced the problem of disordered immunologic regulation in the aging and the autoimmune mouse. Singhal showed that old immunodepressed mice did not lack potentially immunocompetent cells since the antibody response of old spleen could be restored by specifically activated T cells. His results suggested that a rise in the activity of non-T suppressor cells in the spleen and bone marrow may account, in part,

for the depression in humoral immunity in aging mice. Talal presented some
most interesting data concerning the role of female sex hormones in
accelerating the acquisition of the characteristic autoimmune disease of
(NZB/NZW)F_1 (B/W) mice. Strikingly, he demonstrated that castration and
androgen treatment of female B/W mice caused a marked prolongation of life in
this normally short-lived autoimmune strain; this lengthening of life was
associated with a striking amelioration of the immunopathology these mice
normally display.

Closely related to this line of work was the report by Good and his
colleagues that comparable degrees of lengthening of life expectancy in such
strains could be achieved by caloric deprivation. Indeed, caloric deprivation
has been shown to cause quite substantial life prolongation in normal mouse
strains, particularly those with somewhat shorter than average life
expectancies. However, the effects in B/W mice are substantially more
striking and appear to be mediated, at least in part, by a delay in the onset
of autoimmunity. Clearly, these results raise the possibility that the
effects in autoimmune and normal strains have a common mechanism and that
derangements in immune mechanisms are critical determinants of the aging
process. However, one must recall that caloric deprivation can have quite
wide ranging effects; it would be premature to conclude that life prolongation
in normal strains is, in fact, determined by effects on the immune system.

A series of papers considered key elements of immunologic function in aging
animals, most notably susceptibility to tolerance induction which appears to
wane relatively early in the aging process-indeed during what we would
normally call mature life. Weksler discussed the problem of thymic involution
in aging and of the age-dependent diminution in serum thymopoietin levels.
In humans, this appears to occur relatively early in mature life while the
T lymphocytes of aging individuals appear to retain the ability to respond to
thymopoietin. This raises a most provocative possibility for the immunologic
defects of aging individuals. Deficiencies in circulating thymopoietin may
limit the normal development to maturity of individual T lymphocyte types,
leading to the idea that one difficulty of the old individual is that he has
too many young cells. I emphasize this point because we must continuously
be aware that aging of the immune system and aging of individual cells
within the system may be quite unrelated events. The principal changes in
aging could well be an elimination of mature antigen-reactive and effector
cells or major changes in the relative numbers of interacting cells without
any of the cells being intrinsically abnormal. Indeed, Dr. Makinodan's

presentation was aimed at evaluating the relative potency of each of the
cellular elements of the aging immune system and of the general environment
of the aging individual. His results tended to suggest that principal cell
types which he was able to test were relatively normal, although the environment provided by the aging host was not. Perhaps more optimistically, it
appeared that the stem cell pool, at least to the extent it could be tested,
was relatively normal.

Thus, we are left with the beginnings of a picture of immune function in
aging mice and aging humans. Clear abnormalities in the relative proportions
of cell types are found; autoimmunity and disordered regulation can be
demonstrated but their relative contribution to changes in immune reactivity
in aging are not yet certain. No certain evidence for intrinsic cellular
abnormalities in cells of old mice, in contrast to young mice have yet been
shown. In this light, we can have some optimism because it appears that the
cells might continue to function normally if their regulatory problems could
be corrected. Although it may not be immediately possible to make inroads into
the correction of disordered regulatory states, the enormous attention being
given to the analysis of regulation at both the animal and human level suggests
that intelligent intervention may soon be possible.

The relative contribution of the aging of the immune system to the overall
phenomenon of aging is still not clear. Although some have claimed the
immunologic system may be the clock marking our decline with the years, a
more conservative view is that this system is one of the key bodily systems
in which derangements can have wide ranging effects on health. The aging of
this system might clearly have serious effects. The question to resolve is
this. If we can slow the aging of the immune system, what overall effect on
the health and life expectancy of the human population could be expected?

ROUND TABLE DISCUSSION

PAUL: Perhaps Norman Talal would like to comment on suppressor cells and autoimmunity.

TALAL: Harvey discussed the feedback circuitry stating there is no loss of suppressor cells. In fact there is an increase in Ly-2,3 positive cells. Perhaps there are 10 different publications which say "wait a minute – there are problems with B cells", as early as at the stage of fetal liver. It has been shown that fetal liver cells of NZB mice can be polyclonally activated and that NZB's deprived of thymic influence have B cells that can also be polyclonally activated. I think the best and most logical position to take at the moment, is that there is an early abnormality in a stem cell. We do not know if this is a single genetic lesion being transmitted into T cells, B cells, macrophages and K cells or whether it is multiple genetic defects each being expressed in a separate line. I do not know if we will be able to resolve that question easily.

PAUL: If there is an early defect in the stem cell, how can you correct all the immune defects in the NZB mouse?

TALAL: Well, I don't think Bob Good said that they are corrected, but that there is a change.

GOOD: I think this needs a lot more study before we know how much we can correct. Many we can correct, no question about that. Possibly the consequences of an abnormal stem cell defect may be to disorganize an endogenously or exogeneously ordered system. There is no question that a stem cell abnormality exists. Now that we can transplant bone marrow across major histocompatibility barriers without GVH disease, our approach will be to add stem cells from long-lived strains of animals and observe the consequences with respect to resultant disorganizations. I think that the fact that we can manipulate these changes with diet, indicates that whatever the defect is in the stem cells the consequences of its influence are very subtle, being perhaps nodulated by hormonal change.

SISKIND: The data which Marc Wecksler has generated with reference to mice and stimulation of aged human cells, showing that there are not only fewer responsive units but also that the progeny of a cell which does respond has less likelihood to proliferate a second time in culture than the progeny of a cell from a young donor, could be interpreted as implying a defect in the cell. An intrinsic defect in the cells which was expressed in its daughter cells could be another interpretation of that data.

PAUL: Alternatively, one could attempt to explain such data by postulating interactive differences.

CUNNINGHAM: You raised the issue that when one looks at individual effector cells or their precursors in states like aging, often there is nothing dramatic to be seen. Yet it is clear that the homeostatic regulation between the cells is often grossly abnormal. Therefore, it seems to me that when one ruthlessly applies the classical reductionist kind of analysis, only a limited amount can come out of it. That applies, of course, to all highly regulated systems outside immunology. It is easy to make that statement but difficult to propose alternative approaches. Perhaps there is some value in looking at a level above the single cell and not worrying too much about the purified pots of cells that were mentioned earlier in discussion. For example, what is the capacity of a population of lymphocytes to respond to certain kinds of insults at different ages or in different states of disease?

PAUL: This is a valuable approach in the sense it identifies areas to attack. However, I think in the end, one still has to apply analysis in order to determine whether in fact the difficulty lies at an organizational level, or in defects amongst the cullular elements. I would say that immunologists really cannot be accused too much of analysis and of not being phenomenologists. In fact, one might wish to say the opposite. Next I wanted to go back to Norman Talal's point. We have in fact been working on the prematurely aging strains which display very substantial autoimmunity because they have certain features in common with the immunological situation in normal aging, and also because they are very convenient to work with. We essentially assumed that the processes going on there will in fact illuminate normal aging. Would anyone like to comment about how valid an approach this is likely to be?

TALAL: As usual, Bill is making a series of excellent points. I think that NZB mice or the new strains should not be equated with the autoimmunity of aging. In fact it seems to me that one should draw a distinction between successive stages of the response to self. The first I would call physiologic and that involves the MHC antigens and idiotype network and it is, in fact, the way the immune system regulates itself. The third I would call autoimmune disease where we have interesting spontaneous autoimmune models. There is a middle ground where aging falls, and I would call that autoimmunity without disease, because among the characteristics of aged individuals, you will find, for example, that over the age of 80, 40% of them will have rheumatoid factor without rheumatoid arthritis. The same percentage will have antinuclear factor without lupus. They have the serologic expression of autoimmunity without necessarily showing the pathologic consequences. Perhaps an analogous model to the aging situation would be the autoimmunity of chronic infection, which is reversible when the infection is treated.

PAUL: We could take the view of course that the appearance of autoantibodies was a more reliable sign of advancing age than chronological years. Thus the people who have autoantibodies are in fact older than those who do not, and are more likely to die. Yet the autoantibodies are not causative. This view is tenable, in a logical sense. Is there anyone else who would like to make a comment about the utilization of the experimental autoimmune strains as an experimental tool for gaining information about physiology of aging and the immune system in aging?

GOOD: As I stressed earlier, these strains reveal not only classical autoimmunity. As models of susceptibility to certain kinds of malignancy, they are relevant to the aging problem. With respect to their susceptibility to the development of vascular diseases, even coronary disease, they are useful models of reference to the diseases of aging. The most common disease of aging to me is the increasing susceptibility to infection. I do not think that this has been established in these strains and thus is an area for fruitful investigation. I think this susceptibility can be addressed in experimental terms, but no model is perfect.

PAUL: Perhaps we could turn very briefly again to the question which came up so strongly from both Norman Talal's presentation and Bob Good's presentation concerning the ways in which the nutritional and hormonal status of the individual interact. I think, Bob, you may have not wished to speculate too much during the talk, but I would like you to share your thoughts with us about what mechanism may be involved such that reduced calorie intake might, in fact, diminish autoimmune status.

GOOD: When one is in this early phase of phenomenology, there is a tremendous temptation to excessive speculation. It would be pure guess, but I think that our analysis of the immunological apparatus and changes in the immunological apparatus thus far certainly indicates that there are maintenance and inhibitory mechanisms affecting what might otherwise be looked on as a programmed involution. I can only think of that program being resident in the influence of the central nervous system on the endocrinological apparatus. Thus Norman Talal and I may be working much closer together than either of us realized in the beginning. We know it is not a virus. Other possible influences are speculative. There could be substances generated from different diets, or circulating substances could have profound influences. My energies can best be spent looking in detail at the regulatory immunological networks, at issues I might incorrectly have interpreted as evidence of stem cell abnormality in these diseases, and looking at some of the modern ways of examining hormonal regulation.

TALAL: Some additional information from my laboratory that has not yet come out concerns the ability of estrogen to influence marrow dependent cell functions, natural killer cells being one of those. It has been known to people interested in bone metabolism for a long time that one of the effects of giving estrogen is to cause tremendous osteoproliferation. Bill Seamans and I have found that normal mice as well as New Zealand mice implanted with silastic tubes containing estrogen have essentially complete marrow ablation. One of the consequences of this is abrogation of the natural killer cell activity in the spleen after four to six weeks of estrogen administration. Others are now finding that this renders the animal markedly deficient in its defence against certain transplantable malignancies.

PAUL: I suspect we could discuss a good deal longer but I am not certain this would be a good time to start an entirely new topic. May I close by extending my thanks again to Kim, his colleagues, and indeed to the entire group of participants for what has been a very stimulating meeting.

Index